LECTURES

ON

CONSTITUTIONAL LAW,

FOR THE USE OF THE

LAW CLASS

AT THE

UNIVERSITY OF VIRGINIA.

BY HENRY ST. GEORGE TUCKER,

PROFESSOR.

THE LAWBOOK EXCHANGE, LTD.
Clark, New Jersey

ISBN-13: 9781584774532

Lawbook Exchange edition 2004, 2010

The quality of this reprint is equivalent to the quality of the original work.

THE LAWBOOK EXCHANGE, LTD.
33 Terminal Avenue
Clark, New Jersey 07066-1321

Please see our website for a selection of our other publications and fine facsimile reprints of classic works of legal history:
www.lawbookexchange.com

Library of Congress Cataloging-in-Publication Data

Tucker, Henry St. George, 1780-1848.
Lectures on constitutional law : for the use of the law class at the University of Virginia /
by Henry St. George Tucker.
p. cm.
Originally published : Richmond : Printed by Shepherd and Colin, 1843.
Includes bibliographical references.
ISBN 1-58477-453-3 (cloth : alk. paper)
1. Constitutional law—United States. I. Title.

KF4550.Z9T83 2004
342.73—dc22 2004040919

Printed in the United States of America on acid-free paper

LECTURES

ON

CONSTITUTIONAL LAW,

FOR THE USE OF THE

LAW CLASS

AT THE

UNIVERSITY OF VIRGINIA.

BY HENRY ST. GEORGE TUCKER,

PROFESSOR.

RICHMOND:

PRINTED BY SHEPHERD AND COLIN.

1843.

LECTURES

ON THE

CONSTITUTION OF THE UNITED STATES.

LECTURE I.

Having presented to you, young gentlemen, in some former lectures, my views of the character and principles of the several forms of government, and particularly of the representative and confederate, we will now proceed to a more accurate examination of our own political system, which has been professedly constructed upon the combined principles of popular representation and an union of sovereign and independent states. I confidently believe that these enquiries will result in the conviction that whilst we have adopted a system without a prototype, we shall, nevertheless, find it eminently calculated to protect us from foreign aggression, and to secure the rights of life, liberty and property to every citizen of those free and happy republics.

Before we proceed however with our task, it may not be improper to recall to your recollections certain points of our national history with which you are doubtless familiar, but which bear too materially upon our subject to be passed at least without a reference.

The people of the United States, as you all are aware, are composed of the descendants of those subjects of the British crown, who, from various motives, left within the two last centuries their native isles and settled themselves upon this wild and desert continent. It is a principle of British law that if an uninhabited country is discovered and planted by British subjects, the English laws are immediately in force there; for the law is the birthright of every subject: so that wherever they go they carry their laws with them, and the new found country is governed by them.(*a*) The proposition however must be considered as limited by their applicability and their consistency with the local and political circumstances in which the colonists are placed; and, moreover, by those changes which, in the lapse of time may be made by that power which exercises the legislative authority over them.

Such seems, indeed, to be the natural course of things, though the notion has been derided by some of our most distinguished men.(*b*) It could not well have been otherwise. If we imagine a body of emigrants settling in an uninhabited country, we must suppose them to be under the government of *some* laws. Bodies of men cannot subsist without them. And if they must have *some*, what so natural as their recognition, even without adoption, of that system under which they were born, and to which they have been accustomed? Under such circumstances, the laws of the fatherland, so far as they might be applicable, would be looked to as the rule of civil conduct, commanding what is right and prohibiting what is wrong. This would be the natural course of things, if the bond which united the emigrants to the land of their birth was severed forever. It would have been the case with our forefathers, if, when they left the British shores, they could have fled beyond the reach of the keen eye and powerful arm of the monarch who claimed them as his subjects. But this was not their case. They might have exclaimed in the language of the Psalmist, "If I take the wings of the morning and dwell in the uttermost parts of the sea, even there shall thy hand lead me and thy right hand shall hold me."

This indeed was eminently the case with the British subject. Leashed to the footstool of the British crown, no time nor distance could dissolve the tie. The law of allegiance bound him wherever he might go, and "he dragged at each remove a lengthening chain." It was the principle of the law of that land that neither time nor distance could impair its obligation. Allegiance was a *quality* or duty, and as is said in the quaint language of a learned ap-

(*a*) 1 Black. Com. 107.
(*b*) 4 Jeff. Corr. 178.

prentice in Plowden, it was held to be ridiculous to attempt to force the *predicament of quality* into the *predicament* of ubi. Wherever, therefore, the British power reached, the British emigrant would be governed by its laws; and wherever he felt its restraints, or was sensible of its trammels, he would naturally claim as a set-off to its burdens, a full title to its privileges and protection.(*c*) Thus it is that in the declaration of rights drawn up by the continental congress of 1774, we find it declared, "that our ancestors, who first settled these colonies, were, at the time of their emigration from the mother country, entitled to all the rights, liberties and immunities of free and natural born subjects within the realm of England."

But the common law thus brought by the colonists was, it must be observed, very different at the periods of the different settlements. The common law as existing at the settlement of Virginia was very much modified before the settlement of Georgia in the reign of George the second; so that there never has been in the various states the same system of common law in all its ramifications, though its general character throughout the whole was very much the same, except so far as it had been altered by statutes enacted by the legislatures of the respective colonies. For very early after the respective settlements, provincial assemblies were established, composed of the representatives of the freeholders and planters, with whom were associated the governor and council, the last of whom composed an upper house, while the governor was invested with the power of a negative, and of proroguing and dissolving them. Thus constituted they soon acquired a code of their own, and introduced very large and important variations from the common law in all its branches; so that at the date of the revolution, and still more at the date of the present constitution of the United States, the systems of jurisprudence of the several states were so dissimilar that it would have been *impossible*, even if had been desired, to have adopted the common law as the general law of the United States *as such*.

The power of legislation thus exercised by the colonial legislatures, with the restrictions necessarily arising from

(*c*) See Cond. Rep. 204, 211, 212; 10 East. 282, 288, 289.

1*

their dependence on Great Britain was not without control: for in all the colonies, except Maryland, Connecticut and Rhode Island, the king possessed the power of abrogating the laws, and they were not final in their authority until they had passed under his review. (1 Story 158.) The colonies indeed were looked upon as dependencies of the British crown and owing allegiance thereto; the king being their supreme and sovereign lord. (1 Vez. 444; Vaugh. R. 300, 400; Shower's Parl. Ca. 30, &c.) From him the colonial assemblies were considered as deriving their energies, and it was in his power to assent or dissent to all their proceedings. In regard to the authority of parliament, the government of Great Britain maintained the right of that body to bind the colonies in all cases whatsoever; though it was admitted that they were bound by no act of parliament in which they were not expressly named. In America different opinions were entertained on the subject at different times and in different colonies. The power of taxation however was resisted from a very early period; (1 Story 172, 3, 4,) and the allegiance to the crown on the one hand, and the right of exemption from taxes unless imposed by themselves on the other, are equally asserted in a declaration of the colonies assembled at New York in October 1765. (1 Story 175.) And although in the same paper, the power of parliament to bind the colonies by legislation was admitted, yet upon the same principles on which the right of taxation was denied, the people of the colonies at length settled down upon the broad principle, that parliament had no power to bind them by its laws, except by such as might be enacted for the regulation of commerce and of the general concerns of the empire. While allegiance to the crown was, thus admitted, the authority of parliament to legislate in matters of taxation and internal policy was denied; and even the declaration of independence distinctly evinces by its silence as to parliament, that the authority to which they traced their wrongs, and whose action upon them was recognized was the king alone, until the power of taxation was asserted by parliament. This assertion and the wrongs of the crown at length brought revolution, and as soon as its first steps were taken, and even before a final separation was in contemplation, a close union and co-operation of all the colonies were perceived to be essential to the successful vindication of their rights and liberties as British subjects. A congress of delegates from the several colonies accordingly assembled first in 1774, and afterwards in 1775, and by them the necessary measures were adopted for the general defence. We shall hereafter have occasion to consider whether this body was to be looked upon as representing one people or thirteen distinct communities. But in this hasty sketch of the progress of the states to their present condition, it seems only necessary to say, that the congress of 1774 considered itself as invested with power to concert measures for redress of grievances, and that those of 1775 and 1776 were clothed with yet more ample powers; their commissions being sufficiently broad to embrace the right to pass measures of a national character and obligation. Anticipating the eager spirit of the people in resistance of British oppression and claims of dominion, they took measures of national defence; prohibited intercourse and trade with Great Britain, and raised an army and navy and authorized hostilities. They also raised and borrowed money; emitted bills of credit; established a post office, and authorized captures and condemnations of prizes in prize courts, with a reserve of appellate jurisdiction to themselves. At length, by the same body, the United States were declared independent in the most gloomy moments of the contest, and they continued to exercise the powers of a general government under a loose and irregular authority, until the adoption of the articles of confederation by some of the states in 1778. Those articles gave indeed a more firm and decided character to the government, and sustained by patriotism and the ardour of the conflict, bore us at length safely through our arduous struggle with one of the most powerful nations of the globe. On the termination of the war, the pressure of which, like the pressure of the superincumbent atmosphere, gave a principle of solidity to our institutions which did not properly belong to them, every thing became relaxed. The bands which united us seemed loosened, and all perceived how important it was they should be tightened. Years however passed away before the submission of the plan of a new constitution to the people, and the adoption of it by them. No sooner did it go into operation than it placed the states of the Union upon an elevation which even the most sanguine could scarcely have anticipated. We may reiterate the exclamation which Mr. Blackstone has borrowed from father Paul, and terminate our grateful acknowledgments to the giver of all good for our blessed constitution, by the fervent ejaculation "*Esto perpetua.*"

After this rapid sketch let us now proceed to look more closely into the nature and character, not only of our institutions, but of the relation which the several states have borne to each other, whether considered as colonies, or as brethren fighting shoulder to shoulder under the same irregular government, or as members of a great and organized confederacy, or finally as constituting the great and happy Union under which we live, protected against enemies abroad, and carefully secured from the danger of tyranny at home.

In the history of the two great parties which have divided the people of the United States ever since the adoption of the present constitution, a constant struggle is observable in relation to the character of the government. The *federal* party(*d*) (so called by a strange perversion

(*d*) Judge Story tells us: § 286. In this state of things the embarrassments of the country in its financial concerns, the general pecuniary distress among the people from the exhausting operations of the war, the total prostration of commerce, and the languishing unthriftiness of agriculture, gave new impulses to the already marked political divisions in the legislative councils. Efforts were made, on one side, to relieve the pressure of the public calamities by a resort to the issue of paper money, to tender laws, and instalment and other laws, having for their object the postponement of the payment of private debts, and a diminution of the public taxes. On the other side, public as well as private creditors became alarmed from the increased dangers to property, and the increased facility of perpetrating frauds to the destruction of all private faith and credit. And they insisted strenuously upon the establishment of a government, and system of laws, which should preserve the public faith, and redeem the country from that ruin, which always follows upon the violation of the principles of justice, and the moral obligation of contracts. "At length," we are told,* "two great parties were formed in every state, which were distinctly marked, and which pursued distinct objects with systematic arrangement. The one struggled with unabated zeal for the exact observance of public and private engagements. The distresses

* 5 Marshall's Life of Washington, 83.

of the use of the terms) have always been inclined to represent the United States as constituting *one people,* instead of a confederacy of states; while their opponents (formerly called anti-federalists, but more recently known as the democratic or republican party) have ever strenuously contended that the constitution was a compact, or the result of a compact between the *states;* who retain their sovereignty, and all the rights of sovereignty, which they have not expressly transferred to the federal government. Thus we find Mr. Webster, the great champion of the federal party, pronouncing, (and judge Story once, but no longer, supposed to be of the states right party, quotes him with approbation) that "the doctrine that the states are parties to the constitution is refuted by the constitution itself *in its very front.* It declares that it is ordained and established by the PEOPLE of the United States. So far from saying that it is established by the governments of the several states, it does not even say that it is established by the *people of the several states.* But it pronounces that it is established by the people of the United States in the AGGREGATE!! Doubtless the people of the several states taken collectively constitute the people of the United

of individuals were, they thought, to be alleviated by industry and frugality, and not by a relaxation of the laws, or by a sacrifice of the rights of others. They were consequently uniform friends of a regular administration of justice, and of a vigorous course of taxation, which would enable the state to comply with its engagements. By a natural association of ideas, they were also, with very few exceptions, in favour of enlarging the powers of the federal government, and of enabling it to protect the dignity and character of the nation abroad, and its interests at home. The other party marked out for itself a more indulgent course. They were uniformly in favour of relaxing the administration of justice, of affording facilities for the payment of debts, or of suspending their collection, and of remitting taxes. The same course of opinion led them to resist every attempt to transfer from their own hands into those of congress, powers, which were by others deemed essential to the preservation of the Union. In many of the states the party last mentioned constituted a decided majority of the people; and in all of them it was very powerful." Such is the language of one of our best historians in treating of the period immediately preceding the formation of the constitution of the United States.*

* See also 5 Marshall's Life of Washington, 130, 131

States. But it is in this their *collective capacity*, it is, as *all the people of the United States* that they establish the constitution." (Webster's Speeches, pa. 430, cited 1 Story 331, 2.) Similar opinions are delivered in *Martin* v. *Hunter*, 1 Wheat. 324.

The foregoing passage is cited here, not for the purpose of exposing its disingenuous sophisms, but merely to present the views of one of the great parties of the country in relation to our federal constitution. It is their favourite position "that the constitution of the United States was ordained and adopted, *not by the states in their sovereign capacities*, but emphatically, as the *preamble declares by the* people of the United States, and it is this position which it behoves every lover of truth and of the rights of the states most vigorously to assail. Its advocates indeed have maintained it with equal earnestness and ability, but having been foiled on some eminent occasions, and having fallen from power in no small degree from their strenuous maintenance of this political heresy, one of the most distinguished among them has compiled a laborious work with a view to sustain it. In doing this, judge Story has attempted to fortify himself, by shewing that the people of the United States were *always one people:* that the colonies themselves, when subjects of Great Britain, were not distinct and separate from each other, but were *one people:* that during the revolutionary struggle they were still *one people* even anterior to the confederation: that the declaration of independence treated them as *one people*, and that this oneness or unity particularly distinguished them in "ordaining and establishing the constitution of the United States." Such is the general tenor, as it appears to me, of judge Story's doctrine, but as I shall, in proceeding to examine it, quote his very language, I shall have done him no injustice, if what I have just said does not represent him fairly. Let us proceed then to state and examine his several positions.

We will begin with the colonies. In page 164, judge Story remarks that "though the colonies were independent of each other in respect to their domestic concerns, they were not wholly alien to each other. On the contrary they were fellow subjects, and *for many purposes one people.* Every colonist had a right to inhabit if he pleased in any other,(*e*) and, as a British subject, was capable of inheriting lands by descent in every other colony." And he proceeds to cite Ch. Jus. Jay to the same point "that they were in a *variety of respects one people.*"

Let us then enquire whether the colonies before the revolution *were* justly to be regarded in *any respect* or for *any* purpose *one people.* I propose to examine this question shortly, according to the views of the statesmen of the times, and the admissions of judge Story himself; according to the nature of the several political societies; according to historical facts, and upon principle.

First, it is clear, that the colonies were looked upon not as constituting part even of the body politic of the British government, but as subject to it; "not as *part of the mother* country, BUT AS DISTINCT, though dependent dominions." Such is the language of Mr. Blackstone when speaking of these very colonies. (Vol. 1, 107.) So even the kingdom of Scotland, after the union of the two crowns on the accession of James I. continued an *entire, separate and distinct* kingdom for above a century; and so when judge Blackstone wrote, Ireland was *still* a *distinct, though a dependent and subordinate kingdom* (p. 99). So also of Hanover, though it has the same king that sits on the British throne, it is a distinct, independent and unconnected kingdom, (p. 110.)(*f*)

Admitting then that the colonies, though the subjects of the crown, made *no part* of the MOTHER country, but were DISTINCT, though dependent dominions, they were *a fortiori* DISTINCT from each other: For if their being subject to the authority of the crown of England did not make them to any intent one people with England, still less could they be *one people* with other states, that neither were subject to them nor had authority over them.

(*e*) "It *never was considered*," says judge Iredell, "that before the actual signature of the articles of confederation a citizen of one state was to any one purpose a citizen of another. He was, as to all substantial purposes, as a foreigner to their forensic jurisprudence. If rigorous law had been enforced, perhaps, he might have been deemed an *alien* without an express provision of the state to save him." Hence the provisions in the articles of confederation and in the constitution United States.

(*f*) See Vattel, Burlamaque and Hutchinson, quoted Tucker's Black. app. 64, 65.

That the colonies were held to be only subjects, and not as forming part of the British body politic, is fairly to be inferred from the speeches of lord Chatham and Mr. Burke in the passages quoted by Mr. Story himself (p. 153, 4); for they are distinctly considered as the *subjects* of the crown, and their rights and privileges are placed upon the footing of being British subjects, who, though residing in a *distinct* dominion from England, were entitled to the common privileges of every subject of the crown. The colonies themselves they considered *distinct* from the realm of England: and, moreover, "the authority over them was declared by lord Chatham to be sovereign and supreme in every circumstance of government and legislation."(*g*) The statute 6 Geo. III. also declares the colonies *subordinate* to and *dependent* upon the imperial crown and parliament: and so they were not on a footing with British people, but were subject to them, and were not therefore *one with them*. And if not one with *them*, in what manner could they be *one with each other*.

Judge Story indeed himself admits that "for all purposes of domestic and internal regulation the colonial legislatures deemed themselves possessed of entire authority, exclusive of each other," (p. 152): and that with the restrictions necessarily arising from their dependency on Great Britain, "they were sovereign within the limits of their respective territories." (p. 158.) And again he says, "they considered themselves *not as parcel of the realm* of Great Britain, but as dependencies of the British *crown*, and owing allegiance thereto, the *king* being their supreme and sovereign lord." If then they were not *one* with the *realm*, it is difficult indeed to imagine how they could as distinct dependencies be one with each other.

Again, in page 163, he says more distinctly, "though the colonies had a common origin, and owed a common allegiance, and the inhabitants of each were British subjects, they had no direct political connexion with each other. Each was independent of all the others; each in a limited sense was sovereign within its own territory. There was neither alliance nor confederacy between them.

(*g*) This doctrine, however extravagant, shews that Chatham did not look upon the colonies as parts of the realm.

The assembly of one province could not make laws for another, nor confer privileges which were to be enjoyed or exercised in another, farther than they could be in any independent foreign state. They were known only as dependencies." Now all this is orthodox and true, and as such we heartily adopt it. It is not for me indeed to attempt to reconcile it with the position already cited, that they were to *many purposes one people;* (page 164,) and still less with the reasoning attempted, in page 196, to be founded on these narrow premises. We shall have occasion however to view this matter more closely by and by. At present we think judge Story's admissions sufficiently establish, that if the colonies were "not sovereign communities in the most large and general sense," it was because they were subjects of the British crown, and not because they were subjects of or connected with each other. The matter would have been more doubtful had they formed parts of the realm as York and Middlesex do; subject to the same laws, constituting portions of one body politic, and having the *commune vinculum* of the same legislative authority. Then indeed there might have been some pretext for considering the fragments broken off from a common mass as being homogeneous and identical, but it will require more than the *ipse dixit* even of judge Story to establish a unity between peoples(*h*) with different laws, different systems of government, different organizations in all their parts, different revenues, different taxation, different deliberative assemblies in relation to their concerns as "people," and different local executives and judiciaries for the conduct of their affairs and the administration of their varied jurisprudence. This leads me to observe,

Secondly, That the states were *not one* but distinct from the nature of their several political societies. This is apparent, if we look at their origin, their settlements, and their forms of civil polity. They were settled at very different times, Virginia 150 years before Georgia, and the rest at intermediate periods. They came over to these desert countries under different circumstances. Some of the governments were provincial, some proprietary, and some

(*h*) I use the plural as Détoqueville very happily does.

were chartered. Nay, more—some were conquered, as were New York and Jersey, and by the principles of the common law, the laws of the conquered lands prevailed till changed by the stern *fiat* of the conquerors. These various peoples were, therefore, essentially distinct and separate, and utterly incapable of amalgamation or *oneness:* and we must remember that the question is not whether they were sovereign in respect of foreign nations, but whether they were *one* in regard to each other.

But the several colonies were not only different in origin and in organization, but they were perfectly independent in their jurisdiction. No one colony had any pretence of authority or power within the bounds of another. Even under the threatenings of a savage foe one could not call out the militia of another. Hence the early confederations among some of the northern colonies for mutual defence, and hence the abortive attempt shortly anterior to the war of 1756 to establish a more comprehensive union of the colonies.(*i*) These associations and attempts at association successfully repel every notion of *oneness* between them. If they were one already, where was the *necessity* of any farther measure to bind them together? If they were one, why were not all compelled to join in those associations? Why, in the language of chancellor Kent, (vol. 1, pa. 205,) were they destined to remain longer separate, and in a considerable degree alien commonwealths, *jealous* of each other's prosperity, and *divided* by policy, institutions, prejudice and manners? Why was the force of these considerations so strong, as to have induced Dr. Franklin (one of the commissioners to the congress that formed the plan of Union in 1754) to have observed that a union of the colonies was absolutely impossible, or at least without being forced by the most grievous tyranny and oppression? Why did Gov. Pownal concur in the same sentiment, declaring, that the colonies had no one principle of association among them, and that their manner of settlement, diversity of charters, conflicting interests, and mutual rivalships and jealousies rendered union impracticable? (Pownal on the Colonies, 35, 36, 93.)

(*i*) 1 Kent 202, 203.

The colonies, indeed, in some regards, appear not only to have been distinct from each other, but to have exercised distinctly independent acts of sovereignty, under the control indeed of the king of England, whose subjects they were. Thus, anterior to the revolution, many treaties were made by the respective colonies with the Indians within their boundaries, all of whom were admitted to be the rightful occupants of the soil, with a right to use, retain and reside upon it, exercising authority over it, governing themselves by their own laws, and having the privilege of selling their lands or not, at their pleasure, to the civilized people who discovered the country.(*j*) Accordingly the several colonies, by treaties, anterior to the revolution, entered, for themselves and on their separate account, into treaties with the Indians in which no other colony had any participation or concern. Thus it would seem that in all things they acted at pleasure, independently of each other; no *one* could interfere with *another:* when they acted in concert it was either by compact or by command of a common head, and when that head was severed, they were left without any *commune vinculum* to hold them together, and each had a separate and distinct power to supply the loss by creating an executive of its own, according to its own notions of propriety and policy.

If we consider the matter upon principle it is not less clear. What is it which constitutes nationality or the *oneness* of people? A nation or people is a political body united together by common laws and common institutions. To constitute one people, those who compose it must *act* as one people. It is the unity of action which alone makes those one, who, without it, would be several. Several individuals may unite in a body politic, and by this unity of action be held as one man. Without such unity they must remain, what they are by nature, several. No union of *states*, indeed, can ever make one people; for while they continue states, each acts for itself, and that entire unity of action is wanting, which, alone, constitutes oneness. If the power of *separate action* be surrendered, nationality indeed is created, but the *states* are no more. With what

(*j*) 8 Wheat. 543.

propriety can it be affirmed that bodies of people are one people, when they have separate and distinct governments; of separate and distinct forms; with distinct and conflicting systems of jurisprudence; where the judgments of one are held foreign to the other (as was the case in the colonies); when neither can interfere with or control another, and, in short, when each has the power of governing itself without being dependent on the will of the other? Judge Story, himself, tells us (195) that if a state has the sole power of governing itself, and is not dependent on any foreign state, it is called a sovereign state; from which the corollary seems fair, that every state must be held to be independent and distinct from every other state by which it is *not* governed. The law-making power seems peculiarly to give its character in this regard to the society. That which makes for itself *law,* and particularly its *fundamental law*, is so far sovereign. That power of legislation for itself, makes it distinct from others; for legislation is the action of political bodies, and separate legislation is separate action, which is inconsistent with the notion of unity.(*k*) Thus it is that two peoples may have the same king, and yet be separate people: as in the case of Great Britain and Hanover now, and of England and Scotland before the union. The union itself proves that they *were* not *one* before. At this day England and Hanover, with the same king, are not involved in the wars of each other. Ireland, too, before the union, was considered as foreign, and the judgments of her courts, and those of Jamaica, of Canada and of India are looked upon as foreign judgments. Even the judgment of the king's bench is a foreign judgment in Ireland, 2 Str. 1090; 4 Barn. & Cres. 411; and the court of king's bench itself affirms the judgment which so pronounces it. But if these portions of the empire are foreign to England, the thirteen colonies must have been foreign to her, and if foreign to her, how much more foreign to Hindostan, or Antigua, or to one another?

There was then nothing of nationality or *oneness* in the people of the colonies. Each colony was a distinct com-

(*k*) 1 Tuck. Black. app. 64, 65, citing Hutchinson, Vattel and Burlamaque.

munity or body politic; having its own charter, its own government, its own laws and institutions, and its own right of separate action, under the control indeed of the crown, but not of the sister colonies: and hence, I confidently conclude, that they did not in any sense whatever constitute one people.

Unwilling however to leave this important position upon my less forcible arguments, I offer to the student the acute remarks of judge Upshur in his able review of a part of judge Story's work. The learned and sagacious author observes:

"It appears to be a favourite object with the author to impress upon the mind of the reader, at the very commencement of his work, the idea that the people of the several colonies were, as to some objects, which he has not explained, and to some extent, which he has not defined, 'one people.' This is not only plainly inferable from the general scope of the book, but is expressly asserted in the following passage: 'But although the colonies were independent of each other in respect to their domestic concerns, they were not wholly alien to each other. On the contrary, they were fellow subjects, and for many purposes one people. Every colonist had a right to inhabit, if he pleased, in any other colony, and as a British subject he was capable of inheriting lands by descent in every other colony. The commercial intercourse of the colonies too was regulated by the general laws of the British empire, and could not be restrained or obstructed by colonial legislation. The remarks of Mr. chief justice Jay are equally just and striking: 'All the people of this country were then subjects of the king of Great Britain, and owed allegiance to him, and all the civil authority then existing or exercised here flowed from the head of the British empire. They were in a strict sense *fellow subjects*, and in a variety of respects *one people.* When the revolution commenced, the patriots did not assert that only the same affinity and social connexion subsisted between the people of the colonies, which subsisted between the people of Gaul, Britain and Spain, while Roman provinces, to wit, only that affinity and social connexion which results from the mere circumstance of being governed by the same prince.''

"In this passage the author takes his ground distinctly and boldly. The first idea suggested by the perusal of it is, that he discerned very clearly the necessity of establishing his position, but did not discern quite so clearly by what process of reasoning he was to accomplish it. If the passage stood alone, it would be fair to suppose that he did not design to extend the idea of a unity among the people of the colonies beyond the several particulars which he has enumerated. Justice to him requires that we should suppose this; for, if it had been otherwise, he would scarcely have failed to support his opinion by pointing out some one of the 'many purposes,' for which the colonies were, in his view of them, 'one people.' The same may be said of Mr. chief justice Jay. He also has specified several particulars in which he supposed this unity to exist, and arrives at the conclusion, that the people of the several colonies were, 'in a variety of respects, one people.' In what respect they were 'one,' except those which he has enumerated, he does not say, and of course it is fair to presume that he meant to rest the justness of his conclusion upon them alone. The historical facts stated by both of these gentlemen are truly stated; but it is surprising that it did not occur to such cool reasoners, that every one of them is *the result of the relation between the colonies and the mother country, and not the result of the relation between the colonies themselves.* Every British subject, whether born in England proper or in a colony, has a right to reside any where within the British realm; and this *by the force of British laws.* Such is the right of every Englishman, wherever he may be found. As to the right of the colonist to inherit lands by descent in any other colony than his own, our author himself informs us that it belonged to him 'as a British subject.' That right, indeed, is a consequence of his allegiance. By the policy of the British constitution and laws, it is not permitted that the soil of her territory should belong to any from whom she cannot demand all the duties of allegiance. This allegiance is the same in all the colonies as it is in England proper; and, wherever it exists, the correspondent right to own and inherit the soil attaches. The right to regulate commercial intercourse among her colonies belongs, of course, to the parent country, unless she relinquishes it by some act of her own; and no such act is shewn in the present case. On the contrary, although that right was resisted for a time by some of the American colonies, it was finally yielded, as our author himself informs us, by all those of New England, and I am not informed that it was denied by any other. Indeed, the supremacy of parliament, in most matters of legislation which concerned the colonies, was generally—nay, *universally*—admitted, up to the very eve of the revolution. It is true, the right to *tax* the colonies was denied, but this was upon a wholly different principle. It was the right of every British subject to be exempt from taxation, except by his own consent; and as the colonies were not, and from their local situation could not be, represented in parliament, the right of that body to tax them was denied, upon a fundamental principle of English liberty. But the right of the mother country to regulate commerce among her colonies is of a different character, and it never was denied to England by her American colonies, so long as a hope of reconciliation remained to them. In like manner, the facts relied on by Mr. Jay, that 'all the people of this country were then subjects of the king of Great Britain, and owed allegiance to him,' and that 'all the civil authority then existing or exercised here flowed from the head of the British empire,' are but the usual incidents of colonial dependence, and are by no means peculiar to the case he was considering. They do, indeed, prove a unity between all the colonies and *the mother country*, and shew that these, taken altogether, are, in the strictest sense of the terms, 'one people;' but I am at a loss to perceive how they prove, that two or more parts or subdivisions of the same empire necessarily constitute 'one people.' If this be true of the colonies, it is equally true of any two or more geographical sections of England proper; for every one of the reasons assigned applies as strictly to this case as to that of the colonies. Any two countries may be 'one people,' or 'a nation *de facto*,' if they can be made so by the facts that their people are 'subjects of the king of Great Britain, and owe allegiance to him,' and that 'all the civil authority exercised therein flows from the head of the British empire.'

"It is to be regretted that the author has not given us his own views of the sources from which these several rights and powers were derived. If they authorize his conclusion, that there was any sort of unity among the people of the several colonies, distinct from their common connexion with the mother country, as parts of the same empire, it must be because they flowed from something in the relation betwixt the colonies themselves, and not from their common relation to the parent country. Nor is it enough that these rights and powers should, *in point of fact*, flow from the relation of the colonies to one another; they must be the *necessary result of their political condition.* Even admitting, then, that they would, under any state of circumstances, warrant the conclusion which the author has drawn from them, it does not follow that the conclusion is correctly drawn in the present instance. For aught that he has said to the contrary, the right of every colonist to inhabit and inherit lands in every colony, whether his own or not, may have been derived from positive compact and agreement among the colonies themselves; and this presupposes that they were distinct and separate, and not 'one people.' And so far as the rights of the mother country are concerned, they existed in the same form, and to the same extent, over every other colony of the empire. Did this make the people of *all* the colonies 'one people?' If so, the people of Jamaica, the British East Indian possessions and the Canadas are, for the very same reason, 'one people' at this day. If a common allegiance to a common sovereign, and a common subordination to his jurisdiction, are sufficient to make the people of different countries 'one people,' it is not perceived (with all deference to Mr. chief justice Jay) why the people of Gaul, Britain and Spain might not have been 'one people,' while Roman provinces, notwithstanding 'the patriots' did not say so. The *general* relation between colonies and the parent country is as well settled and understood as any other, and it is precisely the same in all cases, except where special consent and agreement may vary it. Whoever, therefore, would prove that any peculiar *unity* existed between the American colonies, is bound to shew something in their charters, or some peculiarity in their condition, to exempt them from the general rule. Judge Story was too well acquainted with the state of the facts to make any such attempt in the present case. The congress of the nine colonies, which assembled at New York, in October 1765, declare, that the colonists 'owe the same allegiance to the crown of Great Britain, that is owing from his subjects born within the realm, and all due subordination to that august body, the parliament of Great Britain.'—'That the colonists are entitled to all the inherent rights and liberties of his [the king's] natural born subjects within the kingdom of Great Britain.' We have here an all-sufficient foundation of the right of the crown to regulate commerce among the colonies, and of the right of the colonists to inhabit and to inherit land in each and all the colonies. They were nothing more than the ordinary rights and liabilities of every British subject; and, indeed, the most that the colonies ever contended for was an equality, in these respects, with the subjects born in England. The facts, therefore, upon which our author's reasoning is founded, spring from a different source from that from which he is compelled to derive them, in order to support his conclusion.

"So far as the author's argument is concerned, the subject might be permitted to rest here. Indeed, one would be tempted to think, from the apparent carelessness and indifference with which the argument is urged, that he himself did not attach to it any particular importance. It is not his habit to dismiss grave matters with such slight examination, nor does it consist with the character of his mind to be satisfied with reasoning which bears even a doubtful relation to his subject. Neither can it be supposed that he would be willing to rely on the simple *ipse dixit* of chief justice Jay, unsupported by argument, unsustained by any references to historical facts, and wholly indefinite in extent and bearing. Why, then, was this passage written? As mere history, apart from its bearing on the constitution of the United States, it is of no value in this work, and is wholly out of place. All doubts upon this point will be removed in the progress of this examination. The great effort of the author, throughout his entire work, is to establish the doctrine, that the constitution of the United States is a government of 'the people of the United States,' as contradistinguished from the people of the several states; or, in other words, that it is a consolidated, and not a federative system. His construction of every contested federal power depends mainly upon this distinction; and hence the necessity of establishing a *oneness* among the people of the several colonies, prior to the revolution. It may well excite our surprise, that a proposition so necessary to the principal design of the work, should be stated with so little precision, and dismissed with so little effort to sustain it by argument. One so well informed as judge Story, of the state of political opinions in this country, could scarcely have supposed that it would be received as an admitted truth, requiring no examination. It enters too deeply into grave questions of constitutional law, to be so summarily disposed of. We should not be content, therefore, with simply proving that the author has assigned no sufficient reason for the opinion he has advanced. The subject demands of us the still farther proof that his opinion is, in fact, erroneous, and that it cannot be sustained by any *other* reasons.

"In order to constitute 'one people,' in a political sense, of the inhabitants of different countries, something more is necessary than that they should owe a common allegiance to a common sovereign. Neither is it sufficient that, in some particulars, they are bound alike, by laws which that sovereign may prescribe: nor does the question depend on geographical relations. The inhabitants of different islands may be one people, and those of contiguous countries may be, as we know they in fact are, different nations. By the term 'people,' as here used, we do not mean merely a number of persons. We mean by it a political corporation, the members of which owe a common allegiance to a common sovereignty, and do not owe any allegiance which is *not* common; who are bound by no laws except such as that sovereignty may prescribe; who owe to one another reciprocal obligations; who possess common political interests; who are liable to common political duties; and who can exert no sovereign power except in the name of the whole. Any thing short of this, would be an imperfect definition of that political corporation which we call 'a people.'

"Tested by this definition, the people of the American colonies were, in no conceivable sense, 'one people.' They owed, indeed, allegiance to the British king, as the head of each colonial government, and as forming a part thereof; but this allegiance was exclusive, in each colony, to its own government, and, consequently, to the king as the head thereof, and was not a common allegiance of the people of all the colonies to a common head.(*l*) These colonial governments were clothed with the sovereign power of making laws, and of enforcing obedience to them from their own people. The people of one colony owed no allegiance to the government of any other colony, and were not bound by its laws. The colonies had no common legislature, no common treasury, no common military power, no common judicatory. The people of one colony were not liable to pay taxes to any other colony, nor to bear arms in its defence; they had no right to vote in its elections; no influence or control in its municipal government, no interest in its municipal institutions. There was no prescribed form by which the colonies could act together, for any purpose whatever; they were not known as 'one people' in any one function of government. Although they were all, alike, dependencies of the British crown, yet, even in the action of the parent country, in regard to them, they were recognized as separate and distinct. They were established at different times, and each under an authority from the crown, which applied to itself alone. They were not even alike in their organization. Some were provincial, some proprietary, and some charter governments. Each derived its form of government from the particular instrument establishing it, or from assumptions of power acquiesced in by the crown, without any connexion with, or relation to, any other. They stood upon the same footing, in every respect, with other British colonies, with nothing to distinguish their relation either to the parent country or to one another. The charter of any one of them might have been destroyed, without in any manner affecting the rest. In point of fact, the charters of nearly all of them were altered, from time to time, and the whole character of their governments changed. These changes were made in each colony for itself alone, some-

(*l*) The resolutions of Virginia, in 1769, shew that she considered herself merely as an appendage of the British crown; that *her* legislature was alone authorized to tax her; and that she had a right to call on *her* king, who was also king of England, to protect her against the usurpations of the British parliament.

times by its own action, sometimes by the power and authority of the crown; but never by the joint agency of any other colony, and never with reference to the wishes or demands of any other colony. Thus they were separate and distinct in their creation; separate and distinct in the forms of their governments; separate and distinct in the changes and modifications of their governments, which were made from time to time; separate and distinct in political functions, in political rights, and in political duties.

"The provincial government of Virginia was the first established. The people of Virginia owed allegiance to the British king, as the head of their own local government. The authority of that government was confined within certain geographical limits, known as Virginia, and all who lived within those limits were 'one people.' When the colony of Plymouth was subsequently settled, were the people of that colony 'one' with the people of Virginia? When, long afterwards, the proprietary government of Pennsylvania was established, were the followers of William Penn 'one' with the people of Plymouth and Virginia? If so, to which government was their allegiance due? Virginia had a government of her own, Pennsylvania a government of her own, and Massachusetts a government of her own. The people of Pennsylvania could not be equally bound by the laws of all three governments, because those laws might happen to conflict; they could not owe the duties of citizenship to all of them alike, because they *might* stand in hostile relations to one another. Either, then, the government of Virginia, which originally extended over the whole territory, continued to be supreme therein, (subject only to its dependence upon the British crown,) or else its supremacy was yielded to the new government. Every one knows that this last was the case; that within the territory of the new government the authority of that government alone prevailed. How then could the people of this new government of Pennsylvania be said to be 'one' with the people of Virginia, when they were not citizens of Virginia, owed her no allegiance and no duty, and when their allegiance to another government might place them in the relation of enemies of Virginia?

"In farther illustration of this point, let us suppose that some one of the colonies had refused to unite in the declaration of independence; what relation would it then have held to the others? Not having disclaimed its allegiance to the British crown, it would still have continued to be a British colony, subject to the authority of the parent country, in all respects as before. Could the other colonies have rightfully compelled it to unite with them in their revolutionary purposes, on the ground that it was part and parcel of the 'one people,' known as the people of the colonies? No such right was ever claimed, or dreamed of, and it will scarcely be contended for now, in the face of the known history of the time. Such recusant colony would have stood precisely as did the Canadas, and every other part of the British empire. The colonies which had declared war, would have considered its people as enemies, but would not have had a right to treat them as traitors, or as disobedient citizens resisting their authority. To what purpose, then, were the people of the colonies 'one people,' if, in a case so important to the common welfare, there was no right in all the people together, to coerce the members of their own community to the performance of a common duty?

"It is thus apparent that the people of the colonies were not 'one people,' as to any purpose involving allegiance on the one hand, or protection on the other. What then, I again ask, are the 'many purposes' to which the author alludes? It is certainly incumbent on him who asserts this identity, against the inferences most naturally deducible from the historical facts, to shew at what time, by what process, and for what purposes, it was effected. He claims too much consideration for his personal authority, when he requires his readers to reject the plain information of history, in favour of his bare assertion. The charters of the colonies prove no identity between them, but the reverse; and it has already been shewn that this identity is not the necessary result of their common relation to the mother country. By what other means they came to be 'one,' in any intelligible and political sense, it remains for the author to explain.

"If these views of the subject be not convincing, the author himself has furnished proof, in all needful abundance, of the incorrectness of his own conclusion. He tells us that, 'though the colonies had a common origin, and owed

3

a common allegiance, and the inhabitants of each were British subjects, they *had no direct political connexion with each other.* Each was independent of all the others; each, in a limited sense was sovereign within its own territory. There was neither alliance nor confederacy between them. The assembly of one province could not make laws for another, nor confer privileges which were to be enjoyed or exercised in another, farther than they could be in any independent foreign state. As colonies they were also excluded from all connexion with foreign states. They were known only as dependencies, and they followed the fate of the parent country, both in peace and war, without having assigned to them, in the intercourse or diplomacy of nations, any distinct or independent existence. *They did not possess the power of forming any league or treaty among themselves, which would acquire an obligatory force, without the assent of the parent state.* And though their mutual wants and necessities often induced them to associate for common purposes of defence, these confederacies were of a casual and temporary nature, and were allowed as an indulgence, rather than as a right. They made several efforts to procure the establishment of some general superintending government over them all; but their own differences of opinion, as well as the jealousy of the crown, made these efforts abortive.'

"The English language affords no terms stronger than those which are here used to convey the idea of separateness, distinctness and independence, among the colonies. No commentary could make the description plainer, or more full and complete. The *unity*, contended for by the author, no where appears, but it is distinctly disaffirmed in every sentence. The colonies were not only distinct in their creation, and in the powers and faculties of their governments, but there was not even 'an alliance or confederacy between them.' They had no 'general superintending government over them all,' and tried in vain to establish one. Each was 'independent of all the others,' having its own legislature, and without power to confer either right or privilege beyond its own territory. 'Each, in a limited sense, was sovereign within its own territory;' and to sum up all, in a single sentence, 'they had no direct political connexion with each other!' The condition of the colonies was, indeed, anomalous, if our author's view of it be correct. They presented the singular spectacle of 'one people,' or political corporation, the members of which had 'no direct political connexion with each other,' and who had not the power to form such connexion, even 'by league or treaty among themselves.'

"This brief review will, it is believed, be sufficient to convince the reader, that our author has greatly mistaken the real condition and relation of the colonies, in supposing that they formed 'one people,' in any sense, or for any purpose whatever. He is entitled to credit, however, for the candour with which he has stated the historical facts. Apart from all other sources of information, his book affords to every reader abundant materials for the formation of his own opinion, and for enabling him to decide satisfactorily whether the author's inferences from the facts, which he himself has stated, be warranted by them, or not."

LECTURE II.

So much, young gentlemen, for the *oneness* of the colonies as such. We will now proceed to another singular position of the learned commentator on the constitution, in furtherance of his favourite theory of the oneness of the American people. After having attempted to sustain his views of the anti-revolutionary state of the colonies, he proceeds to consider their condition during the throes of the revolution, and contends that neither anterior to the declaration of independence, nor subsequent to that event, were the former colonies "sovereign and independent states in the sense in which the term sovereign is applied to states." As the positions of judge Story are very frequently ingeniously insinuated, rather than distinctly announced, and as I am unwilling to misstate his opinions, or do injustice to his arguments, I shall insert the whole of this passage in a note.(*a*)

(*a*) § 200. No redress of grievances having followed upon the many appeals made to the king, and to parliament, by and in behalf of the colonies, either conjointly or separately, it became obvious to them, that a closer union and co-operation were necessary to vindicate their rights and protect their liberties. If a resort to arms should be indispensable, it was impossible to hope for success, but in united efforts. If peaceable redress was to be sought, it was as clear, that the voice of the colonies must be heard, and their power felt in a national organization. In 1774 Massachusetts recommended the assembling of a continental congress to deliberate upon the state of public affairs; and according to her recommendation, delegates were appointed by the colonies for a congress, to be held in Philadelphia in the autumn of the same year. In some of the legislatures of the colonies, which were then in session, delegates were appointed by the popular, or representative branch; and in other cases they were appointed by conventions of the people in the colonies.* The congress of delegates (calling themselves in their more formal acts "the delegates appointed by the *good people* of these colonies," assembled on the 4th of September 1774;† and having chosen officers, they adopted certain fundamental rules for their proceedings.

* 1 Journ. of Cong. 2, 3, &c. 27, 45; 9 Dane's Abridg. App. § 5, p. 16, § 10, p. 21.

† All the states were represented, except Georgia.

In the commencement of this sketch of the state of the colonies during the revolution, we are told (§ 200) that a congress was recommended by Massachusetts in 1774;

§ 201. Thus was organized under the auspices, and with the consent of the people, acting directly in their primary, sovereign capacity, and without the intervention of the functionaries, to whom the ordinary powers of government were delegated in the colonies, the first general or national government, which has been very aptly called "the revolutionary government," since in its origin and progress it was wholly conducted upon revolutionary principles.* The congress, thus assembled, exercised *de facto* and *de jure* a sovereign authority; not as the delegated agents of the governments *de facto* of the colonies, but in virtue of original powers derived from the people. The revolutionary government, thus formed, terminated only, when it was regularly superceded by the confederated government under the articles finally ratified, as we shall hereafter see, in 1781.†

§ 202. The first and most important of their acts was a declaration, that in determining questions in this congress, each colony or province should have one vote; and this became the established course during the revolution. They proposed a general congress to be held at the same place in May, in the next year. They appointed committees to take into consideration their rights and grievances. They passed resolutions, that "after the 1st of December 1774, there shall be no importation into British America from Great Britain or Ireland of any goods, &c. or from any other place, of any such goods, as shall have been exported from Great Britain or Ireland;" that "after the 10th of September 1775, the exportation of all merchandize, &c. to Great Britain, Ireland, and the West Indies ought to cease, unless the grievances of America are redressed before that time."‡ They adopted a declara- of rights, not differing in substance from that of the congress of 1765,|| and affirming, that the respective colonies are entitled to the common law of England and the benefit of such English statutes, as existed at the time of their colonization, and which they have by experience respectively found to be applicable to their local and other circumstances. They also, in behalf of themselves and their constituents, adopted and signed certain articles of association, containing an agreement of non-importation, non-exportation, and non-consumption, in order to carry into effect the preceding resolves; and also an agreement to discontinue the slave-trade. They also adopted addresses to the people of England, to the neighbouring British colonies, and to the king, explaining their grievances, and requesting aid and redress.

§ 203. In May 1775, a second congress of delegates met from all the states.§ These delegates were chosen, as the preceding had

* 9 Dane's Abridg. App. P. 1, § 5, p. 16, § 13, p. 23.
† Sergeant on Const. Introd. 7, 8, (2d ed.)
‡ 1 Jour. of Cong. 21.
|| See ante, note, p. 179.
§ Georgia did not send delegates until the 15th of July, 1775, who did not take their seats until the 13th of September.

which accordingly met on the 4th of September, and (§ 201) that thus was organized under the auspices and with the consent of the *people*, acting directly in their *pri-*

been, partly by the popular branch of the state legislatures, when in session; but principally by conventions of the people in the various states.* In a few instances the choice of the legislative body was confirmed by that of a convention, and *e converso*.† They immediately adopted a resolution, prohibiting all exportations to Quebec, Nova Scotia, St. Johns, Newfoundland, Georgia, except St. Johns Parish, and East and West Florida.‡ This was followed up by a resolution, that the colonies be immediately put into a state of defence. They prohibited the receipt and negotiation of any British government bills, and the supply of any provisions or necessaries for the British army and navy in Massachusetts or transports in their service.§ They recommended to Massachusetts to consider the offices of governor and lieutenant-governor of that province vacant, and to make choice of a counsel by the representatives in assembly, by whom the powers of government should be exercised, until a governor of the king's appointment should consent to govern the colony according to its charter. They authorized the raising of continental troops, and appointed general Washington commander in chief, to whom they gave a commission in the name of the delegates of the united colonies. They had previously authorized certain military measures, and especially the arming of the militia of New York, and the occupation of Crown Point and Ticonderoga. They authorized the emission of two millions of dollars in bills of credit, pledging the colonies to the redemption thereof. They framed rules for the government of the army, they published a solemn declaration of the causes of their taking up arms, an address to the king, entreating a change of measures, and an address to the people of Great Britain, requesting their aid, and admonishing them of the threatening evils of a separation. They erected a general post-office, and organized the department for all the colonies. They apportioned the quota that each colony should pay of the bills emitted by congress.||

§ 204. At a subsequent adjournment, they authorized the equipment of armed vessels to intercept supplies to the British, and the organization of a marine corps. They prohibited all exportations, except from colony to colony under the inspection of committees. They recommended to New Hampshire, Virginia and South Carolina, to call conventions of the people to establish a form of government.¶ They authorized the grant of commissions to capture armed vessels and transports in the British service; and recom-

* See *Penhallow* v. *Doane*, 3 Dall. 54, and particularly the opinions of Iredell J. and Blair J. on this point. Journals of 1775, p. 73 to 79.

† Journals of Congress of 1775, p. 73 to 79.

‡ Journals of Congress of 1775, p. 103.

§ Journals of Congress of 1775, p. 115.

|| Journals of Congress of 1775, p. 177.

¶ Journals of Congress of 1775, p. 231, 235, 279.

mary sovereign capacity, and without the intervention of the functionaries to whom the ordinary powers of government were delegated, the first *general* or *national* government,

mended the creation of prize courts in each colony, reserving a right of appeal to congress.* They adopted rules for the regulation of the navy, and for the division of prizes and prize money.† They denounced, as enemies, all, who should obstruct or discourage the circulation of bills of credit. They authorized further emissions of bills of credit, and created two military departments for the middle and southern colonies. They authorized general reprisals, and the equipment of private armed vessels against British vessels and property.‡ They organized a general treasury department. They authorized the exportation and importation of all goods to and from foreign countries, not subject to Great Britain, with certain exceptions; and prohibited the importation of slaves; and declared a forfeiture of all prohibited goods.§ They recommended to the respective assemblies and conventions of the colonies, where no government, sufficient to the exigencies, had been established, to adopt such government, as in the opinion of the representatives should best conduce to the happiness and safety of their constituents in particular, and America in general, and adopted a preamble, which stated, "that the exercise of every kind of authority under the crown of Great Britain should be totally suppressed."‖

§ 205. These measures, all of which progressively pointed to a separation from the mother country, and evinced a determination to maintain, at every hazard, the liberties of the colonies, were soon followed by more decisive steps. On the 7th of June 1776, certain resolutions respecting independency were moved, which were referred to a committee of the whole. On the tenth of June it was resolved, that a committee be appointed to prepare a declaration, "that these united colonies are, and of right ought to be, free and independent states; that they are absolved from all allegiance to the British crown; and that all political connexion between them and the state of Great Britain is, and ought to be, dissolved."¶ On the 11th of June a committee was appointed to prepare and digest the form of a confederation to be entered into between the colonies, and also a committee to prepare a plan of treaties to be proposed to foreign powers.** On the 28th of June the committee appointed to prepare a Declaration of Independence brought in a draught. On the second of July, congress adopted the resolution for Independence; and on the 4th of July they adopted the Declaration of Independence; and thereby solemnly

* Journals of Congress of 1775, p. 259, 260, &c.
† Journals of Congress of 1776, p. 13.
‡ Journals of Congress of 1776, p. 106, 107, 118, 119.
§ Journals of Congress of 1776, p. 122, 123.
‖ Journals of Congress of 1776, p. 166, 174.
¶ Journals of Congress of 1776, p. 205, 206.
** Journals of Congress of 1776, p. 207.

and "that the congress thus assembled, exercised *de facto* and *de jure* a sovereign authority; not as *the delegated* agents of the governments *de facto* of the colonies, but in

published and declared, "That these united colonies are, and of right ought to be, free and independent states; that they are absolved from all allegiance to the British crown; and that all political connexion between them and the state of Great Britain is, and ought to be, totally dissolved; and that, as free and independent states, they have full power to levy war, conclude peace, contract alliances, establish commerce, and to do all other acts and things, which independent states may of right do."

§ 206. These minute details have been given, not merely, because they present an historical view of the actual and slow progress towards independence; but because they give rise to several very important considerations respecting the political rights and sovereignty of the several colonies, and of the union, which was thus spontaneously formed by the people of the united colonies.

§ 207. In the first place, antecedent to the Declaration of Independence, none of the colonies were, or pretended to be sovereign states, in the sense, in which the term "sovereign" is sometimes applied to states.* The term "sovereign" or "sovereignty" is used in different senses, which often leads to a confusion of ideas, and sometimes to very mischievous and unfounded conclusions. By "sovereignty" in its largest sense is meant, supreme, absolute, uncontrollable power, the *jus summi imperii*,† the absolute right to govern. A state or nation is a body politic, or society of men, united together for the purpose of promoting their mutal safety and advantage by their combined strength.‡ By the very act of civil and political association, each citizen subjects himself to the authority of the whole; and the authority of all over each member essentially belongs to the body politic.§ A state, which possesses this absolute power, without any dependence upon any foreign power or state, is in the largest sense a sovereign state.‖ And it is wholly immaterial, what is the form of the government, or by whose hands this absolute authority is exercised. It may be exercised by the people at large, as in a pure democracy; or by a select few, as in an absolute aristocracy; or by a single person, as in an absolute monarchy.¶ But "sovereignty" is often used in a far more limited sense, than that, of which we have spoken, to designate such political powers, as in the actual organization of the particular state or nation are to be exclusively exercised by certain public functionaries, without the control of any superior authority. It is in this sense, that Blackstone employs it, when he says, that it is of "the very essence of a law, that it is made by the supreme power. Sovereignty and legislature are,

* 3 Dall. 110. Per Blair J.; 9 Dane's Abridg. Appx. § 2, p. 10, § 3, p. 12, § 5, p. 16.
† 1 Bl. Comm. 49; 2 Dall. 471. Per Jay C. J.
‡ Vattel, B. 1, ch. 1, § 1; 2 Dall. 455. Per Wilson J.
§ Vattel, B. 1, ch. 1, § 2.
‖ 2 Dall. 456, 457. Per Wilson J.
¶ Vattel, B. 1, ch. 1, § 2, 3.

virtue of original powers derived from the people." Now in this short passage there is a material misstatement even according to the learned author himself. He *here* says, that

indeed, convertible terms; one cannot subsist without the other."* Now, in every limited government the power of legislation is, or at least may be, limited at the will of the nation; and therefore the legislature is not in an absolute sense sovereign. It is in the same sense, that Blackstone says, "the law ascribes to the king of England the attribute of sovereignty or pre-eminence,"† because in respect to the powers confided to him, he is dependant on no man, and accountable to no man, and subjected to no superior jurisdiction. Yet the king of England cannot make a law; and his acts, beyond the powers assigned to him by the constitution, are utterly void.

§ 208. In like manner the word "state" is used in various senses. In in its most enlarged sense it means the people composing a particular nation or community. In this sense the state means the whole people, united into one body politic; and the state, and the people of the state, are equivalent expressions.‡ Mr. Justice Wilson in his Law Lectures, uses the word "state" in its broadest sense. "In free states," says he, "the people form an artificial person, or body politic, the highest and noblest, that can be known. They form that moral person, which in one of my former lectures,§ I described, as a complete body of free, natural persons, united together for their common benefit; as having an understanding and a will; as deliberating, and resolving, and acting; as possessed of interests, which it ought to manage; as enjoying rights, which it ought to maintain; and as lying under obligations, which it ought to perform. To this moral person, we assign, by way of eminence, the dignified appellation of "STATE."‖ But there is a more limited sense, in which the word is often used, where it expresses merely the positive or actual organization of the legislative, executive, or judicial powers.¶ Thus, the actual government of a state is frequently designated by the name of *the state.* We say, the state has power to do this or that; the state has passed a law,

* 1 Bl. Comm. 46. See also 1 Tucker's Black. Comm. App. note A., a commentary on this clause of the author's text.

† 1 Bl. Comm. 241.

‡ *Penhallow* v. *Doane*, 1 Peters's Cond. Rep. 37, 38, 39; 3 Dall. R. 93, 94. Per Iredell J. *Chisholm* v. *Georgia*, 2 Dall. 455. Per Wilson J. S. C. 2 Cond. Rep. 656, 670; 2 Wilson's Lect. 120; Dane's Appx. § 50, p. 63.

§ 1 Wilson's Lect. 304, 305.

‖ 2 Wilson's Lect. 120, 121.

¶ Mr. Madison, in his elaborate report in the Virginia legislature in January 1800, adverts to the different senses, in which the word "state" is used. He says, "It is indeed true, that the term 'states' is sometimes used in a vague sense, and sometimes in different senses, according to the subject, to which it is applied. Thus it sometimes means the separate sections of territory, occupied by the political societies within each; sometimes the particular *governments* established by those societies; sometimes those societies, as organized into those particular governments; and lastly, it means *the people*, composing those political societies in their highest sovereign capacity."

"the members of the congress acted not as the delegated agents of the governments *de facto*, but in virtue of original powers derived from the people." And yet in the next

or prohibited an act, meaning no more than, that the proper functionaries, organized for that purpose, have power to do the act, or have passed the law, or prohibited the particular action. The sovereignty of a nation or state, considered with reference to its association, as a body politic, may be absolute and uncontrollable in all respects, except the limitations, which it chooses to impose upon itself.* But the sovereignty of the government, organized within the state, may be of a very limited nature. It may extend to few, or to many objects. It may be unlimited, as to some; it may be restrained, as to others. To the extent of the power given, the government may be sovereign, and its acts may be deemed the sovereign acts of the state. Nay the state, by which we mean the people composing the state, may divide its sovereign powers among various functionaries, and each in the limited sense would be sovereign in respect to the powers, confided to each; and dependent in all other cases.† Strictly speaking, in our republican forms of government, the absolute sovereignty of the nation is in the people of the nation; and the residuary sovereignty of each state, not granted to any of its public functionaries, is in the people of the state.‡

§ 209. There is another mode, in which we speak of a state as sovereign, and that is in reference to foreign states. Whatever may be the internal organization of the government of any state, if it has the sole power of governing itself, and is not dependent upon any foreign state, it is called a *sovereign state;* that is, it is a state having the same rights, privileges, and powers, as other independent states. It is in this sense, that the term is generally used in treatises and discussions on the law of nations. A full consideration of this subject will more properly find place in some future page.§

*2 Dall. 433; Iredell J. Id. 455, 456. Per Wilson J.
†3 Dall. 93. Per Iredell J. 2 Dall. 455, 457. Per Wilson J.
‡2 Dall. 471, 472. Per Jay C. J.
Mr. J. Q. Adams, in his Oration on the 4th of July 1831, published after the preparation of these commentaries, uses the following language: "It is not true, that there must reside in all governments an absolute, uncontrollable, irresistible and despotic power; nor is such power in any manner essential to sovereignty. Uncontrollable power exists in no government on earth. The sternest despotisms in any region and in every age of the world, are and have been under perpetual control. Unlimited power belongs not to man; and rotten will be the foundation of every government, leaning upon such a maxim for its support. Least of all can it be predicated of a government, professing to be founded upon an original compact. The pretence of an absolute irresistible, despotic power, existing in every government somewhere, is incompatible with the first principles of natural right."

§Dr. Rush, in a political communication, in 1786, uses the term "sovereignty" in another, and somewhat more limited sense.* He says, "The people of America have mistaken the meaning of the word 'sovereignty.' Hence each state pretends to be *sovereign.* In Europe it is applied to those states, which possess the power of making war and peace, of forming treaties, and the like.

*1 Amer. Museum, 8, 9.

preceding section we are told that "in some of the legislatures of the colonies, which were then in session, delegates *were appointed by the popular or representative*

§ 210. Now it is apparent, that none of the colonies before the revolution were, in the most large and general sense, independent, or sovereign communities. They were all originally settled under, and subjected to the British crown.* Their powers and authorities were derived from, and limited by their respective charters. All, or nearly all, of these charters controlled their legislation by prohibiting them from making laws repugnant, or contrary to those of England. The crown, in many of them, possessed a negative upon their legislation, as well as the exclusive appointment of their superior officers; and a right of revision, by way of appeal, of the judgments of their courts.† In their most solemn declarations of rights, they admitted themselves bound, as British subjects, to allegiance to the British crown; and as such, they claimed to be entitled to all the rights, liberties and immunities of free born British subjects. They denied all power of taxation, except by their own colonial legislatures; but at the same time they admitted themselves bound by acts of the British parliament for the regulation of external commerce, so as to secure the commercial advantages of the whole empire to the mother country, and the commercial benefits of its respective members ‡ So far, as respects foreign states, the colonies were not, in the sense of the laws of nations, sovereign states; but mere dependencies of Great Britain. They could make no treaty, declare no war, send no ambassadors, regulate no intercourse or commerce, nor in any other shape act, as sovereigns, in the negotiations usual between independent states. In respect to each other, they stood in the common relation of British subjects; the legislation of neither could be controlled by any other; but there was a common subjection to the British crown.§ If in any sense they might claim the attributes of sovereignty, it was only in that subordinate sense, to which we have alluded, as exercising within a limited extent certain usual powers of sovereignty. They did not even affect to claim a local allegiance.‖

§ 211. In the next place, the colonies did not severally act for themselves, and proclaim their own independence. It is true, that

As this power belongs only to congress, they are the only sovereign power in the United States. We commit a similar mistake in our ideas of the word 'independent.' No individual state, as such, has any claim to independence. She is independent only in a union with her sister states in congress." Dr. Barton, on the other hand, in a similar essay, explains the operation of the system of the confederation in the manner, which has been given in the text.*

* 2 Dall. 471. Per Jay, C. J.

† See Marshall's Hist. of Colonies, p. 483; Journal of Congress, 1774, p. 29.

‡ Journal of Congress 1774, p. 27, 29, 38, 39; 1775, p. 152, 156; Marshall's Hist. of Colonies, ch. 14, p. 412, 483.

§ 1 Chalmers's Annals, 686, 687; 2 Dall. 470. Per Jay, C. J.

‖ Journal of Congress, 1776, p. 282; 2 Haz. Coll. 591; Marsh. Colonies, App. No. 3, p. 469.

*1 Amer. Museum, 13, 14.

branch, and in other cases they were appointed by conventions of the people in the colonies. How *many* were appointed in one mode, and how many in the other, I have

some of the states had previously formed incipient governments for themselves; but it was done in compliance with the recommendations of congress.* Virginia, on the 29th of June 1776, by a convention of delegates, declared "the government of this country, as formerly exercised under the crown of Great Britain, totally dissolved;" and proceeded to form a new constitution of government. New Hampshire also formed a government in December 1775, which was manifestly intended to be temporary, "during (as they said) the unhappy and unnatural contest with Great Britain."† New Jersey, too, established a frame of government, on the 2d of July 1776; but it was expressly declared that it should be void upon a reconciliation with Great Britain.‡ And South Carolina, in March 1776, adopted a constitution of government; but this was, in like manner, "established until an accommodation between Great Britain and America could be obtained."§ But the declaration of the independence of all the colonies was the united act of all. It was "a declaration by the representatives of the United States of America in congress assembled;"—"by the delegates appointed by the good people of the colonies," as in a prior declaration of rights they were called.‖ It was not an act done by the state governments then organized; nor by persons chosen by them. It was emphatically the act of the whole *people* of the united colonies, by the instrumentality of their representatives, chosen for that, among other purposes.¶ It was an act not competent to the state governments, or any of them, as organized under their charters, to adopt. Those charters neither contemplated the case, nor provided for it. It was an act of original, inherent sovereignty by the people themselves, resulting from their right to change the form of government, and to institute a new government, whenever necessary for their safety and happiness. So the declaration of independence treats it. No state had presumed of itself to form a new government, or to provide for the exigencies of the times, without consulting congress on the subject; and when they acted, it was in pursuance of the recommendation of congress. It was, therefore, the achievement of the whole for the benefit of the whole. The people of the united colonies made the united colonies free and independent states, and absolved them from all allegiance to the British crown. The declaration of independence has accordingly always been treated, as an act of paramount and sovereign authority, complete and perfect *per se*, and *ipso facto* working an entire dis-

* Journal of Congress, 1775, p. 115, 231, 235, 279; 1 Pitk. Hist. 351, 355; Marsh. Colon. ch. 14, p. 441, 447; 9 Hening's Stat. 112, 113; 9 Dane's Abridg. App. § 5, p. 16.

† 2 Belk. N. Hamp. ch. 25, p. 306, 308, 310; 1 Pitk. Hist. 351, 355.

‡ Stokes's Hist. Colon. 51, 75.

§ Stokes's Hist. Colon. 105; 1 Pitk. Hist. 355.

‖ Journal 1776, p. 241; Journal 1774, p. 27, 45.

¶ 2 Dall. 470, 471. Per Jay, C. J.; 9 Dane's Abridg. App. § 12, 13, p. 23, 24.

not at hand the means of ascertaining. It is sufficient that *part* of the members were appointed by the acting governments, to disarm the argument of all its force, if indeed it

solution of all political connexion with and allegiance to Great Britain. And this, not merely as a practical fact, but in a legal and constitutional view of the matter by courts of justice.*

§ 212. In the debates in the South Carolina legislature, in January 1788, respecting the propriety of calling a convention of the people to ratify or reject the constitution, a distinguished statesman† used the following language: "This admirable manifesto (i. e. the declaration of independence) sufficiently refutes the doctrine of the individual sovereignty and independence of the several states. In that declaration the several states are not even enumerated; but after reciting in nervous language, and with convincing arguments, our right to independence, and the tyranny, which compelled us to assert it, the declaration is made in the following words: 'We, therefore, the representatives of the United States, &c. do, in the name, &c. of the good people of these colonies, solemnly publish, &c. that these united colonies are, and of right ought to be, free and independent states.' The separate independence and individual sovereignty of the several states were never thought of by the enlightened band of patriots, who framed this declaration. The several states are not even mentioned by name in any part, as if it was intended to impress the maxim on America, that our freedom and independence arose from our union, and that without it we could never be free or independent. Let us then consider all attempts to weaken this union by maintaining, that each state is separately and individually independent, as a species of political heresy, which can never benefit us, but may bring on us the most serious distresses."‡

* 2 Dallas's R. 470.

† Mr. Charles Cotesworth Pinckney.

‡ Debates in South Carolina, 1788, printed by A. E. Miller, Charleston, 1831, p. 43, 44.—Mr. Adams, in his Oration on the 4th of July 1831, which is valuable for its views of constitutional principles, insists upon the same doctrine at considerable length. Though it has been published since the original preparation of these lectures, I gladly avail myself of an opportunity to use his authority in corroboration of the same views. "The union of the colonies had preceded this declaration, [of independence,] and even the commencement of the war. The declaration was joint, that the united colonies were free and independent states, but not that any one of them was a free and independent state, separate from the rest."—"The declaration of independence was a social compact, by which the whole people covenanted with each citizen, and each citizen with the whole people, that the united colonies were, and of right ought to be, free and independent states. To this compact union was as vital, as freedom or independence."—"The declaration of independence announced the severance of the thirteen united colonies from the rest of the British empire, and the existence of their people from that day forth as an independent nation. The people of all the colonies, speaking by their representatives, constituted themselves one moral person before the face of their fellow men."—"The declaration of independence was not a declaration of liberty merely acquired, nor was it a form of government. The people of the colonies were already free, and their forms of government were various. They were all colonies of a monarchy. The king of Great Britain was their common sovereign."

possessed any. It would be sufficient to demonstrate that the popular branch of the state legislatures were in part at least represented in congress, as political bodies, and that

§ 213. In the next place we have seen, that the power to do this act was not derived from the state governments; nor was it done generally with their co-operation. The question then naturally presents itself, if it is to be considered as a national act, in what manner did the colonies become a nation, and in what manner did congress become possessed of this national power? The true answer must be, that as soon as congress assumed powers and passed measures, which were in their nature national, to that extent the people, from whose acquiescence and consent they took effect, must be considered as agreeing to form a nation.* The congress of 1774, looking at the general terms of the commissions, under which the delegates were appointed, seem to have possessed the power of concerting such measures, as they deemed best, to redress the grievances, and preserve the rights and liberties of all the colonies. Their duties seem to have been principally of an advisory nature; but the exigencies of the times led them rather to follow out the wishes and objects of their constituents, than scrupulously to examine the words, in which their authority was communicated.† The congress of 1775 and 1776 were clothed with more ample powers, and the language of their commissions generally was sufficiently broad to embrace the right to pass measures of a national character and obligation. The caution necessary at that period of the revolutionary struggle rendered that language more guarded, than the objects really in view would justify; but it was foreseen, that the spirit of the people would eagerly second every measure adopted to further a general union and resistance against the British claims. The congress of 1775 accordingly assumed at once (as we have seen) the exercise of some of the highest functions of sovereignty. They took measures for national defence and resistance; they followed up the prohibitions upon trade and intercourse with Great Britain; they raised a national army and navy, and authorized limited national hostilities against Great Britain; they raised money, emitted bills of credit, and contracted debts upon national account; they established a national post office; and finally they authorized captures and condemnation of prizes in prize courts, with a reserve of appellate jurisdiction to themselves.

§ 214. The same body, in 1776, took bolder steps, and exerted powers, which could in no other manner be justified or accounted for, than upon the supposition, that a national union for national purposes already existed, and that the congress was invested with sovereign power over all the colonies for the purpose of preserving the common rights and liberties of all. They accordingly authorized general hostilities against the persons and property of British

* 3 Dall. R. 80, 81, 90, 91, 109, 110, 111, 117.
† 3 Dall. R. 91.

the congress was in fact not national but federative in its character. But this is placed beyond all reasonable question by two considerations, to neither of which has the learned author thought fit to advert.

subjects; they opened an extensive commerce with foreign countries, regulating the whole subject of imports and exports; they authorized the formation of new governments in the colonies; and finally they exercised the sovereign prerogative of dissolving the allegiance of all colonies to the British crown. The validity of these acts was never doubted, or denied by the people. On the contrary, they became the foundation, upon which the superstructure of the liberties and independence of the United States has been erected. Whatever, then, may be the theories of ingenious men on the subject, it is historically true, that before the declaration of independence these colonies were not, in any absolute sense, sovereign states; that that event did not find them or make them such; but that at the moment of their separation they were under the dominion of a superior controlling national government, whose powers were vested in and exercised by the general congress with the consent of the people of all the states.*

§ 215. From the moment of the declaration of independence, if not for most purposes at an antecedent period, the united colonies must be considered as being a nation *de facto*, having a general government over it created, and acting by the general consent of the people of all the colonies. The powers of that government were not, and indeed could not be well defined. But still its exclusive sovereignty, in many cases, was firmly established; and its controlling power over the states was in most, if not in all national measures, universally admitted.† The articles of confederation, of which we shall have occasion to speak more hereafter, were not prepared or adopted by congress until November 1777;‡ they were not signed or ratified by any of the states until July 1778; and they were not ratified, so as to become obligatory upon all the states, until March 1781. In the intermediate time, con-

* This whole subject is very amply discussed by Mr. Dane in his Appendix to the 9th volume of his Abridgement of the Laws; and many of his views coincide with those stated in the text. The whole of that Appendix is worthy of the perusal of every constitutional lawyer, even though he might differ from some of the conclusions of the learned author. He will there find much reasoning from documentary evidence of a public nature, which has not hitherto been presented in a condensed or accurate shape.

Some interesting views of this subject are also presented in president Monroe's message on internal improvements, on the 4th of May 1822, appended to his message respecting the Cumberland road. See, especially, pages 8 and 9.

When Mr. chief justice Marshall, in *Ogden* v. *Gibbons*, (9 Wheat. R. 187,) admits, that the states, before the formation of the constitution, were sovereign and independent, and were connected with each other only by a league, it is manifest, that he uses the word "sovereign" in a very restricted sense. Under the confederation there were many limitations upon the powers of the states.

† See *Penhallow* v. *Doane*, 3 Dall. R. 54; *Ware* v. *Hylton*, 3 Dall. 199, per Chase J. See the Circular Letter of Congress, 13th September 1779; 5 Jour. Cong. 341, 348, 349.

‡ Jour. of Cong. 1777, p. 502.

In the first place, it is an historical fact that these very conventions, which in some of the states elected members to the congress of 1774, constituted at that time the legis-

gress continued to exercise the powers of a general government, whose acts were binding on all the states. And though they constantly admitted the states to be "sovereign and independent communities;"* yet it must be obvious, that the terms were used in the subordinate and limited sense already alluded to; for it was impossible to use them in any other sense, since a majority of the states could by their public acts in congress control and bind the minority. Among the exclusive powers exercised by congress, were the power to declare war and make peace; to authorize captures; to institute appellate prize courts; to direct and control all national, military, and naval operations; to form alliances, and make treaties; to contract debts, and issue bills of credit upon national account. In respect to foreign governments, we were politically known as the United States only; and it was in our national capacity, as such, that we sent and received ambassadors, entered into treaties and alliances, and were admitted into the general community of nations, who might exercise the right of belligerents, and claim an equality of sovereign powers and prerogatives.†

§ 216. In confirmation of these views, it may not be without use to refer to the opinions of some of our most eminent judges, delivered on occasions, which required an exact examination of the subject. In *Chisholm's Executors* v. *The State of Georgia*, (2 Dall. 419, 470,‡) Mr. chief justice Jay, who was equally distinguished as a revolutionary statesman and a general jurist, expressed himself to the following effect: "The revolution, or rather the declaration of independence, found the *people* already united for general purposes, and at the same time providing for their more domestic concerns by state conventions, and other temporary arrangements. From the crown of Great Britian the sovereignty of their country passed to the *people* of it; and it was then not an uncommon opinion, that the unappropriated lands, which belonged to that crown, passed, not to the people of the colony or states, within whose limits they were situated, but to the *whole people*. On whatever principle this opinion rested, it did not give way to the other; and *thirteen sovereignties* were considered as emerging from the principles of the revolution, combined by local convenience and considerations. The people, nevertheless, continued to consider themselves, in a national point of view, as *one people;* and they continued without interruption to manage their national concerns accordingly." In *Penhallow* v. *Doane*, (3 Dall. R. 54,||) Mr. justice Patterson (who was also a revolutionary statesman) said, speaking of the period before the ratification of the confederation:

* See Letter of 17th Nov. 1777, by Congress, recommending the articles of confederation; Journal of 1777, p. 513, 514.

† 1 Amer. Museum, 15; 1 Kent. Comm. 197, 198, 199.

‡ S. C. 1 Peters's Cond. R. 635.

|| S. C. 1 Peters's Cond. Rep. 21.

lative bodies of the respective states. They had been substituted for the legislatures appointed under the crown, and passed laws of a municipal nature as well as of a political

"The powers of congress were revolutionary in their nature, arising out of events adequate to every national emergency, and co-extensive with the object to be attained. Congress was the general, supreme, and controlling council of the nation, the centre of the union, the centre of force, and the sun of the political system. Congress raised armies, fitted out a navy, and prescribed rules for their government, &c. &c. These high acts of sovereignty were submitted to, acquiesced in, and approved of by the *people* of America, &c. &c. The danger being imminent and common, it became necessary for the people or colonies to coalesce and act in concert, in order to divert, or break the violence of the gathering storm. They accordingly grew into union, and formed one great political body, of which congress was the directing principle and soul, &c. &c. The truth is, that the states, individually, were not known, nor recognized as sovereign by foreign nations, nor are they now. The states collectively under congress, as their connecting point or head, were acknowledged by foreign powers, as sovereign, particularly in that acceptation of the term, which is applicable to all great national concerns, and in the exercise of which other sovereigns would be more immediately interested. In *Ware* v. *Hylton*, (3 Dall. 199,*) Mr. justice Chase (himself also a revolutionary statesman) said: "It has been inquired, what powers congress possessed from the first meeting in September 1774, until the ratification of the confederation on the 1st of March 1781. It appears to me, that the powers of congress during that whole period were derived from the *people* they represented, expressly given through the medium of their state conventions or state legislatures; or, that after they were exercised, they were impliedly ratified by the acquiescence and obedience of the *people*, &c. The powers of congress originated from necessity, and arose out of it, and were only limited by events; or, in other words, they were revolutionary in their nature. Their extent depended on the exigencies and necessities of public affairs. I entertain this general idea, that the several states retained all internal sovereignty; and that congress properly possessed the rights of external sovereignty. In deciding on the powers of congress, and of the several states before the confederation, I see but one safe rule, namely, that all the powers actually exercised by congress before that period were rightfully exercised, on the presumption not to be controverted, that they were so authorized by the people they represented, by an express or implied grant; and that all the powers exercised by the state conventions or state legislatures were also rightfully exercised, on the same presumption of authority from the people."†

* S. C. 1 Peters's Cond. R. 99.

† See also 1 Kent. Comm. Lect. 10, p. 196; President Monroe's Exposition and Message, 4th of May 1822, p. 8, 9, 10, 11.

character. They were as much the government *de facto*, then, as the legislature at ordinary periods, and in the appointment of delegates to congress, they no more acted in virtue of original powers, derived from the people, than the ordinary legislature in ordinary times. They constituted, indeed, the legislature for those extraordinary times; for the interregnum; for the revolutionary struggle. The appointment of members of congress by them was therefore no more the direct action of the people, as contradistinguished from the government, than that appointment by the legislatures in other states. Still less was any such appointment the act of the people in a national character, as one people, as contradistinguished from their act in their distinct political characters, as independent states. This brings me to observe,

Secondly, that on the question whether the appointment of members of congress was an act of the people, as constituting one nation or not, it is utterly unimportant whether it was made by legislature or convention,—by the representatives of the people, or even by the people themselves *in plenis commitiis*. Justice Story tells us they were acting "in their primary sovereign capacity, and with-

§ 217. In respect to the powers of the continental congress exercised before the adoption of the articles of confederation, few questions were judicialy discussed during the revolutionary contest; for men had not leisure in the heat of war nicely to scrutinize or weigh such subjects; *inter arma silent leges*. The people, relying on the wisdom and patriotism of congress, silently acquiesced in whatever authority they assumed. But soon after the organization of the present government, the question was most elaborately discussed before the supreme court of the United States, in a case calling for an exposition of the appellate jurisdiction of congress in prize causes before the ratification of the confederation.* The result of that examination was, as the opinions already cited indicate, that congress, before the confederation, possessed, by the consent of the people of the United States, sovereign and supreme powers for national purposes; and among others, the supreme powers of peace and war, and, as an incident, the right of entertaining appeals in the last resort in prize causes, even in opposition to state legislation. And that the actual powers exercised by congress, in respect to national objects, furnished the best exposition of its constitutional authority, since they emanated from the representatives of the people, and were acquiesced in by the people.

* *Penhallow* v. *Doane*, 3 Dall. 54, 80, 83, 90, 91, 94, 109, 110, 111, 112, 117; Journals of Congress, March 1779, p. 86 to 88; 1 Kent. Comm. 198, 199.

out the intervention of the ordinary functionaries." Admit it. But in what sovereign capacity? In the capacity of *one* people, composing *one* political society, and *one* sovereignty throughout British America, or as *separate* people of *distinct* political societies, uniting together as such for common defence and the maintenance of rights which were common to them all? This is the true issue, and history leaves no doubt how it should be decided. The colonies had always been independent of each other, though subject to the crown. The king was the only knot which bound them together. Did the cutting off the common head unite them into one body? Did cutting the knot have the effect of binding them more closely instead of leaving, to each, entire sovereignty and independence, except so far as it might be voluntarily vested in a common agent, the congress of the United States? Surely not. By cutting the only bond which served to hold them together, they became separate and independent states. Their rebellion was not as one people, but as thirteen states. They were not bound to rebel together; for Canada, which stood in the same position with themselves, never did rebel, and the thirteen states had no right to compel her to do so.(*b*) We can look upon them as acting in no other manner than as communities distinct and independent of each other, each resolving for itself, judging for itself, acting for itself. And so they looked upon themselves. They were *commanded* by no authority to assemble in congress. The measure was simply recommended by one of the sister states. The members were appointed in each state according to its own

(*b*) "When the obnoxious acts passed," says judge Iredell, 3 Dall. 92, "if the people in each province had chosen to resist *separately*, they undoubtedly had equal right to do so as to join in general measures of resistance with the people of the other provinces, however unwise and destructive such a policy might and undoubtedly would have been."—"If congress previously to the articles of confederation possesed any authority, it was an authority derived from the people of *each* province in the first instance." "I conclude, therefore, that every particle of authority which originally resided either in congress, or in any branch of the state governments, was derived from the *people of each province*: that this authority was conveyed by *each body politic separately*, and *not by all the people* in the several provinces or states *jointly*, and of course that no authority could be conveyed to the whole but that which previously was possessed by the several parts," &c.

pleasure, under its own electoral regulations, and with powers and discretion prescribed by each, and were, moreover, liable to recall. The members when elected voted by states ;(c) giving to the smallest state in the Union the same weight in the deliberations of the body with the largest. This is of itself conclusive of the character of the body, as representing, not one great people, but thirteen independent states, who thus united in action and in council for common benefit. But this is not all :—every thing in our revolutionary annals distinctly proves, that congress represented states alone, and acted only upon states. Its wants were supplied by requisitions : its commissions were countersigned by the states. It powers were at first little more than advisory, though the exigencies of the revolution compelled them on many occasions to extend them. 3 Dall. 91. As soon as the provinces took up arms, *each* state stood of itself as rebel, or *quasi* sovereign : each in that character assumed upon itself to act ; each in that character might have treated and made peace. That character they held before a congress was appointed. In that character they stood when it was created. It was the creature of those who were *de facto* sovereign ; and all its powers were not only derivative, but derivative from bodies politic, or societies of people distinct and separate, in the assumed character of sovereign, during the convulsions of the time. Notwithstanding the existence, also, of the congress, the states exercised every attribute of sovereignty. Among the memorable instances of this was the act of this venerable commonwealth, the common mother of us all, in declaring herself independent anterior to the 4th of July 1776, and before that measure had been adopted by the thirteen states in congress assembled. Such was assuredly the effect of the resolutions of the Virginia convention on the 15th day of May 1776. By those resolutions it was distinctly declared, that " there was no alternative left but abject submission or total separation ;" it was therefore recommended to congress to make a general declaration of independence for all the states, and a committee was appointed to prepare a declaration of rights and a plan of government ; all of which was equivalent to an assertion by the state of

(c) 1 Story, § 202.

her right to self-government, and to take her stand as an independent power among the nations of the earth. And so the ablest minds have ever regarded it. Postponing for a while, a quotation from judge Upshur's Review of a most interesting passage upon this subject, I shall here offer the vigorous remarks of a very able judge in support of my positions. They were delivered in the celebrated case of *Ware* v. *Hylton*, 3 Dall. 199. In that case, it is said by Mr. Marshall, (afterwards chief justice of the United States,) that it had been *conceded* in the argument that Virginia in 1777 was an independent state, and as such, competent to pass confiscation laws. In delivering his opinion in the case, judge Chase declares the right of confiscation (which is a *jus belli*, belonging to the sovereign alone,) to have resided only in the legislature of Virginia in relation to the claims of her enemy's people within her territories. He then proceeds: "It is worthy of remembrance, that delegates and representatives were elected by the people of the several counties and corporations of Virginia, to meet in *general convention*, for the purpose of framing a NEW government, by the authority of *the people only;* and that the said convention met on the 6th of May, and continued in session until the 5th of July 1776; and, in virtue of their *delegated* power, established a constitution, or form of government, to regulate and determine by *whom*, and in *what manner*, the authority of *the people* of Virginia was *thereafter* to be executed. As *the people* of that country were the genuine source and fountain of *all* power, that could be *rightfully* exercised within its limits; they had therefore an unquestionable *right* to grant it to whom they pleased, and under what restrictions or limitations they thought proper. *The people* of Virginia, by their constitution or *fundamental* law, granted and delegated all their supreme civil power to a *legislature*, an *executive* and a *judiciary;* The *first* to make; the *second* to execute; and the last to declare or expound, the laws of the commonwealth. This abolition of the *old* government, and this establishment of a *new* one, was the highest act of power that any people can exercise. From the moment *the people* of Virginia exercised *this power*, all dependence on, and connexion with, Great Britain, absolutely and forever ceased; and no *formal* declaration of independence was necessary, although a decent respect for the opinions of mankind required a declaration of the causes, which impelled the separation; and was proper to give notice of the event to the nations of Europe. I hold it as unquestionable, that the *legislature* of Virginia, established as I have stated by the authority of the people, was forever thereafter invested with the *supreme and sovereign power of the state*, and with authority to make any *laws* in their discretion, to affect the *lives, liberties* and *property* of all the citizens of that commonwealth, *with this exception only*, that such laws should not be repugnant to the *constitution* or *fundamental* law, which could be subject only to the control of the *body of the nation*, in cases not to be defined, and which *will always* provide for themselves. The *legislative* power of every nation can only be restrained by its *own constitution:* and it is the duty of its courts of justice not to question the *validity* of any law made in pursuance of the constitution. There is no question but the act of the Virginia legislature (of the 20th of October 1777) was within the authority granted to them by *the people* of that country; and this being admitted, it is a necessary result, that the law is obligatory on the courts of Virginia, and, in my opinion, on the courts of the United States. If Virginia, as a sovereign state, violated the ancient or modern law of nations, in making the law of the 20th of October 1777, she was answerable in her *political* capacity to the British nation, whose subjects have been injured in consequence of that law. Suppose a general right to confiscate British property, is admitted to be in congress, and congress had confiscated all British property within the United States, including private debts, would it be permitted to contend in any court of the United States, that congress had no power to confiscate such *debts*, by the *modern* law of nations? If the *right* is conceded to be in congress, it necessarily follows, that she is the judge of the exercise of the right, as to the *extent, mode* and *manner*. The same reasoning is strictly applicable to Virginia, if considered a *sovereign nation;* provided she had not delegated such power to congress, before the making of the law of October 1777, which I will hereafter consider.

"In June 1776, the convention of Virginia *formally* declared, that Virginia was a free, sovereign and independent state; and on the 4th of July 1776, following, the United States in congress assembled, declared the thirteen united colonies free and independent states; and that as *such*, they had full power to levy war, conclude peace, &c. I consider this as a declaration, not that the united colonies *jointly*, in a *collective* capacity, were independent states, &c., but that *each* of them was a sovereign and independent state; that is, that *each* of them had a right to govern itself by its own authority, and its own laws, without any control from any other power upon earth.

"*Before* these solemn acts of separation from the crown of Great Britain, the war between Great Britian and the united colonies, *jointly* and *separately*, was *a civil* war; but *instantly*, on that great and ever memorable event, the war changed its *nature*, and became a PUBLIC war between *independent governments;* and immediately thereupon ALL the *rights* of *public* war (and all the other rights of an independent nation) attached to the government of Virginia; and all the *former political* connexion between Great Britian and Virginia, and also between their respective subjects, were totally dissolved; and not only the *two nations*, but all the subjects of each, were in a state of war; precisely as in the present war between Great Britain and France. Vatt. Lib. 3, c. 18, s. 292 to 295; lib. 3, c. 5, s. 70, 72 and 73.

"From the 4th of July 1776, the American states were *de facto*, as well as *de jure*, in the possession and actual exercise of *all* the *rights* of independent governments. On the 6th of February 1778, the king of France entered into a treaty of *alliance* with the United States; and on the 8th of October 1782, a treaty of amity and commerce was concluded between the United States and the states general of the United Provinces. I have ever considered it as the established doctrine of the United States, that their independence originated from, and commenced with, the declaration of congress, on the 4th of July 1776; and that *no other period* can be fixed on for its commencement; and that all laws made by the legislatures of the several states, *after* the declaration of independence, were the laws of sovereign and independent governments."

To these remarks of judge Chase, it may be added that in *Penhallow* v. *Doane*,(*d*) judge Iredell very clearly sustains the same positions, contending that the *jus belli* belonged at first to the states as sovereign, and was not possessed by congress unless given by all the states.

Notwithstanding these strong judicial opinions, and the historical facts on which they rest, we find Mr. Story reiterating the remark "that antecedent to the declaration of independence, none of the colonies *pretended* to be sovereign states in the sense in which the term sovereign is sometimes applied to states:" and again, "before the revolution none were independent or sovereign communities;" and again, "from the moment of the declaration of independence, *if not for most purposes*, at an antecedent period, the United Colonies must be considered as a *nation de facto*, having a general government over it created, and acting by the general consent of the people of all the colonies;" obviously meaning as one nation. And again, "Before the declaration of independence the colonies were not, in any absolute sense, sovereign states. That event did not find or make them such; but at the moment of separation,(*e*) they were under the dominion of a superior controlling national government, whose powers were vested in and exercised by the general congress with the consent of the people of all the states;" meaning obviously as *one people*.

These opinions are utterly at war with the first principles of our federal government, as they have been received and handed down to us by the wisest and purest statesmen of both parties. According to these views, the states never have been sovereign and independent! According to these views, "at the moment of the separation of the colonies from Great Britain, they were under the dominion of a superior controlling *national government*(*f*) *whose powers*

(*d*) 3 Dall. 92, 93, 94.

(*e*) "From the crown of Great Britain the sovereignty of this country passed to the people of it," says chief justice Jay very truly. But to what people? Not to the whole people of the United States as one people, for there was none such, but to the people of the respective states. See *post*.

(*f*) Anterior to the declaration of independence the states still recognized the supremacy of England, and still looked to her as their sovereign. Congress was in no sense a sovereign or a go-

were vested in and exercised by the general congress with the consent of the *people of all the states!!!*" The states then are not the fountains of power; they are not the grantors, but the grantees; not the dispensers, but the recipients; and as a fair corollary, from these positions, all powers not granted TO the states, are reserved to the general government!!!

It is obvious that these startling principles should be carefully examined before they are adopted. However great the name under which they are put forth, it is not greater than those of the wise and good who have gone before him, who have ever looked upon the states as great political bodies, endued with all the attributes of sovereignty, and the source from whence the general government of the Union draws all its powers.

Let us then first examine the position that at the moment of the separation, in other words, at the date of the declaration of independence, "the colonies were under the dominion of a superior controlling national government, whose powers were vested in and exercised by the general congress with the consent of the people of all the states."

I have already sufficiently shewn that under British domination, the colonies, though subject to the crown, were independent of each other; and that the cutting the only bond which in any manner connected them, could not have the effect of binding them more closely than they had been bound before under their common head. Its obvious effect, on the contrary, was to separate entirely the thirteen distinct political societies, until by some act of their own they should form a connexion, more or less close, according to their pleasure. If this was so, it implies the existence of *sovereignty* in *each* from the moment of separation. Judge Story quotes Ch. justice Jay, who says that

vernment, but the great organ of a revolution, whose termination was yet hidden from mortal ken. The war was, until July 4, 1776, a civil war, and congress was not looked upon by foreign powers as competent to be treated with until that date, nor did the states indeed consider themselves as individually or collectively constituting a nation. At the moment of the declaration each state emerged into sovereignty and independence, and from that moment till the confederation congress was their organ, and had no legitimate authority but that which their commissions gave to the delegates of each.

from the crown of Great Britain the sovereignty of this country passed to the *people* of it. And this is true when properly understood. A revolting colony in throwing off the authority of the mother country, becomes itself invested with the attributes of sovereignty. *Each* of the thirteen revolting colonies, therefore, in throwing off the authority of Great-Britain became itself a sovereign. The crown had the sovereignty over each, but as they were communities independent of each other, the sovereignty when thrown off passed to the *people of each*, and not to the people of the *whole*, for they never had constituted *one whole*. The *whole* continent was not *our* country. Virginia was *our* country, and the government of Virginia passed of course to the people of Virginia, and, accordingly, in this same passage we find chief justice Jay admitting that "*thirteen sovereigns* were considered as emerging from the principles of the revolution, combined by local convenience and considerations." They were indeed combined, but combined as states or sovereigns, investing in a general congress formed by their respective delegates (representing them as states) a government for the conduct of their combined interests amid the throes of a revolution. What was the character of this government, of this national authority, vested in the general congress? First, in regard to its formation, was it national or confederate? The answer is easy; it was confederate as far as it was a government at all. The delegates were appointed by the *states*, not by the people; sometimes, indeed, by conventions, but they were conventions, who as much represented the state as the legislatures could do. Moreover, in the deliberations of congress they voted by states, the smallest having equal weight with the largest; a test of confederate character which has been universally admitted. Moreover, each delegation obeyed its own state; each was removable by its own state, so that the congress partook in no small degree of the character of a congress of ambassadors. But, secondly, this general congress, (if government it could be called) was merely revolutionary. It grew up out of the necessities of the times. It was not constituted or established as a government. It was assembled upon recommendation merely, which no state was bound to obey. It acted by recommendation mainly. It had no prescribed authority. Its powers were not, and could not, well indeed be defined. It continued to exercise the powers of a general government, whose acts were respected and concurred in by the states. It *constantly* admitted the states to be sovereign and independent communities. (1 Story, p. 204.) It exercised its powers by a *sufferance* growing out of the situation of the country, which had not yet been able to form any regular government; and the *acquiescence* of the *states* constituted its justification for the broad powers it often found itself compelled to exercise. Such were the powers of war and peace; of forming treaties and alliances; authorizing captures; establishing courts of prizes, &c. None of these were *conferred*, but they were exercised and *acquiesced* in, because the exigencies of the cause in which we were engaged in common, imperiously demanded it. Lastly, this revolutionary government was ephemeral. The withdrawal of the delegates would have dissolved it, and any state at pleasure might have withdrawn its own, and then it would have been no longer bound by the acts of congress. Moreover, being merely revolutionary, it may be considered as limited at farthest by the continuance of hostilities. Peace would have withered it forever, for it had grown only out of the necessities of revolution and war. It lasted not indeed till peace. It was found but a rope of sand, and in June 1778 the confederation was adopted by all the states except Maryland and Delaware. Justly then has it been admitted by judge Story, that the union of the states, anterior to that time, "grew out of the exigencies of the times; and from its nature and objects might be deemed temporary, extending only to the maintenance of the common liberties and independence of the states, and to *terminate* with the return of peace with Great Britain and the accomplishment of the ends of the revolutionary contest." It was under this ephemeral government—this government of *sufferance;* this government, the creature of their own will, and capable of being dissolved at a moment by their own breath, that the states are said to have been at the time of the separation. With what propriety could it be intimated by judge Story that they were "under the dominion of a *superior controlling national government,*" at the time of the adoption of the declaration of independence?

It is, indeed, most singular that judge Story should so obstinately contend for the existence of this superior controlling power, when he admits that the powers of congress were *assumed* in most instances, and only acquiesced in by the tacit consent of the states. Can this exercise of the powers of government by *sufferance* constitute sovereignty or supreme controlling power? Were not the acts of congress, indeed, the acts of the states themselves through their own servants, their delegates? How could that be a controlling power *over* them, which was exerted *by* them, and not by others having authority over them. In other words, how could the delegates of the states, who were their servants, have supreme control over those who were confessedly their masters. Judge Story indeed contends that it was impossible to consider the states as sovereign, because the majority of the states could bind the minority. But when was it ever otherwise in any confederacy or union of states, however cautiously they may have guarded their sovereign powers? In every confederacy that ever existed, whether formal or informal, this has been the case. Yet who ever dreamed that the sovereignty of the states was swallowed up in their *confederacy?* *That* sovereignty is essential to *its existence.* It may, indeed, invest the exercise of certain powers in a congress of ambassadors or delegates, but the sovereignty itself is unimpaired, since the power which is given is vicarious, and but the emanation of its own free will. Thus it is even under our constitution which has so many features of nationality, judge Story himself acknowledges the states to be still sovereign,(*g*) notwithstanding the national character he attributes to the constitution. And thus it was, too, under the confederation. The second section of the articles expressly declares the sovereignty and independence of each of the states; and yet in all its action a minority of states was bound by the decision of a majority. It is then no proof of the loss of their sovereignty that each state was bound by its own consent, by the decision of the majority of all the states in congress assembled. It was necessary

(*g*) In *Martin* v. *Hunter*, 1 Wheat. 304.

that the states should coalesce,(*h*) or act in concert, and this action could never have been expected had unanimity been made necessary.

It is also often remarked, with an air of triumph, that during the revolutionary war, the states *individually* were not known nor recognized as sovereign by foreign nations. But the answer is plain: The *states*, collectively, under congress, as their connecting point or head, were acknowledged by foreign powers as sovereign, and treated with as such; and the states, even under our present constitution, are acknowledged to be sovereign states, though they are not recognized by foreign nations in their intercourse as such.

Judge Story, after quoting judges Patterson and Jay, proceeds to quote judge Chase in page 206, on this subject of the sovereignty of the states, anterior to the final adoption of the articles of confederation; but, unfortunately, he has omitted the most forcible passages in the opinion of that able judge, militating against the positions he himself so zealously maintains. This may be seen by comparing the opinion already cited, *ante*, pa. 46, with the extract in judge Story's work. "I consider," says judge Chase "the declaration of independence as a declaration, *not that the United Colonies jointly, in a collective capacity, were independent states, but that* EACH *of them was an* INDEPENDENT STATE; that is, that each of them had a right to govern itself by its own authority, and its own laws, *without any control from any other power upon earth*."

It seems to me not unworthy of remark, that the learned commentator, in the frequent use of the term "union," seems never to have duly adverted to its only legitimate use in its application to political societies. He speaks familiarly of the union existing anterior to the declaration of independence. He says, "the *union* might be deemed temporary, extending only to the maintenance of common liberty and independence of the states." "Union!" What does it imply? Previous separation and disunion of parts? If so, then the proposition is surrendered as to the original

(*h*) Per Patterson, justice. The idea of coalescing between political bodies implies sovereignty in each, and admits they were not coalesced before.

unity or *oneness* of the colonies. And of *what* was this *union?* Was it of individuals or of political bodies? If used in relation to the last, it is intelligible, but if applied to the former, it is entirely unrecognized by the political vocabulary. We speak of forming or dissolving a union in reference to states, but no one ever dreamed of calling a national government a union, or of breaking up the very foundations of society itself, when he speaks of dissolution of an union.

After thus presenting some of my own views on this interesting topic, I beg leave to add from the author before cited, his much more satisfactory refutation of the heretical notion of the *oneness* of the colonies and of the states anterior to the declaration of independence:

"In the execution of the second division of his plan, very little was required of the author either as a historian or as a commentator. Accordingly, he has alluded but slightly to the condition of the colonies, during the existence of the revolutionary government, and has sketched with great rapidity, yet sufficiently in detail, the rise, decline and fall of the confederation. Even here, however, he has fallen into some errors, and has ventured to express decisive and important opinions without due warrant. The desire to make 'the people of the United States' one consolidated nation, is so strong and predominant, that it breaks forth, often uncalled for, in every part of his work. He tells us that the first congress of the revolution was 'a general or national government;' that it 'was organized under the auspices and with the consent of *the people*, acting directly in their primary, sovereign capacity, and without the intervention of the functionaries to whom the ordinary powers of government were delegated in the colonies.' He acknowledges that the powers of this congress were but ill-defined; that many of them were exercised by mere usurpation, and were acquiesced in by the people, only from the confidence reposed in the wisdom and patriotism of its members, and because there was no proper opportunity, during the pressure of the war, to raise nice questions of the powers of government. And yet he infers, from the exercise of powers thus ill-defined, and in great part, usurped, that 'from the moment of the declaration of independence, if not for most purposes, at an antecedent period, the united colonies must be considered as being a nation *de facto*,' &c.

"A very slight attention to the history of the times will place this subject in its true light. The colonies complained of oppressions from the mother country, and were anxious to devise some means by which their grievances might be redressed. These grievances were common to all of them; for England made no discrimination between them, in the general course of her colonial policy. Their rights, as British subjects, had never been well defined; and some of the most important of those rights, as asserted by themselves, had been denied by the British crown. As early as 1765 a majority of the colonies had met together in congress, or convention, in New York, for the purpose of deliberating on these grave matters of common concern; and they then made a formal declaration of what they considered their rights, as colonists and British subjects. This measure, however, led to no redress of their grievances. On the contrary, the subsequent measures of the British government gave new and just causes of complaint; so that, in 1774, it was deemed necessary that the colonies should again meet together, in order to consult upon their general condition, and provide for the safety of their common rights. Hence the congress which met at Carpenter's hall, in Philadelphia, on the 5th of September 1774. It consisted of delegates from New Hampshire, Massachusetts Bay, Rhode Island and Providence Plantations, Connecticut, *from the city and county of New York, and other counties in the province of New York*, New Jersey, Pennsylvania, *Newcastle, Kent and Sussex in Delaware*, Maryland, Virginia and South Carolina. North Carolina was not represented until the 14th September, and Georgia not at all. It is also apparent, that New York was not represented *as a colony*, but only through certain portions of her people;(*i*) in like manner, Lyman Hall

(*i*) The historical fact here stated, is perfectly authenticated, and has never been disputed; nevertheless, the following extracts from the journals of congress, may not be out of place:

"Wednesday, September 14, 1774. Henry Wisner, a delegate from *the county of Orange*, in the colony of New York, appeared at congress, and produced a certificate of his election *by the said county*, which being read and approved, he took his seat in congress as a deputy from the colony of New York."

was admitted to his seat, in the succeeding congress, as a delegate from the parish of St. Johns, in Georgia, although he declined to vote on any question requiring a majority of *the colonies* to carry it, because he was not the representative of a colony. This congress passed a variety of important resolutions, between September 1774, and the 22d October, in the same year; during all which time Georgia was not represented at all; for even the parish of St. Johns did not appoint a representative till May 1775. In point of fact, the congress was a *deliberative and advisory* body, and nothing more; and, for this reason, it was not deemed important, or, at least, not *indispensable*, that all the colonies should be represented, since the resolutions of congress had no obligatory force whatever. It was appointed for the sole purpose of taking into consideration the general condition of the colonies, and of devising and recommending proper measures, for the security of their rights and interests. For these objects no precise powers and instructions were necessary, and *beyond* them none were given. Neither does it appear that any precise time was assigned for the duration of congress. The duty with which it was charged was extremely simple; and it was taken for granted that it would dissolve itself as soon as that duty should be performed.(*k*)

"Monday, September 26, 1774. John Hening, Esq., a deputy from *Orange county*, in the colony of New York, appeared this morning, and took his seat as a deputy from that colony."

"Saturday, October 1, 1774. Simon Bocrum, Esq., appeared in congress as a deputy from King's county, in the colony of New York, and produced the credentials of his election, which being read and approved, he took his seat as a delegate from that colony."

It is evident from these extracts, that although the delegates from certain portions of the people of New York were admitted to seats in congress as delegates *from the colony*, yet, in point of fact, they were not *elected* as such, neither were they ever recognized as such, by New York herself. The truth is, as will presently appear, the majority of her people were not ripe for the measures pursued by congress, and would not have agreed to appoint delegates for the whole colony.

(*k*) A reference to the credentials of the congress of 1774 will shew, beyond all doubt, the true character of that assembly. The following are extracts from them:

New Hampshire. "To *devise, consult and adopt* such measures as may have the most likely tendency to extricate the colonies from

"It is perfectly apparent that the mere *appointment* of this congress did not make the people of all the colonies 'one people,' nor 'a nation *de facto*.' All the colonies

their present difficulties; to secure and perpetuate their rights, liberties and privileges, and to restore that peace, harmony and mutual confidence, which once happily subsisted between the parent country and her colonies."

Massachusetts. "To *consult* on the present state of the colonies, and the miseries to which they are, and must be reduced, by the operation of certain acts of parliament respecting America; and to deliberate and determine upon wise and proper measures *to be by them recommended to all the colonies*, for the recovery and establishment of their just rights and liberties, civil and religious, and the restoration of union and harmony between Great Britain and the colonies, most ardently desired by all good men."

Rhode Island. "To consult on proper measures to obtain a repeal of the several acts of the British parliament for levying taxes on his majesty's subjects in America without their consent, and upon proper measures to establish the rights and liberties of the colonies upon a just and solid foundation, *agreeably to instructions given by the general assembly*."

Connecticut. "To *consult and advise* on proper measures for advancing the best good of the colonies, and such conferences to report, from time to time, to the colonial house of representatives."

New York. Only a few of her counties were represented, some by deputies authorized to "represent," and some by deputies authorized to "attend congress."

New Jersey. "To represent the colony in the general congress."

Pennsylvania. "To form and adopt a plan for the purposes of obtaining redress of American grievances, ascertaining American rights upon the most solid and constitutional principles, and for establishing that union and harmony between Great Britain and the colonies which is indispensably necessary to the welfare and happiness of both."

Delaware. "To consult and advise with the deputies from the other colonies, to determine upon all such prudent and lawful measures as may be judged most expedient for the colonies immediately and unitedly to adopt, in order to obtain relief for an oppressed people,* and the redress of our general grievances."

Maryland. "To attend a general congress, to effect one general plan of conduct, operating on the commercial connexion of the colonies with the mother country, for the relief of Boston and the preservation of American liberty."

Virginia. "To consider of the most proper and effectual manner of so operating on the commercial connexion of the colonies with the mother country, as to procure redress for the much injured province of Massachusetts Bay, to secure British America

* Massachusetts, the particular wrongs of which are just before recited at large.

did not unite in the appointment, neither as colonies nor by any portion of their people acting in their primary assemblies, as has already been shewn. The colonies were

from the ravage and ruin of arbitrary taxes, and speedily to procure the return of that harmony and union, so beneficial to the whole empire, and so ardently desired by all British America."

North Carolina. "To take such measures as they may deem prudent to effect the purpose of describing with certainty the rights of Americans, repairing the breach made in those rights, and for guarding them for the future from any such violations done under the sanction of public authority." For these purposes the delegates are "invested with such powers as may make any acts done by them *obligatory in honour*, on every inhabitant hereof, who is not an alien to his country's good, and an apostate to the liberties of America."

South Carolina. "To consider the acts lately passed, and bills depending in parliament with regard to the port of Boston and colony of Massachusetts Bay; which acts and bills, in the precedent and consequences, affect the whole continent of America. Also the grievances under which America labours, by reason of the several acts of parliament that impose taxes or duties for raising a revenue, and lay unnecessary restraints and burdens on trade; and of the statutes, parliamentary acts and royal instructions, which make an invidious distinction between his majesty's subjects in Great Britain and America, with full power and authority to concert, agree to and prosecute such legal measures, as in the opinion of the said deputies, so to be assembled, shall be most likely to obtain a repeal of the said acts, and a redress of those grievances."

[The above extracts are made from the credentials of the deputies of the several colonies, as spread upon the journal of congress, according to a copy of that journal bound (as appears by a gilt label on the back thereof) for the use of the president of congress; now in possession of B. Tucker esq.]

It is perfectly clear from these extracts, 1. That the colonies did not consider themselves as "one people," and that they were therefore bound to consider the quarrel of Boston as their own; but that they made common cause with Massachusetts, only because the *principles* asserted in regard to her, equally affected the other colonies. 2. That each colony appointed its own delegates, giving them precisely such power and authority as suited its own views. 3. That no colony gave any power or authority except for advisement only. 4. That so far from designing to establish "a general or national government," and to form themselves into "a nation *de facto*," their great purpose was to bring about a reconciliation and harmony with the mother country. This is still farther apparent from the tone of the public addresses of congress. 5. That this congress was not "organized under the auspices and with the consent of the people, acting directly in their primary, sovereign capacity, and without the intervention of the functionaries to whom the ordinary powers of government were delegated in the

not independent, and had not even resolved to declare themselves so at any future time. On the contrary, they were extremely desirous to preserve and continue their connexion with the parent country, and congress was charged with the duty of devising such measures as would enable them to do so, without involving a surrender of their rights as British subjects. It is equally clear, that the powers with which congress was clothed, did not flow from, nor *constitute* 'one people,' or 'nation *de facto*,' and that that body was not 'a general or national government,' nor a government of any kind whatever. The existence of such government was absolutely inconsistent with the allegiance which the colonies still acknowledged to the British crown. Our author himself informs us, in a passage already quoted, that they had no power to form such government, nor to enter into 'any league or treaty among themselves.' Indeed, congress did not claim any legislative power whatever, nor could it have done so consistently with the political relations which the colonies still acknowledged and desired to preserve. Its acts were in the form of *resolutions*, and not in the form of *laws*; it *recommended* to its constituents whatever it believed to be for their advantage, but it *commanded* nothing. Each colony, and the people thereof, were at perfect liberty to act upon such recommendation or not, as they might think proper.(*l*)

colonies," but, on the contrary, that it was organized by the colonies *as such*, and generally through their ordinary legislatures; and *always* with careful regard to their separate and independent rights and powers.

If the congress of 1774 was "a general or national governvernment," neither New York nor Georgia was a party it; for neither of them was represented in that congress. It is also worthy of remark that the congress of 1774 had no agents of its own in foreign countries, but employed those of the several colonies. See the resolution for delivering the address to the king, passed October 25, 1774, and the letter to the agents, approved on the following day.

(*l*) The journals of congress afford the most abundant and conclusive proofs of this. In order to shew the general character of their proceedings, it is enough for me to refer to the following:

On the 11th October 1774, it was "Resolved unanimously, That a memorial be prepared to the people of British America, stating to them the necessity of a firm, united and invariable ob-

"On the 22d October 1774, this congress dissolved itself, having recommended to the several colonies to appoint delegates to another congress, to be held in Philadelphia in the following May. Accordingly delegates were chosen, as they had been chosen to the preceding congress, each colony and the people thereof acting for themselves, and by themselves; and the delegates thus chosen were clothed with substantially the same powers, for precisely the same objects, as in the former congress. Indeed, it could not have been otherwise; for the relations of the colonies were still unchanged, and any measure establishing 'a general or national government,' or uniting the colonies so as to constitute them 'a nation *de facto*,' would have been an act of open rebellion, and would have

servation of the measures *recommended* by the congress, as they tender the invaluable rights and liberties derived to them from the laws and constitution of their country." The memorial was accordingly prepared, in conformity with the resolution.

Congress having previously had under consideration the plan of an association for establishing non-importation &c. finally adopted it, October 20, 1774. After reciting their grievances, they say, "And, therefore, we do, for ourselves and the inhabitants of the several colonies whom we represent, firmly agree and associate, *under the sacred ties of virtue, honour and love of our country*, as follows." They then proceed to recommend a certain course of proceeding, such as non-importation and non-consumption of certain British productions. They recommend the appointment of a committee in every county, city and town, to watch their fellow-citizens, in order to ascertain whether or not "any person within the limits of their appointment has violated this association;" and if they should find any such, it is their duty to report them, "to the end, that all such foes to the rights of British America may be publicly known, and *universally contemned as the enemies of American liberty; and, thenceforth, we respectively will break off all dealings with him or her*." They also resolve that they will "have no trade, commerce, dealings or intercourse whatsoever, with any colony or province in North America, which shall not accede to, or which shall hereafter violate this association, but will hold them as unworthy of the rights of freemen, and as inimical to the liberties of their country."

This looks very little like the legislation of the "general or national government" of "a nation *de facto*." The most important measures of general concern are rested upon no stronger foundation than "the sacred ties of virtue, honour, and the love of our country," and have no higher sanction than public contempt and exclusion from the ordinary intercourse of society!

severed at once all the ties which bound them to the mother country, and which they were still anxious to preserve. New York was represented in this congress precisely as she had been in the former one, that is, by delegates chosen by a part of her people; for the royal party was so strong in that colony, that it would have been impossible to obtain from the legislature an expression of approbation of any measure of resistance to British authority. The accession of Georgia to the general association was not made known till the 20th of July, and her delegates did not take their seats till the 13th of September. In the mean time congress had proceeded in the discharge of its duties, and some of its most important acts, and among the rest, the appointment of a commander-in-chief of their armies, were performed while those two colonies were unrepresented. Its acts, like those of the former congress, were in the form of resolution and recommendation; for, as it still held out the hope of reconciliation with the parent country, it did not venture to assume the function of authoritative legislation. It continued to hold this attitude and to act in this mode till the 4th of July 1776, when it declared that the colonies there represented (including New York, which had acceded after the battle of Lexington) were, and of right ought to be, free and independent states.(*m*)

(*m*) That the powers granted to the delegates to the second congress were substantially the same with those granted to the delegates to the first, will appear from the following extracts from their credentials:

New Hampshire. "To consent and agree to all measures which said congress shall deem necessary to obtain redress of American grievances." Delegates appointed by a *convention*.

Massachusetts. "To concert, agree upon, direct and order" (in concert with the delegates of the other colonies) "such further measures as to them shall appear to be best calculated for the recovery and establishment of American rights and liberties, and for restoring harmony between Great Britain and the colonies." Delegates appointed by provincial congress.

Connecticut. "To join, consult and advise with the other colonies in British America, on proper measures for advancing the best good of the colonies." Delegates appointed by the colonial house of representatives.

The *colony* of New York was not represented in this congress, but delegates were appointed by a convention of deputies from the

"It is to be remarked, that no new powers were conferred on congress after the declaration of independence. Strictly speaking, they had no authority to make that de-

city and county of New York, the city and county of Albany, and the counties of Dutchess, Ulster, Orange, West Chester, King's, and Suffolk. They gave their delegates power to "concert and determine upon such measures as shall be judged most effectual for the preservation and re-establishment of American rights and privileges, and for the restoration of harmony between Great Britain and the colonies." Queen's county approved of the proceeding.

Pennsylvania. Simply to "attend the general congress." Delegates appointed by provincial assembly.

New Jersey. "To attend the continental congress, and to report their proceedings to the next session of general assembly." Delegates appointed by the colonial assembly.

Delaware. "To concert and agree upon such farther measures as shall appear to them best calculated for the accommodation of the unhappy differences between Great Britain and the colonies on a constitutional foundation, which the house most ardently wish for, and that they report their proceedings to the next session of general assembly." Delegates appointed by the assembly.

Maryland. "To consent and agree to all measures which said congress shall deem necessary and effectual to obtain a redress of American grievances; and this province bind themselves to execute, to the utmost of their power, all resolutions which the said congress may adopt." Delegates appointed by convention, and subsequently approved by the general assembly.

Virginia. "To represent this colony in general congress, to be held &c." Delegates appointed by convention.

North Carolina. "Such powers as may make any acts done by them, or any of them, or consent given in behalf of this province, obligatory in honour upon every inhabitant thereof." Delegates appointed by convention, and approved in general assembly.

South Carolina. "To concert, agree to, and effectually prosecute such measures as, in the opinion of the said deputies and the deputies to be assembled, shall be most likely to obtain a redress of American grievances." Delegates appointed by provincial congress.

In the copy of the journals of congress now before me, I do not find the credentials of the delegates from Rhode Island. They did not attend at the first meeting of congress, although they did at a subsequent period. Georgia was not represented in this congress until September 1775. On the 13th May 1775, Lyman Hall appeared as a delegate from the parish of St. John's, and he was admitted to his seat, "subject to such regulations, as the congress shall determine, relative to his voting." He was never regarded as the representative of Georgia, nor was that colony then considered as a party to the proceedings of congress. This is evident from

claration. They were not appointed for any such purpose, but precisely the reverse; and although some of them were expressly authorized to agree to it, yet others were not. Indeed, we are informed by Mr. Jefferson, that the declaration was opposed by some of the firmest patriots of the body, and among the rest, by R. R. Livingston, Dickenson, Wilson and E. Rutledge, on the ground that it was premature; that the people of New York, New Jersey, Maryland and Delaware, were not *yet ripe for it*, but would soon unite with the rest, if not indiscreetly urged. In venturing upon so bold a step, congress acted precisely as they did in all other cases, in the name of the states whose representatives they were, and with a full reliance that those states would confirm whatever they might do for the general good. They were, strictly, agents or ministers of independent states, acting each under the authority and instructions of his own state, and having no power whatever, except what those instructions conferred. The states themselves were not bound by the resolves of congress, except so far as they respectively authorized their own delegates to bind them. There was no original grant of powers to that body, except for deliberation and advisement; there was no constitution, no law, no agreement, to which they could refer, in order to ascertain the extent of their powers. The members did not all act under the same instructions, nor with the same extent of au-

the fact that, in the address to the inhabitants of Great Britain, they use the style, "The *twelve* United Colonies, by their delegates in congress, to the inhabitants of Great Britain," adopted on the 8th July 1775. On the 20th of that month, congress were notified that a convention of Georgia had appointed delegates to attend them, but none of them took their seats till the 13th of September following. They were authorized "to do, transact, join, and concur with the several delegates from the other colonies and provinces upon this continent, on all such matters and things as shall appear eligible and fit, at this alarming time, for the preservation and defence of our rights and liberties, and for the restoration of harmony, upon constitutional principles, between Great Britain and America."

Some of the colonies appointed their delegates only for limited times, at the expiration of which, they were replaced by others, but without any material change in their powers. The delegates were, in all things, subject to the orders of their respective colonies.

thority. The different states gave different instructions, each according to its own views of right and policy, and without reference to any general scheme to which they were all bound to conform. Congress had in fact *no power of government at all*, nor had it that character of *permanency* which is implied in the idea of government. It could not pass an obligatory law, nor devise an obligatory sanction, by virtue of any inherent power in itself. It was, as already remarked, precisely the same body *after* the declaration of independence as *before*. As it was not then a government, and could not establish any new and valid relations between the colonies, so long as they acknowledged themselves dependencies of the British crown, they certainly could not do so after the declaration of independence, without some new grant of power. The dependent colonies had then become independent states; their political condition and relations were necessarily changed by that circumstance; the deliberative and advisory body, through whom they had consulted together as colonies, was *functus officio;* the authority which appointed them had ceased to exist, or was superseded by a higher authority. Every thing which they did, after this period, and before the articles of confederation, was without any other right or authority than what was derived from the mere consent and acquiescence of the several states. In the ordinary business of that government *de facto*, which the occasion had called into existence, they did whatever the public interest seemed to require, upon the secure reliance that their acts would be approved and confirmed. In other cases, however, they called for specific grants of power; and in such cases, each representative applied to his own state alone, and not to any other state or people. Indeed, as they were called into existence by the *colonies* in 1775, and as they continued in existence without any new election or new grant of power, it is difficult to perceive how they could form 'a general or national government, organized by *the people*.' They were *elected* by subjects of the king of England; subjects who had no right, as they themselves admitted, to establish any government whatever; and when those subjects became citizens of independent states, they gave no instructions to establish any such government. The government *exer-*

6*

cised was, as already remarked, merely a government *de facto*, and no farther *de jure* than the subsequent approval of its acts by the several states made it so.

"This brief review will enable us to determine how far the author is supported in the inferences he has drawn, in the passages last quoted. We have reason to regret that in these, as in many others, he has not been sufficiently specific, either in stating his proposition or in citing his proof. To what people does he allude, when he tells us that the 'first general or national government' was organized 'by the people?' The first and every recommendation to send deputies to a general congress was addressed to the colonies *as such;* in the choice of those deputies each colony acted for itself, without mingling in any way with the people or government of any other colony; and when the deputies met in congress, they voted on all questions of public and general concern by colonies, each colony having one vote, whatever was its population or number of deputies. If, then, this government was organized by 'the people' at all, it was clearly the people of the *several* colonies, and not the *joint* people of *all* the colonies. And where is the author's warrant for the assertion, that they acted 'directly in their primary sovereign capacity, and without the intervention of the functionaries, to whom the ordinary powers of government were delegated in the colonies.' He is in most respects a close follower of Marshall, and he could scarcely have failed to see the following passage, which is found in a note in the 168th page of the second volume of the Life of Washington. Speaking of the congress of 1774, Marshall says: 'The members of this congress were *generally* elected by the authority of the colonial legislatures, but in *some* instances a different system had been pursued. In New Jersey and Maryland the elections were made by committees chosen in the several counties for that particular purpose; and in New York, where the royal party was very strong, and where it is probable that no legislative act, authorizing an election of members to represent that colony in congress, could have been obtained, the people themselves assembled in those places, where the spirit of opposition to the claims of parliament prevailed, and elected deputies, who were readily received into congress.' Here the *general rule* is stated to be, that the deputies were elected by the 'colonial legislatures,' and the instances in which the people acted 'directly in their primary sovereign capacity, without the intervention of the ordinary functionaries of government,' are given as *exceptions*. And even in those cases, in which delegates were appointed by conventions of the people, it was deemed necessary in many instances, as we have already seen, that the appointment should be approved and confirmed by the ordinary legislature. As to New York, neither her people nor her government had so far lost their attachment to the mother country as to concur in any measure of opposition until after the battle of Lexington, in April 1775; and the only representatives which New York had in the congress of 1774 were those of a comparatively small portion of her people. It is well known—and, indeed, the author himself so informs us—that the members of the congress of 1775 were elected substantially as were those of the preceding congress; so that there were very few of the colonies, in which the people performed that act in their 'primary sovereign capacity,' without the intervention of their constituted authorities. It is of little consequence, however, to the present enquiry, whether the deputies were chosen by the colonial legislatures, as was done in most of the colonies, or by conventions, as was done in Georgia and some others, or by committees appointed for the purpose, as was done in one or two instances, or by the people in primary assemblies, as was done in *part* of New York. All these modes were resorted to, according as the one or the other appeared most convenient or proper in each particular case. But, whichever mode was adopted, the members were chosen by each colony in and for itself, and were the representatives of *that* colony alone, and not of any other colony, or any nation *de facto* or *de jure*. The assertion, therefore, that 'the congress thus assembled exercised *de facto* and *de jure* a sovereign authority, not as the delegated agents of the governments *de facto* of the colonies, but in virtue of original powers derived from the people,' is, to say the least of it, *very* bold, in one who had undoubtedly explored all the sources of information upon the subject. Until the adoption of the articles of confederation congress had no 'original powers,' except only for deliberation and advisement, and claimed no 'sovereign authority' whatever. It was an occasional, and not a permanent body, or one renewable from time to time. Although they did, in many instances, 'exercise *de facto*' a power of legislation to a certain extent, yet they never held that power '*de jure*,' by any grant from the colonies or the people; and their acts became valid only by subsequent confirmation of them, and not because they had any delegated authority to perform them. The whole history of the period proves this, and not a single instance can be cited to the contrary. The course of the revolutionary government throughout attests the fact, that, however the people may have occasionally acted, in pressing emergencies, without the intervention of the authorities of their respective colonial governments, they never lost sight of the fact that they were citizens of separate colonies, and never, even impliedly, surrendered that character, or acknowledged a different allegiance. In all the acts of congress, reference was had to the colonies, and never to the people. That body had no power to act directly upon the people, and could not execute its own resolves as to most purposes, except by the aid and intervention of the colonial authorities. Its measures were adopted by the votes of the colonies *as such*, and not by the rule of mere numerical majority, which prevails in every legislative assembly of an entire nation. This fact alone is decisive to prove, that the members were not the representatives of the people of *all* the colonies, for the judgment of each colony was pronounced by its *own* members only, and no others had any right to mingle in their deliberations. What, then, was this 'sovereign authority?' What was the nature, what the extent, of its 'original powers?' From what 'people' were those powers derived? I look in vain for answers to these questions to any historical record which has yet met my view, and have only to regret that the author has not directed me to better guides.

"The author's conclusion is not better sustained by the nature and extent of the powers *exercised* by the revolutionary government. It has already been stated, that no original powers of legislation were granted to the congresses of 1774 and 1775; and it is only from their acts that we can determine what powers they actually exercised. The circumstances under which they were called into existence precluded the possibility of any precise limitations of their powers, even if it had been designed to clothe them with the functions of government. The colonies were suffering under common oppressions, and were threatened with common dangers, from the mother country. The great object which they had in view was to produce that concert of action among themselves which would best enable them to resist their common enemy, and best secure the safety and liberties of all. Great confidence must necessarily be reposed in public rulers under circumstances of this sort. We may well suppose, therefore, that the revolutionary government exercised every power which appeared to be necessary for the successful prosecution of the great contest in which they were engaged; and we may, with equal propriety, suppose that neither the people nor the colonial governments felt any disposition to scrutinize very narrowly any measure which promised protection and safety to themselves. They knew that the government was temporary only; that it was permitted only for a particular and temporary object, and that they could at any time recall any and every power which it had assumed. It would be a violent and forced inference, from the powers of such an *agency*, (for it was not a government, although I have sometimes, for convenience, called it so,) however great they might be, to say that the people, or states, which established it, meant thereby to merge their distinctive character, to surrender all the rights and privileges which belonged to them as separate communities, and to consolidate themselves into one nation.

"In point of fact, however, there was nothing in the powers exercised by the revolutionary government, so far as they can be known from their acts, inconsistent with the perfect sovereignty and independence of the states. These were always admitted in *terms*, and were never denied in *practice*. So far as external relations were concerned, congress seems to have exercised every power of a supreme government. They assumed the right to 'declare war and to make peace; to authorize captures; to institute appellate prize courts; to direct and control all national, military and naval operations; to form alliances and make treaties; to contract debts and issue bills of credit on national account.' These powers were not 'exclusive,' however, as our author supposes. On the contrary, troops were raised, vessels of war were commissioned, and various military operations were conducted by the colonies, on their own separate means and authority. Ticonderoga was taken by the troops of Connecticut before the declaration of independence; Massachusetts and Connecticut fitted out armed vessels to cruise against those of England, in October 1775; South Carolina soon followed their example. In 1776, New Hampshire authorized her executive to issue letters of marque and reprisal.

"These instances are selected out of many, as sufficient to shew that in the conduct of war congress possessed no 'exclusive' power, and that the colonies (or states) retained, and actually asserted, their own sovereign right and power as to that matter. And not as to that matter alone, for New Hampshire established post offices. The words of our author may, indeed, import that the power of congress over the subject of war was 'exclusive' only as to such military and naval operations as he considers national, that is, such as were undertaken by the joint power of all the colonies; and if so, he is correct. But the comma after the word 'national' suggests a different interpretation. At all events, the facts which I have mentioned prove that congress exercised no power which was considered as abridging the absolute sovereignty and independence of the states.

"Many of those powers which, for greater convenience, were entrusted exclusively to congress, could not be effectually exerted except by the aid of the state authorities. The troops required by congress were raised by the states, and the commissions of their officers were countersigned by the governors of the states. Congress were allowed to issue bills of credit, but they could not make them a legal tender, nor punish the counterfeiter of them. Neither could they bind the states to redeem them, nor raise by their own authority the necessary funds for that purpose. Congress received ambassadors and other public ministers, yet they had no power to extend to them that protection which they receive from the government of every sovereign nation. A man by the name of De Longchamps entered the house of the French minister plenipotentiary in Philadelphia, and there threatened violence to the person of Francis Barbe Marbois, secretary of the French legation, consul general of France, and consul for the state of Pennsylvania: he afterwards assaulted and beat him in the public street. For this offence, he was indicted and tried in *the court of oyer and terminer of Philadelphia*, and punished under its sentence. The case turned chiefly upon the law of nations, with reference to the protection which it secures to foreign ministers. A question was made, whether *the authorities of Pennsylvania* should not deliver up De Longchamps to the French government to be dealt with at their pleasure. It does not appear that the federal government was considered to possess any power over the subject, or that it was deemed proper to invoke its counsel or authority in any form. This case occurred in 1784, after the adoption of the articles of confederation; but if the powers of the federal government were *less* under those articles than before, it only proves that, however great its previous powers may have been, they were held at the will of the states, and were actually recalled by the articles of confederation. Thus it appears that, in the important functions of raising an army, of providing a public revenue, of paying public debts, and giving security to the persons of foreign ministers, the boasted 'sovereignty' of the federal government was merely nominal, and owed its entire efficiency to the co-operation and aid of the state governments. Congress had no power to coerce those governments; nor could it exercise any direct authority over their individual citizens.

"Although the powers actually assumed and exercised by congress were certainly very great, they were not always acquiesced in, or allowed, by the states. Thus, the power to lay an embargo was earnestly desired by them, but was denied by the states. And in order the more clearly to indicate that many of their powers were exercised merely by sufferance, and at the same time to lend a sanction to their authority so far as they chose to allow it, it was deemed necessary, by at least *one* of the states, to pass laws indemnifying those who might act in obedience to the resolutions of that body.(*n*)

(*n*) This was done by Pennsylvania. See 2 *Dallas's Col. L. of Penn.* 3.

"A conclusive proof, however, of the true relation which the colonies held to the revolutionary government, even in the opinion of congress itself, is furnished by their own journals. In June 1776, that body recommended the passing of laws for the punishment of treason; and they declare that the crime shall be considered as committed against *the colonies individually*, and not against them all, as united or confederated together. This could scarcely have been so, if they had considered themselves 'a government *de facto* and *de jure*,' clothed with 'sovereign authority.' The author, however, is not satisfied to rest his opinion upon historical facts; he seeks also to fortify himself by a judicial decision. He informs us that, 'soon after the organization of the present government, the question [of the powers of the continental congress] was most elaborately discussed before the supreme court of the United States, in a case calling for an exposition of the appellate jurisdiction of congress in prize causes, before the ratification of the confederation. The result of that examination was, that congress before the confederation possessed, by the *consent of the people of the United States*, sovereign and supreme powers for national purposes; and, among others, the supreme powers of peace and war, and, as an incident, the right of entertaining appeals in the last resort, in prize causes, even in opposition to state legislation. And that the actual powers exercised by congress, in respect to national objects, furnished the best exposition of its constitutional authority, since they emanated from *the people*, and were acquiesced in by *the people*.'

"There is in this passage great want of accuracy, and perhaps some want of candour. The author, as usual, neglects to cite the judicial decision to which he alludes, but it must be the case of Penhallow and others against Doane's administrators. (3 Dallas's Reports 54.) Congress, in November 1775, passed a resolution, recommending to the several colonies to establish prize courts, with a right of appeal from their decisions to congress. In 1776, New Hampshire accordingly passed a law upon the subject, by which an appeal to congress was allowed in cases of capture by vessels in the service of the united colonies; but where the capture was made by 'a vessel in the service of the united colonies and of any particular colony or person together, the appeal was allowed to the superior court of New Hampshire. The brigantine Susanna was captured by a vessel owned and commanded by citizens of New Hampshire, and was duly condemned as prize by her own court of admiralty. An appeal was prayed to congress and denied; and thereupon an appeal to the superior court of New Hampshire was prayed and allowed. From the decision of this court an appeal was taken to congress, in the mode prescribed by their resolution, and the case was disposed of by the court of appeals, appointed by congress to take cognizance of such cases. After the adoption of the present constitution and the organization of the judiciary system under it, a libel was filed in the district court of New Hampshire, to carry into effect the sentence of the court of appeals above mentioned. The cause being legally transferred to the circuit court, was decided there, and an appeal allowed to the supreme court. That court, in its decision, sustains the jurisdiction of the court of appeals established by congress. Mr. justice Paterson's opinion is founded mainly upon these grounds: That the powers actually exercised by congress ought to be considered as legitimate, because they were such as the occasion absolutely required, and were approved and acquiesced in by 'the people;' that the authority ultimately and finally to decide on all matters and questions touching the law of nations does reside and is vested in the sovereign supreme power of war and peace;' that this power was lodged in the continental congress by the consent and acquiescence of 'the people;' that the legality of all captures on the high seas must be determined by the law of nations; that New Hampshire had committed herself upon this subject by voting in favour of the exercise of the same power by congress in the case of the brig Active; that as the commission, under which the capture in the case under consideration was made, was issued by congress, it resulted, of necessity, that the validity of all captures made by virtue of that commission should be judged of by congress, or its constituted authority, because 'every one must be amenable to the authority under which he acts.' It is evident that this opinion, while it sustains the authority of congress in the particular case, does not prove its general supremacy, nor that the states had surrendered to it any part of their sovereignty and independence. On the contrary, it affirms that the 'sovereign and supreme power of war and peace,' was *assumed* by congress, and that the exercise of it became legitimate, only because it was approved and acquiesced in; and that being thus legitimated, the appellate jurisdiction in prize cases followed as a necessary incident. All the powers, which Paterson contends for as exercised by congress, may well be conceded, without in the slightest degree affecting the question before us; they were as consistent with the character of a federative, as with that of a consolidated government. He does not tell us to what people he alludes, when he says that the powers exercised by congress were approved and ratified by 'the people.' He does not, in any part of his opinion, authorize the idea of the author, that 'congress possessed, before the confederation, by the consent of *the people of United States*, sovereign and supreme powers for national purposes.' On the contrary, as to one of those powers, he holds the opposite language; and therefore it is fair to presume, that he intended to be so understood in regard to all the rest. This is his language: 'The authority exercised by congress, in granting commissions to privateers, was approved and ratified by *the several colonies or states*, because they received and filled up the commissions and bonds, and returned the latter to congress.' This approval and ratification alone rendered, in his opinion, the exercise of this, and other similar powers assumed by congress, legitimate.

"Judge Iredell, in delivering his opinion, goes much more fully into the examination of the powers of the revolutionary government. He thinks that, as the power of peace and war was entrusted to congress, they held, as a necessary incident, the power to establish prize courts; and that whatever powers they did in fact exercise, were acquiesced in and consented to, and, consequently legitimated and confirmed. But he leaves no room to doubt as to the source whence this confirmation was derived. After proving that the several colonies were, to all intents and purposes, separate and distinct, and that they did not form 'one people' in any sense of the term, he says, 'If congress, previous to the articles of confederation, possessed any authority, it was an authority, as I have shewn, derived from the people of each province, in the first instance.'

'The authority was not possessed by congress, unless given by all the states.'—'I conclude, therefore, that every particle of authority, which originally resided either in congress or in any branch of the state governments, was derived from the people who were permanent inhabitants of each province, in the first instance, and afterwards became citizens of each state; that this authority was conveyed by each body politic separately, *and not by all the people in the several provinces or states* jointly.' No language could be stronger than this, to disaffirm the author's conclusion, that the powers exercised by congress were exercised 'by the consent of *the people of the United States.*' Certainly Iredell did not think so.

"The other two judges, Blair and Cushing, affirm the general propositions upon which Paterson and Iredell sustained the power of congress in the particular case, but lend no support to the idea of any such unity among the people of the several colonies or states, as our author supposes to have existed. Cushing, without formally discussing the question, expressly says that 'he has no doubt of the sovereignty of the states.'

"This decision, then, merely affirms, what no one has ever thought of denying, that the revolutionary government exercised every power which the occasion required; that, among these, the powers of peace and war were most important, because congress, alone, represented *all* the colonies, and could, alone, express the general will, and wield the general strength; that wherever the powers of peace and war are lodged, belongs also the right to decide all questions touching the laws of nations; that prize causes are of this character; and, finally, that all these powers were not derived from any original grant, but are to be considered as belonging to congress, *merely because congress exercised them*, and because they were sustained in so doing by the approbation of the several colonies or states, whose representatives they were. Surely, then, our author was neither very accurate nor very candid, in so stating this decision as to give rise to the idea that, in the opinion of the supreme court, congress possessed original sovereign powers, by the consent of 'the people of the United States.' Even, however, if the court had so decided, in express terms, it would have been of no value in the present enquiry, as will by-and-by be shewn."

LECTURE III.

We come next to the declaration of independence, and to the novel and original idea, that it did not operate the separate independence and individual sovereignty of the several states, but, that, as the declaration was the united act of all, so it operated to make the united colonies free and independent as one people, and in that character only. This, it is very clear, is the position industriously insinuated by the learned author, although, as usual, he is by no means very specific in stating his proposition, lest, perhaps, it might be the more startling from being more clearly discerned in its first announcement.

"§ 211. In the next place," says judge Story, "the colonies did not severally act for themselves, and proclaim their own independence. It is true, that some of the states had previously formed incipient governments for themselves; but it was done in compliance with the recommendations of congress.(*a*) Virginia, on the 29th of June 1776, by a convention of delegates, declared 'the government of this country, as formerly exercised under the crown of Great Britain, totally dissolved;' and proceeded to form a new constitution of government. New Hampshire also formed a government, in December, 1775, which was manifestly intended to be temporary, 'during (as they said) the unhappy and unnatural contest with Great Britain.'(*b*) New Jersey, too, established a frame of government, on the 2d of July 1776; but it was expressly declared, that it should be void upon a reconciliation with Great Brirain.(*c*) And South Carolina, in March 1776, adopted a constitution of government; but this was, in like manner, 'established until an accommodation between Great Britain and America could be ob-

(*a*) Journal of Congress, 1775, p. 115, 231, 235, 279; 1 Pitk. Hist. 351, 355; Marsh. Colon. ch. 14, p. 441, 447; 9 Hening's Stat. 112, 113; 9 Dane's Abridg. App. § 5, p. 16.

(*b*) 2 Belk. N. Hamp. ch. 25, p. 306, 308, 310; 1 Pitk. Hist. 351, 355.

(*c*) Stokes's Hist. Colon. 51, 75.

tained.'(*d*) But the declaration of the independence of all the colonies was the united act of all. It was 'a declaration by the representatives of the United States of America in congress assembled;'—'by the delegates appointed by the good people of the colonies,' as in a prior declaration of rights they were called.(*e*) It was not an act done by the state governments then organized; nor by persons chosen by them. It was emphatically the act of the whole *people* of the united colonies, by the instrumentality of their representatives, chosen for that, among other purposes.(*f*.) It was an act not competent to the state governments, or any of them as organized under their charters, to adopt. Those charters neither contemplated the case, nor provided for it. It was an act of original, inherent sovereignty by the people themselves, resulting from their right to change the form of government, and to institute a new government, whenever necessary for their safety and happiness. So the declaration of independence treats it. No state had presumed of itself to form a new government, or to provide for the exigencies of the times, without consulting congress on the subject; and when they acted, it was in pursuance of the recommendation of congress. It was, therefore, the achievement of the whole for the benefit of the whole. The people of the united colonies made the united colonies free and independent states, and absolved them from all allegiance to the British crown. The declaration of independence has accordingly always been treated, as an act of paramount and sovereign authority, complete and perfect *per se*, and *ipso facto* working an entire dissolution of all political connexion with and allegiance to Great Britain. And this not merely as a practical fact, but in a legal and constitutional view of the matter by courts of justice.(*g*)

"§ 212. In the debates in the South Carolina legislature, in January 1788, respecting the propriety of calling a convention of the people to ratify or reject the constitution, a distinguished statesman(*h*) used the following lan-

(*d*) Stokes's Hist. Colon. 105; 1 Pitk. Hist. 355.

(*e*) Journal 1776, p. 241; Journal 1774, p. 27, 45.

(*f*) 2 Dall. 470, 471. Per Jay, C. J.; 9 Dane's Abridg. App. § 12, 13, p. 23, 24.

(*g*) 2 Dallas's R. 470.

(*h*) Mr. Charles Cotesworth Pinckney.

guage: 'This admirable manifesto (i. e. the declaration of independence) sufficiently refutes the doctrine of the individual sovereignty and independence of the several states. In that declaration the several states are not even enumerated; but after reciting in nervous language, and with convincing arguments our right to independence, and the tyranny, which compelled us to assert it, the declaration is made in the following words: 'We, therefore, the representatives of the United States, &c. do, in the name, &c. of the good people of these colonies, solemnly publish, &c. that these united colonies are, and of right ought to be, free and independent states.' The separate independence and individual sovereignty of the several states were never thought of by the enlightened band of patriots, who framed this declaration. The several states are not even mentioned by name in any part, as if it was intended to impress the maxim on America, that our freedom and independence arose from our union, and that without it we could never be free or independent. Let us then consider all attempts to weaken this union by maintaining, that each state is separately and individually independent, as a species of political heresy, which can never benefit us, but may bring on us the most serious distresses."(*i*)

(*i*) Debates in South Carolina, 1788, printed by A. E. Miller, Charleston, 1831, p. 43, 44.—Mr. Adams, in his Oration on the 4th of July 1831, which is valuable for its views of constitutional principles, insists upon the same doctrine at considerable length. Though it has been published since the original preparation of these lectures, I gladly avail myself of an opportunity to use his authority in corroboration of the same views. "The union of the colonies had preceded this declaration, [of independence,] and even the commencement of the war. The declaration was joint, that the united colonies were free and independent states, but not that any one of them was a free and independent state, separate from the rest."—"The declaration of independence was a social compact, by which the whole people covenanted with each citizen, and each citizen with the whole people, that the united colonies were, and of right ought to be, free and independent states. To this compact union was as vital, as freedom or independence."—"The declaration of independence announced the severance of the thirteen united colonies from the rest of the British empire, and the existence of their people from that day forth as an independent nation. The people of all the colonies, speaking by their representatives, constituted themselves one moral person before the face of their fellow men."—"The declaration of independence was not a

"§213. In the next place we have seen, that the power to do this act was not derived from the state governments; nor was it done generally with their co-operation. The question then naturally presents itself, if it is to be considered as a national act, in what manner did the colonies become a nation, and in what manner did congress become possessed of this national power? The true answer must be, that as soon as congress assumed powers and passed measures, which were in their nature national, to that extent the people, from whose acquiescence and consent they took effect, must be considered as agreeing to form a nation.(*k*) The congress of 1774, looking at the general terms of the commissions, under which the delegates were appointed, seemed to have possessed the power of concerting such measures, as they deemed best, to redress the grievances, and preserve the rights and liberties of all the colonies. Their duties seem to have been principally of an advisory nature; but the exigencies of the times led them rather to follow out the wishes and objects of their constituents, than scrupulously to examine the words, in which their authority was communicated.(*l*) The congress of 1775 and 1776, were clothed with more ample powers, and the language of their commissions generally, was sufficiently broad to embrace the right to pass measures of a national character and obligation. The caution necessary at that period of the revolutionary struggle, rendered that language more guarded than the objects really in view would justify; but it was foreseen, that the spirit of the people would eagerly second every measure adopted to further a general union and resistance against the British claims. The congress of 1775, accordingly assumed at once (as we have seen) the exercise of some of the highest functions of sovereignty. They took measures for national defence and resistance; they followed up the prohibitions upon trade and intercourse with Great Bri-

declaration of liberty merely acquired, nor was it a form of government. The people of the colonies were already free, and their forms of government were various. They were all colonies of a monarchy. The king of Great Britain was their common sovereign."

(*k*) 3 Dall. R. 80, 81, 90, 91, 109, 110, 111, 117.

(*l*) 3 Dall. R. 91.

tain; they raised a national army and navy, and authorized limited national hostilities against Great Britain; they raised money, emitted bills of credit, and contracted debts upon national account; they established a national post office; and, finally, they authorized captures and condemnation of prizes in prize courts, with a reserve of appellate jurisdiction to themselves.

"§ 214. The same body, in 1776, took bolder steps, and exerted powers, which could in no other manner be justified or accounted for, than upon the supposition, that a national union for national purposes already existed, and that the congress was invested with sovereign power over all the colonies for the purpose of preserving the common rights and liberties of all. They accordingly authorized general hostilities against the persons and property of British subjects; they opened an extensive commerce with foreign countries, regulating the whole subject of imports and exports; they authorized the formation of new governments in the colonies; and, finally, they exercised the sovereign prerogative of dissolving the allegiance of all colonies to the British crown. The validity of these acts was never doubted or denied by the people. On the contrary, they became the foundation upon which the superstructure of the liberties and independence of the United States has been erected. Whatever, then, may be the theories of ingenious men on the subject, it is historically true, that before the declaration of independence, these colonies were not, in any absolute sense, sovereign states; that that event did not find them or make them such, but that at the moment of their separation, they were under the dominion of a superior controlling national government, whose powers were vested in and exercised by the general congress with the consent of the people of all the states.(*m*)

(*m*) This whole subject is very amply discussed by Mr. Dane in his Appendix to the 9th volume of his Abridgment of the Laws; and many of his views coincide with those stated in the text. The whole of that Appendix is worthy of the perusal of every constitutional lawyer, even though he might differ from some of the conclusions of the learned author. He will there find much reasoning from documentary evidence of a public nature, which has not hitherto been presented in a condensed or accurate shape.

"§ 215. From the moment of the declaration of independence, if not for most purposes at an antecedent period, the united colonies must be considered as being a nation *de facto*, having a general government over it created, and acting by the general consent of the people of all the colonies. The powers of that government were not, and indeed could not be well defined. But still its exclusive sovereignty, in many cases, was firmly established; and its controlling power over the states was in most, if not in all national measures, universally admitted.(n) The articles of confederation, of which we shall have occasion to speak more hereafter, were not prepared or adopted by congress until November 1777,(o) they were not signed or ratified by any of the states until July 1778; and they were not ratified, so as to become obligatory upon all the states, until March 1781. In the intermediate time, congress continued to exercise the powers of a general government, whose acts were binding on all the states. And though they constantly admitted the states to be 'sovereign and independent communities;'(p) yet it must be obvious, that the terms were used in the subordinate and limited sense already alluded to; for it was impossible to use them in any other sense, since a majority of the states could, by their public acts in congress, control and bind the minority. Among the exclusive powers exercised by congress, were the power to declare war and make peace; to authorize captures; to institute appellate prize courts; to di-

Some interesting views of this subject are also presented in president Monroe's message on internal improvements, on the 4th of May 1822, appended to his message respecting the Cumberland road. See, especially, pages 8 and 9.

When Mr. chief justice Marshall, in *Ogden* v. *Gibbons*, (9 Wheat. R. 187,) admits, that the states, before the formation of the constitution, were sovereign and independent, and were connected with each other only by a league, it is manifest, that he uses the word "sovereign" in a very restricted sense. Under the confederation, there were many limitations upon the powers of the states.

(n) See *Penhallow* v. *Doane*, 3 Dall. R. 54; *Ware* v. *Hylton*, 3 Dall. 199, per Chase, J. See the circular letter of congress, 13th September 1779; 5 Jour. Cong. 341, 348, 349.

(o) Jour. of Cong. 1777, p. 502.

(p) See letter of 17th Nov. 1777, by congress, recommending the articles of confederation; Jour. of 1777, p. 513, 514.

rect and control all national, military, and naval operations; to form alliances and make treaties; to contract debts and issue bills of credit upon national account. In respect to foreign governments, we were politically known as the United States only; and it was in our national capacity, as such, that we sent and received ambassadors, entered into treaties and alliances, and were admitted into the general community of nations, who might exercise the right of belligerents, and claim an equality of sovereign powers and prerogatives.(*q*)

"§ 216. In confirmation of these views, it may not be without use to refer to the opinions of some of our most eminent judges, delivered on occasions which required an exact examination of the subject. In ***Chisholm's Executors*** v. ***The State of Georgia***, (2 Dall. 419, 470,)(*r*) Mr. chief justice Jay, who was equally distinguished as a revolutionary statesman and a general jurist, expressed himself to the following effect: 'The revolution, or rather the declaration of independence, found the *people* already united for general purposes, and at the same time providing for their more domestic concerns by state conventions and other temporary arrangements. From the crown of Great Britain, the sovereignty of their country passed to the *people* of it; and it was then not an uncommon opinion, that the unappropriated lands, which belonged to that crown, passed, not to the people of the colony or states within whose limits they were situated, but to the *whole people*. On whatever principle this opinion rested, it did not give way to the other; and ***thirteen sovereignties*** were considered as emerging from the principles of the revolution, combined by local convenience and considerations. The people, nevertheless, continued to consider themselves, in a national point of view, as *one people;* and they continued without interruption to manage their national concerns accordingly.' In ***Penhallow*** v. ***Doane***, (3 Dall. R. 54,)(*s*) Mr. justice Patterson (who was also a revolutionary statesman) said, speaking of the period before the ratification of the confederation: 'The powers of congress were revolutionary in their nature, arising out of

(*q*) 1 Amer. Museum, 15; 1 Kent. Comm. 197, 198, 199.
(*r*) S. C. 1 Peters's Cond. R. 635.
(*s*) S. C. 1 Peters's Cond. R. 21.

events adequate to every national emergency, and coextensive with the object to be attained. Congress was the general, supreme, and controlling council of the nation, the centre of the union, the centre of force, and the sun of the political system. Congress raised armies, fitted out a navy, and prescribed rules for their government, &c. &c. These high acts of sovereignty were submitted to, acquiesced in, and approved of by the *people* of America, &c. &c. The danger being imminent and common, it became necessary for the people or colonies to coalesce and act in concert, in order to divert, or break the violence of the gathering storm. They accordingly grew into union, and formed one great political body, of which congress was the directing principle and soul, &c. &c. The truth is, that the states, individually, were not known, nor recognized as sovereign by foreign nations, nor are they now. The states collectively, under congress, as their connecting point or head, were acknowledged by foreign powers, as sovereign, particularly in that acceptation of the term, which is applicable to all great national concerns, and in the exercise of which, other sovereigns would be more immediately interested.' In *Ware* v. *Hyltcn*, (3 Dall. 199,)(*t*) Mr. justice Chase (himself also a revolutionary statesman) said: 'It has been enquired, what powers congress possessed from the first meeting in September 1774, until the ratification of the confederation on the first of March 1781. It appears to me, that the powers of congress during that whole period were derived from the *people* they represented, expressly given through the medium of their state conventions or state legislatures; or that after they were exercised, they were impliedly ratified by the acquiescence and obedience of the *people*, &c. The powers of congress originated from necessity, and arose out of it, and were only limited by events; or, in other words, they were revolutionary in their nature. Their extent depended on the exigencies and necessities of public affairs. I entertain this general idea, that the several states retained all internal sovereignty; and that congress properly possessed the rights of external sovereignty. In deciding on the powers of congress, and of the several states before the confederation, I see but one safe rule, namely,

(*t*) S. C. 1 Peters's Cond. R. 99.

that all the powers actually exercised by congress before that period were rightfully exercised, on the presumption not to be controverted, that they were so authorized by the people they represented, by an express or implied grant; and that all the powers exercised by the state conventions or state legislatures, were also rightfully exercised on the same presumption of authority from the people.'(*u*)

"§ 217. In respect to the powers of the continental congress exercised before the adoption of the articles of confederation, few questions were judicially discussed during the revolutionary contest; for men had not leisure in the heat of war, nicely to scrutinize or weigh such subjects; *inter arma silent leges.* The people, relying on the wisdom and patriotism of congress, silently acquiesced in whatever authority they assumed. But soon after the organization of the present government, the question was most elaborately discussed before the supreme court of the United States, in a case calling for an exposition of the appellate jurisdiction of congress in prize causes before the ratification of the confederation.(*v*) The result of that examination was, as the opinions already cited indicate, that congress, before the confederation, possessed, by the consent of the people of the United States, sovereign and supreme powers for national purposes; and among others, the supreme powers of peace and war, and, as an incident, the right of entertaining appeals in the last resort in prize causes, even in opposition to state legislation. And that the actual powers exercised by congress, in respect to national objects, furnished the best exposition of its constitutional authority, since they emanated from the representatives of the people, and were acquiesced in by the people."

I have here, as before, inserted the whole passage which relates to this remarkable opinion, as to the effect of the declaration of independence, both because I am unwilling

(*u*) See also 1 Kent. Comm. Lect. 10, p. 196; President Monroe's Exposition and Message, 4th of May 1822, p. 8, 9, 10, 11.

(*v*) *Penhallow* v. *Doane*, 3 Dall. 54, 80, 83, 90, 91, 94, 109, 110, 111, 112, 117; Journals of Congress, March 1779, p. 86 to 88; 1 Kent. Comm. 198, 199.

to misstate the positions of the author, and because I am well content to give to it all the benefit of that ability with which it is presented. I shall now proceed to remark very succinctly upon several passages which more particularly demand our scrutiny and observation.

In a preceding passage, § 201, the learned author remarks: "Thus was organized under the auspices, and with the consent of the *people, acting* directly in their primary, sovereign capacity, and without the intervention of the functionaries to whom the ordinary powers of the government were delegated in the colonies, the first *national* government, which has been very aptly called the revolutionary government, since in its origin and progress it was wholly conducted upon revolutionary principles." Now here, in the first place, we have a misstatement of the fact, as is manifest from the next preceding section, in which it is distinctly said that *in some* of the states where the legislatures were in session, delegates to the congress of 1774 *were* appointed "by them; that is, by the functionaries to whom the ordinary powers of the government were entrusted." So that this congress was composed of members chosen indifferently in the several states, either by the legislatures or conventions, as each state thought proper; a fact going far to establish the independent sovereign action of each state, in appointing those who were to represent them in this great congress of nations. But in the second place, it would have made no difference as to the matter in question, whether all or none of the states had made the appointment by conventions, instead of by the ordinary functionaries of government. For the question here is, whether this appointment of delegates was *state* action, or the action of the great body of the American people *composing one nation.* Now, whether the appointments were made by legislatures or conventions, they were equally the result of *state* action.(*w*) The legislature

(*w*) "A distinction has been taken at the bar," says judge Iredell, "between a *state*, and the *people of a state.* It is a distinction I am not capable of comprehending. By a *state* forming a republic (speaking of it as a moral person,) *I do not mean* the *legislature* of the state, the executive or the judiciary, but all the *citizens which compose that state, and are*, if I may so express myself, *integral parts of it*, all together forming a body politic." Of course whe-

no more represented the individual state than the convention. The convention in each state was the representative of that state, *quoad* the matter on which it acted. It represented no other state. It was amenable to none other. It was itself the impersonation of that sovereignty. It was appointed indeed "by the people acting in their primary, sovereign capacity," but yet as *separate communities*, and not as forming one great whole. It was, therefore, sovereign within its own limits, but not beyond them. Accordingly, their delegates looked only to them; obeyed them alone; submitted to their instructions, and were removable by them: all which demonstrably proves that the conventions of the states were as distinct from each other as the "ordinary functionaries," and that the acts of each was in behalf and by authority of its own state, as a distinct sovereign, and not in right of any other part of the confederated states, or of the whole people of America as constituting *one* people. In accordance with this character, each delegation voted together, and the majority of the delegation determined the vote of the state. Each state had but one vote, whether large or small, and thus, in these important features, the congress assumed the character of an assembly of ambassadors, rather than that of the legislature of a single nation.

Such was the character of that body which declared independence; a body composed of delegates from separate political societies, who had only united their common efforts for common defence, and for the severance of the chain that bound them to a common tyrant, without an act indicating a design on the part of any, to surrender their separate political character. Thus acting, they declared independence. In that declaration the representatives of the several colonies pronounced that the United Colonies were and of right ought to be free and independent *states*, *not* that they constituted *a* free and independent *state*. Then plurality is acknowledged and asserted by the declaration itself, and that plurality is decisive of the fact, that the independence of the states themselves, as *several* political bodies, was distinctly asserted. It is not true then that

ther the action be by a legislature or convention, it is the same thing, since *neither* constitutes the state, but on the other hand *either* represents it.

the states did "not severally act for themselves;" for the delegates of each, in congress assembled, acted for their respective states, though in conjunction, it is true, with the delegates from other states acting equally for theirs. And accordingly, we find when the treaty of peace was made, each state is distinctly named in the treaty, and the independence of all is as distinctly acknowledged.

But this is not all. Before the declaration of July 4, the commonwealth of Virginia had formed a government for herself. Not an *incipient* government, as our author says, but a permanent and independent one, which lasted until changed by her own *fiat* in the year 1832. This creation of an independent government by the state of Virginia, *ipso facto* constituted her an independent state, and according to the notion of Mr. Jay,(*x*) the sovereignty over the state must instantly have passed from the crown of Great Britain to the people of the *state*. It could not pass to the people of the United States; for there were none such, since *they* had not yet declared independence. The first steps towards establishing the government of Virginia were taken on the 6th day of May, and the act was consummated on the 29th of June 1776. It was her *own* act, done of her own free will, and not by command, or even by the recommendation of congress. Congress, before the declaration, recommended only provisional governments, like that of New Hampshire, to continue "during the unhappy and unnatural contest with Great Britain." They could not, with any consistency, recommend the erection of a permanent government by any state, before they had themselves resolved on a declaration of independence; about which, it is notorious there was much division of opinion. But the new government of Virginia was permanent, and cut her loose from Great Britain. It is therefore gratuitous in judge Story to say that "no state had presumed of itself to form a new government without consulting congress on the subject;" for Virginia did form such a government without congressional recommendation, and did "declare the former government under Great Britain *totally dissolved*," before the congress of the United States had resolved on independence. From

(*x*) See note, p. 49.

that moment, as judge Chase very justly observes, (3 Dall. 224,) "Virginia was a free, sovereign and independent state." Nay, this learned judge goes farther, and expressly says of the declaration of independence itself, that "he considered it as a declaration not that the United Colonies *jointly* in a collective capacity were independent states, but that *each* of them was a sovereign and independent state; that is, that *each* of them had a right to govern itself by its own authority and its own laws, *without any control from any other power upon earth.*"(y)

But our learned author seems to conceive that he settles the question by saying, that "the declaration was the united act of all;"—"that it was the act of the whole people of the United Colonies, exercising original inherent sovereignty, resulting from their right to change the form of government," &c. But the question is, in what character was it the united act of all? It was in their character of separate communities, dependent on each other only so far as common danger and their own consent had made them so. It was the act, indeed, of all America; but not as forming one nation, but as separate communities, all uniting in the common object of securing sovereignty and independence to each. How did they vote? Not by individuals, as representing parts of one whole, but by states, as representing separate communities. If any one state had refused to concur in the declaration, the vote of all the rest could not have bound her. Delaware could no more have been included if she had declined to assent, than Canada or Vermont, who did not send delegates to the body. It was then the joint act, indeed, of the United Colonies, but it was the joint act of communities independent of each other, and uniting in one common measure for the benefit of each. And this seems to have been the understanding of those who had themselves been actors in the stirring scenes of the revolution. It is distinctly avowed in the Federalist, (p. 213,) a work which we all know was published but a few years after the close of the war, and came from the hands of some of our wisest and purest pa-

(y) The case of Vermont was peculiar. She had no representative in the congress which declared independence, though she joined her arms with ours. She declared her own independence in 1777.

triots, least liable to be biassed in favour of the sovereignty of the states. One of its authors, too, at a future day, from the elevated station of the supreme court, distinctly declared, "that by the declaration of independence *thirteen* sovereignties were considered as emerged from the principles of the revolution;" so that reason and authority concur in rejecting the conclusions of our author.

It is to be regretted that in a work intended for the instruction of our youth, any passage should occur which is calculated to mislead, or may be regarded as a sophism. An instance, however, is found in that which we have been examining. Our author says, a declaration of independence "was an act not competent to the state governments, *as organized under their charters*, to adopt." (p. 198.) This is, indeed, undeniable. Their *charters* did not authorize them to adopt such a measure; but what was there to prevent the "original inherent sovereignty of the people" themselves in *each state* from such adoption. It was the right of revolution which belonged to each of the separate communities, as much as to the whole, and which each might assert independent of the others. It was this right of *each*, which, in general congress, was asserted by the whole, for the benefit of *each*, and in that sense only for the benefit of the whole. With these views, I look upon the positions of judge Story, and the *ipse dixits* of Mr. Pinckney and Mr. Adams, on whose authority he relies, as heretical and false, as I am equally well assured they are dangerous and pernicious.

If, indeed, there could be any doubt that thirteen independent communities sprung into existence with the declaration of independence, that doubt would be removed, by the manner in which the states themselves, looked upon their position. Their view of the matter is distinctly disclosed in the articles of confederation. Those articles profess to be between the *states* of New Hampshire, Massachusetts, &c. [naming *each state* in the confederacy.] They profess to be articles of confederation, (a term only applicable to an association of *states*) and perpetual *union*, which *implies* an *anterior state* in which there was *no such union*. And such was the fact; for until that confederation, the congress of the United States constituted only a revolutionary government, not regularly organized, but existing by tacit consent and acquiescence of the several states, who coalesced and acted in concert from a sense of common danger. There was between them no express agreement. The confederation was, therefore, intended to bind together the states, who were, till then, unbound; and to unite those who had never before been united, but by the bond of common safety. But in its very formation, they were careful to retain that which to every nation is sweet—its sovereignty and independence. The style of the confederacy was the *United States* of America, a name which very plainly indicates the union of political bodies, and not the *oneness* of a single republic. But to place the matter beyond question, the second section is devoted to the declaration "that EACH state *retains* its *sovereignty, freedom* and *independence,* and every power, jurisdiction and right, which is not by this confederation expressly delegated to the United States in congress assembled." They not only declare, that *thenceforth* EACH state shall be held to be sovereign and independent, but they avow their anterior independence and sovereignty, by the declaration that they *retained* them. They could not *retain* that which they had not before enjoyed. Nay, more;—EACH state in making this declaration, *uno flatu,* asserts its own rights, and recognizes the rights of others. EACH, therefore, recognized the anterior sovereignty and independence of every other.

It is much to be regretted that our distinguished author has no where, (so far as I can discover) in the examination of the question of the independence of the states, thought fit to present us with *his* views of the effect of these articles in throwing light upon the matter. Had he done so, we may hope that he would never have arrived at the conclusion which he gives in the language of Mr. Pinckney, that "the *separate* independence and *individual sovereignty of the several states* were NEVER THOUGHT OF *by the enlightened band of patriots who framed the declaration.*" Now it happens that Hancock, Adams and Gerry from Massachusetts, Ellery from Rhode Island, Sherman, Huntingdon and Wolcott from Connecticut, Lewis from New York, Witherspoon from Jersey, Robert Morris from Pennsylvania, Thomas M'Kean from Delaware, Carroll from Maryland, the two Lees from Virginia, Penn from North Carolina, and Hayward from South Carolina, who signed the declaration of independence, were signers of the confederation in which the sovereignty of each was declared to be *retained;* and we have already seen the opinion of judge Chase, another signer of the declaration, of his views of the same interesting matter. I feel myself, therefore, justified in repelling the position, that "the separate independence and individual sovereignty of the several states, were never thought of by the patriot signers of the declaration of independence.

It is also to be regretted that the able commentator, in citing judicial opinions in confirmation of his views, has given us, among others, the portion of judge Chase's opinion in *Ware* v. *Hylton*, 3 Dall. p. 231, which is least at variance with his own theories, and has *omitted* to present to the student the strong remarks of that able judge in conflict with his own views. In these, as we have already seen, he declares, that he considers the declaration of independence (which *he himself had signed;*) "as a declaration NOT that the United States *jointly*, in a *collective capacity*, were independent states, but that EACH OF THEM was a *sovereign and independent state.*" It would, also, have been deeply interesting to his readers to have learned, that Mr. Marshall (afterwards chief justice), was of counsel in that cause, and strenuously maintained the independence and sovereignty of Virginia in 1777; a position in irreconcilable conflict with the opinions of the commentator.

LECTURE IV.

From what has been advanced, I hope the separate sovereignties of the states upon the adoption of the declaration of independence, is sufficiently apparent. I have devoted more time to these investigations, because the opposite opinion has been so industriously maintained by an able writer, obviously with the view of influencing certain great political questions which have arisen under our constitution. If, indeed, judge Story means nothing more than that the revolutionary congress, both before and after the declaration of independence, *exercised* large powers by the acquiescence and consent of the *states*, in relation to national concerns, there could be no difference between us. The matter of fact is beyond question. But judge Story seems to be of opinion that the states were not sovereign during this period, but that the sovereignty was in the general government, and that the people were one.(*a*) Those on the other hand who maintain the rights of the states, regard the sovereignty as having existed and continued in the *states*, though the exercise of certain powers in relation to foreign concerns was permitted by *them* on the part of congress. But this very permission, this acquiescence and tacit consent so frequently spoken of by the commentator, is itself decisive of state supremacy. Congress had no power but by state acquiescence. In whom then was the sovereignty? In those assuredly who *gave* the authority to the general government, and without whose assent that authority could not exist. Such is the case in every league, where powers are vested in a general council, for the conduct of the foreign affairs of the associated nations. Such was the case in our own confederacy, in which, as we have seen, very large powers were given, but the "freedom, sovereignty and independence" of

(*a*) He quotes too, with apparent acquiescence, the extravagances of Mr. Dane, which it might well have been hoped would have found no place save in his own pages. Judge Story has transplanted them into his. They are hereafter adverted to.

the states were scrupulously reserved, and congress was confined to the powers expressly granted by the articles of confederation. From the moment of the adoption of *that* compact, at least, the sovereignty of the states must be admitted, as each expressly asserted its own, while it as clearly acknowledged the independence of others. They treated too, with other nations, in the character of a confederacy of states, and not in that of a single nation. Accordingly, in the treaty of peace, his Britannic majesty acknowledges "the United States, viz: New Hampshire, Massachusetts," &c. [naming them EACH *individually*] "to be free, sovereign and independent STATES; that he treats with them as such, and for himself relinquishes," &c. So too the compact itself admits the distinct anterior sovereignty of each state in this, that though ratified by twelve states, it was not held binding on the thirteenth; whereas, if as judge Story observes, "congress was invested with sovereign power over all the colonies, for the purpose of preserving the rights and liberties of all," (page 202,) what hindered a majority of that body from binding every state to enter into the confederacy, whether they approved it or not? What would have hindered the abolition of the state governments, and the substitution of one general government for all purposes whatever. Yet such sweeping powers were never dreamed of, since in fact the congress was the creature of the states, and existed by their sufferance. Its powers were limited, and limited by those who gave them. *They* therefore were the masters; *they* were the sovereigns, while the general government could exercise no authority but that which they had expressly given. *Its* act was *their* act, and derived its force from them, and the sovereign power which it exercised was *their* sovereign power. While it possessed those powers, it was, it may be said, sovereign as to them, and the states were respectively sovereign as to all powers not granted. As it has been well expressed by judge Iredell, (2 Dall. 435,) in relation to the present constitution, "Every state in the Union, in every instance where its sovereignty has not been delegated to the United States, I consider to be as completely sovereign as the United States are in relation to the powers surrendered. The United States are sovereign *as to all* the powers of government actually surrendered; *each* state in the Union is sovereign as to all the powers reserved; the part not surrendered must remain as it was before."

In strictness, according to the theory of our government, the *people* are the sovereign. And they have delegated a part of their power to the general government, and part to the state governments, and each exercise the respective portions of the sovereign powers allotted to them. Each may in this sense be said to be sovereign, though the sovereignty in fact still resides in the people. In what people? The people of each state, distinct from the other states, and the people of *each* state accordingly delegates the power. For as there is no people of the United States, considered aggregately, the sovereignty must be in the people of *each state*. "I conclude," says judge Iredell, "that every particle of authority which originally resided either in congress, or in any branch of the state governments, was derived from the people, who were permanent inhabitants of *each province* in the first instance, and afterwards became citizens of each state; that this authority was conveyed by *each body politic separately*, and NOT by *all* the people in the several provinces or states, *jointly*, and of course that no authority could be conveyed to the whole, but that which previously was possessed by the several parts," &c.

We now come to the consideration of the condition of the states under the articles of confederation,(*b*) and here we shall find that however successful the commentator may have been in insinuating doubts of their sovereignty before, every thing conspires with that instrument to establish that sovereignty beyond all question. I shall present the different evidences of it as succinctly as possible, as they are so numerous that to expatiate on each would unnecessarily consume our time.

1. And first let it be remarked that the articles are declared to be articles of *confederation;* a term which in its ordinary as well as in its radical signification, implies a league or union between states, as contradistinguished from a national government over one people.

2. They are declared to be articles of confederation *between the states* of New Hampshire, &c., [naming each,] thus recognizing each as a *state,* and as such capable of

(*b*) See the articles, 1 L. U. S. 13.

contracting with other states, which is one of the highest attributes of sovereignty.

3. They are declared also to be articles of perpetual *union;* an expression which strongly negatives the favourite notion of *oneness*, since *union* implies the connection of those who *before were separate.*

4. The act of uniting is styled a confederacy, and the 3d article declares that "the said states hereby SEVERALLY enter into a firm LEAGUE of friendship for common defence, &c., binding themselves to assist *each other*, and thus distinctly recognizing their separateness and independence of each other.

5. The confederacy is styled "The United *States* of America," still keeping in view the fact of its component parts being different bodies politic.

6. The second article declares that each state RETAINS its sovereignty, freedom and independence, and all powers not expressly granted; thus asserting anterior sovereignty in each, and conceding it to every other.

7. Various provisions shew that the parties kept in view, throughout, the distinctness of their several communities, and their attributes of sovereignty; thus

8. "The better to secure and perpetuate mutual friendship and intercourse between the people of the DIFFERENT states in this Union, it is provided, that the free inhabitants of each shall be entitled to all the privileges of citizens in the several states;" a provision utterly unnecessary, if they formed but one people.

9. The states are restricted from sending ambassadors, entering into treaties, engaging in war, or keeping troops or navies; thus clearly admitting, that but for this restriction, every state would possess these important attributes of sovereignty.

10. In assenting to the articles of confederation, the states acted independently of each other, and the *legislatures* of the several states, through their delegates, declared their respective assents.

11. No state was held bound which did not expressly assent, and no change was to be made in the articles at any time without the consent of *every state.*

12. The congress under this confederation was composed of delegates *not* elected by the *people*, but by the *legislatures* in each state.

13. Those delegates might be *recalled* by the legislatures, and were liable to be instructed by them.

14. The ratification of the articles by the states was by delegates acting under instructions of the state legislatures.

15. And every delegate in signing expressly declared that he did so "on the part and behalf of the state" he represented.

Lastly. Several of the states at first declared their assent to the articles which were drawn up in 1778. Maryland withheld her assent till 1781; a fact which distinctly negatives all notion of the nationality of the act.

It is time that I should now lay before the student judge Upshur's remarks on the subject, of which I have been treating:

"The examination of this part of the subject has probably been already drawn out to too great an extent; but it would not be complete without some notice of another ground, upon which our author rests his favourite idea—that the people of the colonies formed 'one people' or nation. Even if this unity was not produced by the appointment of the revolutionary government, or by the nature of the powers exercised by them, and acquiesced in by the people, he thinks there can be no doubt that this was the necessary result of the declaration of independence. In order that he may be fully understood upon this point, I will transcribe the entire passage relating to it:

"'In the next place, the colonies did not severally act for themselves and proclaim their own independence. It is true that some of the states had previously formed incipient governments for themselves; but it was done in compliance with the recommendations of congress. Virginia, on the 29th of June 1776, by a convention of delegates, declared 'the government of this country, as formerly exercised under the crown of Great Britain, totally dissolved,' and proceeded to form a new constitution of government. New Hampshire also formed a new government in December 1775, which was manifestly intended to be temporary, 'during (as they said) the unhappy and unnatural contest with Great Britain.' New Jersey, too, established a frame of government on the 2d July 1776; but it was expressly declared that it should be void upon a reconciliation with Great Britain. And South Carolina, in March 1776, adopted a constitution of government; but this was in like manner 'established until an accommodation between Great Britain and America could be obtained.' But the declaration of the independence of all the colonies was the united act of all. It was 'a declaration by the representatives of the United States of America, in congress assembled;'—'by the delegates appointed by the good people of the colonies,' as, in a prior declaration of rights, they were called. It was not an act done by the state governments then organized, nor by persons chosen by them. It was emphatically the act of the whole *people* of the United Colonies, by the instrumentality of their representatives, chosen for that, among other purposes. It was an act not competent to the state governments, or any of them, as organized under their charters, to adopt. Those charters neither contemplated the case nor provided for it. It was an act of original, inherent sovereignty by the people themselves, resulting from their right to change the form of government, and to institute a new government, whenever necessary for their safety and happiness. So the declaration of independence treats it. No state had presumed, of itself, to form a new government, or provide for the exigencies of the times, without consulting congress on the subject; and when they acted, it was in pursuance of the recommendation of congress. It was, therefore, the achievement of the whole for the benefit of the whole. The people of the United Colonies made the United Colonies free and independent states, and absolved them from allegiance to the British crown. The declaration of independence has, accordingly, always been treated as an act of paramount and sovereign authority, complete and perfect *per se;* and *ipso facto* working an entire dissolution of all political connexion with, and allegiance to, Great Britain. And this, not merely as a practical fact, but in a legal and constitutional view of the matter by courts of justice.'

"The first question which this passage naturally suggests to the mind of the reader is this: if two or more nations or people, confessedly separate, distinct and independent, each having its own peculiar government, without any 'direct political connexion with each other,' yet owing the same allegiance to one common superior, should unite in a declaration of rights which they believed belonged to all of them alike, would that circumstance alone make them 'one people?' Stripped of the circumstances with which the author has surrounded it, this is, at last, the only proposition involved. If Spain, Naples and Holland, while they were 'dependencies' of the imperial crown of France, had united in declaring that they were oppressed, in the same mode and degree, by the measures of that crown, and that they did, for that reason, disclaim all allegiance to it, and assume the station of 'free and independent states,' would they thereby have become one people? Surely this will not be asserted by any one. We should see, in that act, nothing more than the union of several independent sovereignties, for the purpose of effecting a common object, which each felt itself too weak to effect, alone. Nothing would be more natural, than that nations so situated should establish a common military power, a common treasury, and a common agency, through which to carry on their intercourse with other powers; but that all this should unite them together, so as to form them into one nation, is a consequence not readily perceived. The case here supposed, is precisely that of the American colonies, if those colonies were, in point of fact, separate, distinct, and independent of one another. If they were so, (and I think it has been shewn that they were,) then the fact that they united in the declaration of independence, does not make them 'one people,' any more than a similar declaration would have made Spain, Naples and Holland one people; if they were not so, then they were one people already, and the declaration of independence did not render them either more or less identical. It is true, the analogy here supposed does not hold in every particular; the relations of the colonies to one another were certainly closer, in many respects, than those of Spain, Naples and Holland, to one another. But as to all purposes involved in the present enquiry, the analogy is perfect. The effect attributed to the declaration of independence, presupposes that the colonies were not 'one people' before; an effect which is in no manner changed or modified by any other circumstance in their relation to one another. That fact, alone, is necessary to be enquired into; and until that fact is ascertained, the author's reasoning as to the effect of the declaration of independence, in making them 'one people,' does not apply. He is obliged, therefore, to abandon the ground previously taken, to wit, that the colonies were one people *before* the declaration of independence. And having abandoned it, he places the colonies, as to this question, upon the footing of any other separate and distinct nations; and, as to these, it is quite evident that the conclusion which he has drawn in the case of the colonies, could not be correct, unless it would be equally correct in the case of Spain, Naples and Holland, above supposed.

"The mere fact, then, that the colonies united in the declaration of independence, did not *necessarily* make them one people. But it may be said that this fact ought, at least, to be received as proof that they considered themselves as one people already. The argument is fair, and I freely let it go for what it is worth. The opinion of the congress of 1775, whatever it may have been, and however strongly expressed, could not possibly change the historical facts. It depended upon those facts, alone, whether the colonies were one people or not. They might, by their agreement, expressed through their agents in congress, make themselves one people through all time to come; but their power, as to this matter, could not extend to the time past. Indeed, it is contended, not only by our author, but by others, that the colonies did, *by and in that act*, agree to become 'one people' for the future. They suppose that such agreement is implied, if not expressed, in the following passages: 'We, therefore, the representatives of the United States of America,'—'do, in the name and by the authority of the good people of these colonies, solemnly publish and declare that these United Colonies are, and of right ought to be, free and independent states.' Let us test the correctness of this opinion, by the history of the time, and by the rules of fair criticism.

"The congress of 1775, by which independence was declared, was appointed, as has been before shewn, by the colonies in their separate and distinct capacity, each acting for itself, and not conjointly with any other. They were the representatives, each of his own colony, and not of any other; each had authority to act in the name of his own colony, and not in that of any other; each colony gave its own vote by its own representatives, and not by those of any other colony. Of course, it was as separate and distinct colonies that they deliberated on the declaration of independence. When, therefore, they declare, in the adoption of that measure, that they act as 'the representatives of the United States of America,' and 'in the name and by the authority of the good people of these colonies,' they must of course be understood as speaking in the character in which they had all along acted; that is, as the representatives of separate and distinct colonies, and not as the joint representatives of any one people. A decisive proof of this, is found in the fact, that the colonies voted on the adoption of that measure in their separate character, each giving one vote by all its own representatives, who acted in strict obedience to specific instructions from their respective colonies, and the members signed the declaration in that way. So, also, when they declared that 'these United Colonies are, and of right ought to be, free and independent states,' they meant only that their respective communities, which until then had been dependent colonies, should thereafter be independent states, and that the same union which existed between them as colonies, should be continued between them as states. The measure under consideration looked only to their relation to the mother country, and not to their relation to one another; and the sole question before them was, whether they should continue in a state of dependence on the British crown, or not. Having determined that they would not, they from that moment ceased to be colonies, and became states; united, precisely as before, for the common purpose of achieving their common liberty. The idea of forming a closer union, by the mere act of declaring themselves independent, could scarcely have occurred to any one of them. The necessity of such a measure must have been apparent to all, and it had long before engaged their attention in a different form. Men, of their wisdom and forecast, meditating a measure so necessary to their common safety, would not have left it as a mere matter of *inference* from another measure. In point of fact, it was already before them, in the form of a distinct proposition, and had been so ever since their first meeting in May

1775.(*c*) It is impossible to suppose, therefore, in common justice to the sagacity of congress, that they meant any thing more by the declaration of independence, than simply to sever the tie which had theretofore bound them to England, and to assert the rights of the separate and distinct colonies, as separate and independent states; particularly as the language which they use is fairly susceptible of this construction. The instrument itself is entitled, 'the unanimous declaration of the thirteen United States of America;' of *states*, separate and distinct bodies politic, and not of 'one people' or nation, composed of all of them together; 'united,' as independent states may be, by compact or agreement, and not *amalgamated*, as they would be, if they formed *one* nation or body politic.

(*c*) A document which I have not met with elsewhere, but which may be found in the Appendix to professor Tucker's elaborate and instructive Life of Jefferson, affords important evidence upon this point. As early as May 1775, the plan of a "confederation and perpetual union" among the colonies, was prepared and proposed for adoption. It was not in fact adopted, but its provisions shew, in the strongest manner, in what light the colonies regarded their relation to one another. The proposed union was called "a firm *league* of friendship;" each colony reserved to itself "as much as it might think proper of its own present laws, customs, rights, privileges and peculiar jurisdictions, within its own limits; and may amend its own constitution as may seem best to its own assembly or convention;" the external relations of the colonies were to be managed by their general government alone, and all amendments of their "constitution," as they termed it, were to be proposed by congress and "approved by a majority of the colony assemblies." It can scarcely be contended that this "league of friendship," this "confederation and perpetual union," would, if it had been adopted, have rendered the people of the several colonies less identical than they were before. If, in their own opinion, they were "one people" already, no league or confederation was necessary, and no one would have thought of proposing it. The very fact, therefore, that it was proposed as a necessary measure "for their common defence against their enemies, for the security of their liberties and their properties, the safety of their persons and families, and their mutual and general welfare," proves that they did not consider themselves as already "one people," in any sense or to any extent which would enable them to effect those important objects.

This proposition was depending and undetermined at the time of the declaration of independence.

"Is it true then, as the author supposes, that the 'colonies did not severally act for themselves, and proclaim their own independence? It is true that they acted *together;* but is it not equally true that each *acted for itself alone*, without pretending to any right or authority to bind any other? Their declaration was simply their *joint expression* of their separate wills; each expressing its own will, and not that of any other; each bound by its own act, and not responsible for the act of any other. If the colonies had severally declared their independence through their own legislatures, and had afterwards agreed to unite their forces together, to make a common cause of their contest, and to submit their common interests to the management of a common council chosen by themselves, wherein would their situation have been different? And is it true that this declaration of independence 'was not an act done by the state governments then organized, nor by persons chosen by them?' that 'it was emphatically the act of the whole *people* of the United Colonies, by the instrumentality of their representatives chosen for that among other purposes?' What representatives were those that were chosen by 'the people of the United Colonies? When and how were they chosen? Those who declared the colonies independent were chosen more than a year before that event; they were chosen by the colonies separately, and, as has already been shewn, through the instrumentality of their own 'governments then organized;' they were chosen, not for the 'purpose' of declaring the colonies independent, but of protecting them against oppression, and bringing about a reconciliation with the parent country, upon fair terms, if possible. (Jefferson's Notes, 1st ed. 128, 129.) If there were any other representatives than these concerned in the declaration of independence, if that act was performed by representatives chosen by 'the whole people of the colonies,' for that or any other purpose, if any such representatives *could possibly have been chosen* by the colonies as then organized, no historical record, that has yet met my view, contains one syllable of the matter.

"The author seems to attach but little importance to the fact, that several of the colonies had established separate governments for themselves, prior to the declaration of independence. He regards this as of little consequence; because he thinks that the colonies so acted only in pursuance of the recommendation of congress, and would not have 'presumed' to do it, 'without consulting congress upon the subject;' and because the governments so established were, for the most part, designed to be temporary, and to continue only during the contest with England. Such recommendation was given, in express terms, to New Hampshire and South Carolina, in November 1775, and to Virginia, in December of that year; and on the 10th May 1776, 'it was resolved to *recommend* to the respective assemblies and conventions of the United Colonies, where no government sufficient to the exigencies of their affairs had been established, to adopt such a government as should, in the opinion of the representatives of the people, best conduce to the happiness and safety of their constituents in particular, and of America in general.' The preamble to this resolution was not adopted till the 15th May. (1 Elliott's Debates, 80, 83.) It is evident, from the language here employed, that congress claimed no power over the colonies as to this matter, and no right to influence or control them in the exercise of the important function of forming their own governments. It *recommended* only; and, contemplating the colonies as separate and distinct, referred it to the assembly or convention of each, to establish any form of government which might be acceptable to its own people. Of what consequence was it, whether the colonies acted upon the recommendation and advice of others, or merely upon their own will and counsels? With whatever *motive* the act was performed, it was one of supreme and sovereign power, and such as could not have been performed except by a sovereign people. And whether the government so established was intended to last for ever, or only for a limited time, did not affect its character as an act of sovereign power. In point of fact, then, the colonies which established such governments did, by that very act, assert their sovereignty and independence. They had no power, under their charters, to change their governments. They could do so only by setting their charters aside, and acting upon their inherent, sovereign right: and this was *revolution*. In effect, therefore, many of the colonies had declared their independence prior to the 4th July, 1776; they had commenced the revolution, and were considered by England as in a state of rebellion. Of Virginia this is emphatically true. Her declaration of rights was made on the 12th of June 1776; and her constitution was adopted on the 29th of the same month. This constitution continued until 1829. Her subsequent declaration of independence, on the 4th of July, in common with the other colonies, was but a more public, though not a more solemn affirmation of what she had previously done; a pledge to the whole world, that what she had resolved on in her separate character, she would unite with the other colonies in performing. She could not declare herself free and independent more distinctly, in that form, than she had already done, by asserting her sovereign and irresponsible power, in throwing off her former government, and establishing a new one for herself.(*d*)

(*d*) In point of fact, Virginia declared her independence on the 15*th of May* 1776. The following beautiful allusion to that scene is extracted from an address delivered by judge Beverly Tucker, of William and Mary college, before the Petersburg lyceum on the 15th May 1839:

"That spectacle, on this day sixty-three years, Virginia exhibited to the world; and the memory of that majestic scene it is now my task to rescue from oblivion. It was on that day that she renounced her colonial dependence on Great Britain, and separated herself forever from that kingdom. Then it was that, bursting the manacles of a foreign tyranny, she, in the same moment, imposed upon herself the salutary restraints of law and order. In that moment she commenced the work of forming a government, complete within itself; and having perfected that work, she, on the 29th of June in the same year, performed the highest function of independent sovereignty, by adopting, ordaining and establishing the constitution under which all of us were born. Then it was that, sufficient to herself for all the purposes of government, she prescribed that oath of fealty and allegiance to her sole and separate sovereignty, which all of us, who have held any office under her authority, have solemnly called upon the Searcher of hearts to witness and record. In that hour, gentlemen, it could not be certainly known, that the other colonies would take the same decisive step. It was, indeed, expected. In the same breath in which she had declared her own independence, Virginia had advised it. She had instructed her delegates in the general congress to urge it; and it was by the voice of one of her sons, whose name will ever proudly live in her history, that the word of power was spoken, at which the chain that bound the colonies to the parent kingdom fell asunder, 'as flax that severs at the touch of fire.' But even then, and while the terms of the *general* declaration of independence

"There is yet another view of this subject, which cannot be properly omitted. It has already been shewn that, prior to the revolution, the colonies were separate and dis-

were yet unsettled, hers had already gone forth. The voice of her defiance was already ringing in the tyrant's ears; hers was the cry that summoned him to the strife; hers was the shout that invited his vengeance: '*Me! me! Adsum qui feci; in me, convertite ferrum.*'"

This beautiful address, abounding in patriotic sentiments, and sound political doctrines, clothed in the richest language, ought to be in the hands of every citizen, and particularly of those of Virginia. The following extract from the journals of the convention, containing the history of this interesting event, cannot fail to be acceptable to every American reader:

"*Wednesday, May* 15*th*, 1776.

"The convention, then, according to the order of the day, resolved itself into a committee on the state of the colony, and, after some time spent therein, Mr. President resumed the chair, and Mr. Cary reported that the committee had, according to order, had under their consideration the state of the colony, and had come to the following resolutions thereupon; which he read in his place, and afterwards delivered in at the clerk's table, where the same were again twice read, and unanimously agreed to; one hundred and twelve members being present.

"For as much as all the endeavours of the United Colonies, by the most decent representations and petitions to the king and parliament of Great Britain, to restore peace and security to America under the British government, and a reunion with that people, upon just and liberal terms, instead of a redress of grievances, have produced, from an imperious and vindictive administration, increased insult, oppression, and a vigorous attempt to effect our total destruction. By a late act, all these colonies are declared to be in rebellion, and out of the protection of the British crown, our properties subjected to confiscation, our people, when captivated, compelled to join in the plunder and murder of their relations and countrymen, and all former rapine and oppression of Americans declared legal and just. Fleets and armies are raised, and the aid of foreign troops engaged to assist these destructive purposes. The king's representative in this colony hath not only withheld all the powers of government from operating for our safety, but, having retired on board an armed ship, is carrying on a piratical and savage war against us; tempting our slaves by every artifice to resort to him, and training and employing them against their masters.

"In this state of extreme danger, we have no alternative left, but an abject submission to the will of those overbearing tyrants, or a total separation from the crown and government of Great Britain, uniting and exerting the strength of all America for defence,

tinct, and were not, in any political sense, or for any purpose of government, 'one people.' The *sovereignty* over them was in the British crown; but that sovereignty was not *jointly over all*, but *separately over each*, and might have been abandoned as to some, and retained as to others. The declaration of independence broke this connexion. By that act, and not by the subsequent recognition of their independence, the colonies became free states. What then became of the *sovereignty* of which we speak? It could not be in *abeyance;* the moment it was lost by the British crown it must have vested somewhere else. Doubtless it vested in the states themselves. But as they were separate and distinct as colonies, the sovereignty over one

and forming alliances with foreign powers for commerce and aid in war. Wherefore, appealing to the Searcher of all hearts for the sincerity of former declarations, expressing our desire to preserve our connexion with that nation, and that we are driven from that inclination by their wicked councils, and the eternal laws of self-preservation; resolved unanimously, that the delegates appointed to represent this colony in general congress, be instructed to propose to that respectable body, to declare the United Colonies free and independent states, absolved from all allegiance to, or dependence upon, the crown or parliament of Great Britain; and that they give the assent of this colony to that declaration, and to whatever measures may be thought proper and necessary by the congress, for forming foreign alliances, and a confederation of the colonies, at such time and in such manner as to them may seem best. Provided, that the power of forming government for, and the regulations of the internal concerns of each colony, be left to the respective colonial legislatures.

"Resolved, unanimously, that a committee be appointed to prepare a declaration of rights, and such a plan of government, as will be most likely to maintain peace and order in this colony, and secure substantial and equal liberty to the people.

"And a committee was appointed of the following gentlemen: Mr. Archibald Cary, Mr. Meriwether Smith, Mr. Mercer, Mr. Henry Lee, Mr. Treasurer, Mr. Henry, Mr. Dandridge, Mr. Edmund Randolph, Mr. Gilmer, Mr. Bland, Mr. Digges, Mr. Carrington, Mr. Thomas Ludwell Lee, Mr. Cabell, Mr. Jones, Mr. Blair, Mr. Fleming, Mr. Tazewell, Mr. Richard Cary, Mr. Bullit, Mr. Watts, Mr. Banister, Mr. Page, Mr. Starke, Mr. David Mason, Mr. Adams, Mr. Read and Mr. Thomas Lewis."

It is impossible to contemplate this proceeding on the part of Virginia, without being convinced that she acted from her own free and sovereign will; and that *she*, at least, *did* "presume" to establish a government for herself, without the least regard to the recommendation or the pleasure of congress.

could not vest, either in whole or in part, in any other. Each took to itself that sovereignty which applied *to* itself, and for which alone it had contended with the British crown, to wit, the sovereignty *over* itself. Thus each colony became a free and sovereign state. This is the character which they claim in the very terms of the declaration of independence; in this character they formed the colonial government, and in this character that government always regarded them. Indeed, even in the earlier treaties with foreign powers, the distinct sovereignty of the states is carefully recognized. Thus, the treaty of alliance with France, in 1778, is made between 'the most Christian king and the United States of North America, to wit: New Hampshire, Massachusetts Bay, Rhode Island, Connecticut,' &c., enumerating them all by name. The same form is observed in the treaty of amity and commerce with the states general of the United Netherlands, in 1782, and in the treaty with Sweden, in 1783. In the convention with the Netherlands, in 1782, concerning recaptured vessels, the names of the states are *not* recited, but 'the United States of America' is the style adopted; and so also in some others. This circumstance shews that the two forms of expression were considered equipollent; and that foreign nations, in treating with the revolutionary government, considered that they treated with distinct sovereignties, through their common agent, and not with a new nation, composed of all those sovereign countries together. It is true, they treated with them jointly, and not severally; they considered them all bound to the observance of their stipulations, and they believed that the common authority, which was established between and among them, was sufficient to secure that object. The provisional articles with Great Britain, in 1782, by which our independence was acknowledged, proceed upon the same idea. The first article declares, that 'His Britannic Majesty acknowledges the said United States, *to wit:* New Hampshire, Massachusetts Bay, Rhode Island and Providence Plantations, Connecticut, New York, New Jersey, Pennsylvania, Delaware, Maryland, Virginia, North Carolina, South Carolina and Georgia, to be free, sovereign and independent states; that he treats with them as such,' &c. Thus the very act, by which their former sovereign releases them from their allegiance to him, confirms to each one by name the sovereignty within its own limits, and acknowledges it to be a 'free, sovereign and independent state;' *united*, indeed, with all the others, but not as forming with them any new and separate nation. The language employed is not suited to convey any other idea. If it had been in the contemplation of the parties, that the states had merged themselves into a single nation, something like the following formula would naturally have suggested itself as proper. 'His Britannic Majesty acknowledges that New Hampshire, Massachusetts Bay, &c., former colonies of Great Britain, and now united together as one people, are *a* free, sovereign and *independent state*,' &c. The difference between the two forms of expression, and the strict adaptation of each to the state of things which it contemplates, will be apparent to every reader.

"It requires strong and plain proof to authorize us to say, that a nation once sovereign has ceased to be so. And yet our author requires us to believe this of the colonies, although he acknowledges that he cannot tell, with any degree of confidence or precision, when, how, or to what extent the sovereignty, which they acquired by declaring their independence, was surrendered. According to him, the colonies are to be *presumed* to have yielded this sovereignty to a government established by themselves for a special and temporary purpose, which existed only at their will, and by their aid and support; whose powers were wholly undefined, and, for the most part, exercised by usurpation on its part, and legitimated only by the acquiescence of those who appointed it; whose authority was without any adequate sanction which it could itself apply, and which, as to all the important functions of sovereignty, was a mere name—the shadow of power without its substance! If the fact was really so, I venture to affirm that the history of the world affords no similar instance of folly and infatuation.

"But, whatever may have been the condition of the colonies prior to 1781, there is no room for doubt on the subject, after the final ratification of the articles of confederation in that year. Those articles declare that 'each state retains its sovereignty, freedom and independence, and every power, jurisdiction and right, which is not, by this confederation, expressly delegated to the United States, in congress assembled.' The obvious construction of this clause requires that we should apply these latter words, only to 'powers, jurisdiction and rights;' some of which, as enjoyed by the states under the previous government, were clearly surrendered by the articles of confederation. But their *entire* sovereignty, their *entire* freedom, and their *entire* independence, are reserved, for these are not partible. Indeed, this is clear enough, from the provisions of that instrument, which, throughout, contemplate the states as free, sovereign and independent. It is singular, too, that it should escape the observation of any one, that the very fact of adopting those articles, and the course pursued in doing so, attest, with equal clearness and strength, the *previous* sovereignty and independence of the states. What had the states in their separate character to do with that act, if they formed altogether 'one people?' And yet the states, and the states alone, performed it, each acting for itself, and binding itself. The articles were confirmed by ten states, as early as 1778, by another in 1779, and by another in 1780; and yet they were not obligatory until Maryland acceded to them, 1781. Nothing less than the ratification of them by *all* the states, each acting separately for itself, was deemed sufficient to give them any binding force or authority.

"There is much force and meaning in the word 'retains,' as it occurs in the clause above quoted. Nothing can properly be said to be *retained*, which was not *possessed* before; and, of course, the states possessed before 'sovereignty, freedom and independence.' These they retained without any qualification, or limitation, and they also retained every 'power, jurisdiction and right,' which they did not then *expressly* surrender.

"If these views of the subject be not wholly deceptive, our author has hazarded, without due caution, the opinion that the colonies formed 'one people,' either before or after the declaration of independence; and that they are not to be regarded as sovereign states, after that event. For myself, I profess my utter inability to perceive, in their condition, any nearer approach to 'political personality or individuality,' than may be found in a mere league or confederation between sovereign and independent states; and a very *loose* confederation theirs undoubtedly was."

LECTURE V.

Before I proceed to any examination of the present constitution, which was the next step in the political progress of the United States, it may not be unprofitable to look back to the confederation, and take a rapid view of the causes which led to the adoption of another form of government.

Whatever may be the truth, in a speculative point of view, as to the American colonies having constituted one people, history leaves us no doubt, that long anterior to the revolution, efforts had been made in vain for the formation of associations among them, for their mutual support and protection. They are said to have been jealous of each other's prosperity, and divided by policy, institutions, prejudice and manners;(*a*) and even after the commencement of the revolution, when the pressure of British power made some league or association essential, they seem to have felt that it was the true path of safety, to retain all sovereign powers in their own hands, except those, which imperious necessity demanded should be placed in the hands of the irregular revolutionary government. From the batttle of Lexington in 1775, to the month of August 1778, a war with one of the most powerful nations of the globe, was waged by a congress composed of delegates from the states, appointed either by state legislatures, or conventions; and deriving its powers partly from the commissions of its members, but mainly from the necessities of the time.(*b*) The desperate struggle at length led to the projection of a league or confederation, which was not however ratified by all the states till 1781. By the articles of confederation, congress was invested with the powers of peace and war, of sending and receiving ambassadors, of making treaties with certain restrictions, of coining and borrowing money, of emitting bills of credit, of *ascertaining* the necessary sums, and troops and ships required for

(*a*) 1 Kent. 205.
(*b*) 3 Dall. 91.

the public service, and of appropriating money; together with some other powers of minor character. But the most important of those above mentioned, were unaccompanied by any power to carry them into execution. Most of the granted powers, required for their exercise, the assent of nine states; and when they *were* exercised, they depended altogether upon the faith and punctuality of the states, in complying with requisitions. There was no power to raise a revenue or lay a tax; for the authority as to this matter, only extended to "ascertaining" the sums that each state was to pay. They could enforce *no* law, secure no right, and though entitled to send ambassadors, they had no authority to raise the means of paying them. They could contract debts, but had no means of discharging them. They could pledge the public faith, but could not redeem it. They could make treaties, but not enforce them, and every power which did not execute itself, might be trampled upon with impunity. In short, in the language of general Washington, "the confederation was a shadow without the substance;" congress could declare every thing, but do nothing; borrow money, but not repay a dollar; coin money without the ability of purchasing bullion, and make requisitions which were not complied with, or very unequally, if at all. It has been justly observed,(*c*) "that a government authorized to declare war, but relying on independent states for the means of prosecuting it, capable of contracting debts, and of pledging the public faith for their payment, but depending on thirteen distinct sovereignties for the preservation of that faith, could only be rescued from ignominy and contempt by finding those sovereignties administered by men exempt from the passions incident to human nature!" A hopeless expectation surely! and experience soon demonstrated(*d*) that the great and radical vice in the construction of the confederation, was in the principle of legislation for states and governments in their corporate or collective capacities, as contradistinguished from the individuals of whom they consist. A consequence of this was the want of power in congress to give a *sanction* to its laws. They had no power to ex-

(*c*) 5 Mars. Life of Wash. 31.
(*d*) See the Fed. No. 15.

act obedience or to punish infraction, for they had no *express* authority to exercise force, and they had no power except what *was expressly* given. Hence when they made requisitions, it depended upon the good will or the energy of the state legislatures, whether they complied at all; and as congress had no power to lay or levy taxes, or to raise the revenues necessary for the ordinary expenses of the government, a noncompliance by the states left empty the treasury of the Union. Thus it appears, that the requisitions for the payment of the interest on the domestic debt from 1782 to 1786, amounted to more than six millions, and up to March 1787, only one million was paid: and from November 1784, to January 1786, only 483,000 dollars had been paid into the national treasury.

Another and most important defect of the confederation, was the want of power in congress to regulate foreign and domestic commerce; thus making no provision against one of the most fruitful sources of dissention between the states. Nor was this all. Without some general power over the subject, the commerce of the Union was fated to embarrassment and to languishing. During the war, it had been nearly annihilated by the superior naval power of Great Britain, and the return of peace enabled her in a great measure to monopolize all the benefits of our trade. British ships, with their commodities, had free admission into our ports, while American ships and exports were loaded with heavy exactions, or were prohibited from entry into British ports. In April 1784, congress asked the power for fifteen years only to prohibit the importation and exportation of goods in the ships of nations with whom we had no commercial treaties, and to prohibit subjects of foreign nations from importing any goods not the produce or manufacture of the dominions of their own sovereign. It was refused, as was also a subsequent proposal to grant the power of regulating commerce and laying duties, though those duties were to be collected by and paid over to the states. This proposition did not find sufficient countenance even in congress itself for its passage by that body, and thus the regulation of commerce by congress, which under our present constitution has been found to contribute so largely to our national prosperity, was rejected, even in its least objectionable and least alarming form.

10*

There were other defects seriously urged against the confederation, which justified doubts of its efficacy as a bond of union, or as an enduring scheme of government. At length commissioners were appointed by the state of Virginia,(*e*) to meet commissioners from other states, to take into consideration the trade of the United States, and the relative situation of the trade of the states; and to report such an act on the subject, as when ratified would enable congress to provide the necessary regulations. The commissioners of five states only, met at Annapolis in September 1786, and recommended the appointment of other commissioners, to meet at Philadelphia in May thereafter, "to take into consideration the situation of the United States, and to devise such further provisions as should appear to them necessary to render the constitution of the federal government adequate to the exigencies of the Union; and to report also such an act to congress as when agreed to by it, and ratified by the states, would effectually provide for the same." In February 1787, a motion was accordingly moved, and carried in congress, recommending a convention in Philadelphia, for the purpose of revising and amending the articles of confederation. The convention met in May, (Rhode Island alone having declined to send representatives,) and in September 1787, adopted the present constitution; and directed it to be laid before congress, recommending, at the same time, that it should be submitted to *conventions* of delegates chosen in each state by the *people* THEREOF, under a recommendation of *its legislature* for *their assent and ratification.* Conventions accordingly met, and the constitution was at length finally adopted with amendments, though the ratification of North Carolina was delayed till November 1789, and that of Rhode Island until May 1790. During the respective intervals, those states were altogether sovereign and independent. For nine states having adopted the constitution, the old confederation was at an end, and the new government went into operation on the 4th of March 1789, at which date, neither of those states were members of the Union. General Washington was sworn into office on the 30th of April 1789.

(*e*) The commissioners for Virginia who acted, were Edmund Randolph, James Madison and St. George Tucker.

After this rapid sketch of the origin and adoption of the constitution of the United States, I shall now proceed to the consideration of its nature, presenting the student, however, in the first instance, with judge Story's view of the same matter, as he has given it to us in the 3d chapter of the 3d book of his Commentaries:

"§ 308. In the first place," says he, "what is the true nature and import of the instrument? Is it a treaty, a convention, a league, a contract, or a compact? Who are the parties to it? By whom was it made? By whom was it ratified? What are its obligations? By whom, and in what manner may it be dissolved? Who are to determine its validity and construction? Who are to decide upon the supposed infractions and violations of it? These are questions often asked, and often discussed, not merely for the purpose of theoretical speculation, but as matters of practical importance, and of earnest and even of vehement debate.

"§ 310. It has been asserted by a learned commentator(*f*) that the constitution of the United States is an original, written, federal, and social compact, freely, voluntarily, and solemnly entered into by the several states, and ratified by the people thereof respectively; whereby the several states, and the people thereof, respectively have bound themselves to each other, and to the federal government of the United States, and by which the federal government is bound to the several states and to every citizen of the United States. The author proceeds to expound every part of this definition at large. It is (says he) a compact, by which it is distinguished from a charter or grant, which is either the act of a superior to an inferior, or is founded upon some consideration moving from one of the parties to the other, and operates as an exchange or sale.(*g*) But here the contracting parties, whether considered as states in their political capacity and character, or as individuals, are all equal; nor is there any thing granted from one to another; but each stipulates to

(*f*) 1 Tucker's Black. Comm. App. note D, p. 140 et seq *
(*g*) 1 Tucker's Black. Comm. App. note D, p. 141.

[* The views of judge Tucker, as here presented, have generally the concurrence of that party in the United States which is usually denominated the state-rights party.]

part with, and receive the same thing precisely without any distinction or difference between any of the parties.

"§ 311. It is a federal compact.(*h*) Several sovereign and independent states may unite themselves together by a perpetual confederation, without each ceasing to be a perfect state. They will together form a federal republic. The deliberations in common will offer no violence to each member, though they may in certain respects put some constraint on the exercise of it in virtue of voluntary engagements. The extent, modifications, and objects of the federal authority are mere matters of discretion.(*i*) So long as the separate organization of the members remains, and, from the nature of the compact, must continue to exist both for local and domestic, and for federal purposes, the union is in fact, as well as in theory, an association of states, or a confederacy.

"§ 313. It may be proper to illustrate the distinction between federal compacts and obligations, and such as are social, by one or two examples.(*k*) A federal compact, alliance, or treaty, is an act of the state or body politic,

(*h*) Mr. Jefferson asserts, that the constitution of the United States is a compact between the states. "They entered into a compact," says he, (in a paper designed to be adopted by the legislature of Virginia, as a solemn protest,) "which is called the Constitution of the United States of America, by which they agreed to unite in a single government, as to their relations with each, and with foreign nations, and as to certain other articles particularly specified."* It would, I imagine, be very difficult to point out when, and in what manner, any such compact was made. The constitution was neither made, nor ratified by the states, as sovereignties, or political communities. It was framed by a convention† proposed to the people of the states for their adoption by congress; and was adopted by state conventions—the immediate representatives of the people.

(*i*) 1 Tucker's Black. Comm. Appx. note D, p. 141.

(*k*) Id. 145.

* 4 Jefferson's Corresp. 415.

[† To prove that the constitution was not made by the states, our author says it was framed by a convention. A convention of whom? Of the delegates of thirteen separate and distinct communities, each responsible to its own state only, voting by states, and each state having but one vote. These delegates were appointed by the state legislatures, and were subject to their control. This convention was called at the suggestion of *five states*, by the congress of the United States, which represented *states*. The constitution was recommended by it to the states, and the *states* each called a convention of their own, representing itself only, and ratified the constitution. Throughout the whole the action was *state* action. There was no nationality about it. See the remarks, Lectures, p. 43, 86, 87.]

and not of an individual. On the contrary, a social compact is understood to mean the act of individuals about to create and establish a state or body politic among themselves. If one nation binds itself by treaty to pay a certain tribute to another; or if all the members of the same confederacy oblige themselves to furnish their quotas of a common expense, when required; in either of these cases, the state or body politic only, and not the individual, is answerable for this tribute or quota. This is, therefore, a federal obligation. But, where by any compact, express or implied; a number of persons are bound to contribute their proportions of the common expenses, or to submit to all laws made by the common consent; and where in default of compliance with these engagements the society is authorized to levy the contribution, or to punish the person of the delinquent; this seems to be understood to be more in the nature of a social, than a federal obligation.(*l*)

"§ 314. It is an original compact. Whatever political relation existed between the American colonies antecedent to the revolution, as constituent parts of the British empire, or as dependencies upon it, that relation was completely dissolved, and annihilated from that period. From the moment of the revolution they became severally independent and sovereign states, possessing all the rights, jurisdictions, and authority that other sovereign states, however constituted, or by whatever title denominated, possess; and bound by no ties, but of their own creation, except such, as all other civilized nations are equally bound by, and which together constitute the customary law of nations.(*m*)*

(*l*) 1 Tucker's Black. Comm. App. note D, p. 145.

(*m*) Id. 150.—These views are very different from those which Mr. Dane has, with so much force and perspicuity, urged in his Appendix to his Abridgment to the Law, § 2, p. 10, &c.

" In order correctly to ascertain this rank, this linking together, and this subordination, we must go back as far as January 1774,

[* This seems to me strictly true. Judge Story obviously sides with Mr. Dane, whose notions I deem as unsound as they are novel. Such absurdities scarcely admit of a grave and calm refutation. I shall content myself, therefore, with referring to what is said *ante*, p. 36, and *seq.*, 86, and *seq.*, and with contrasting with these notions, the authoritative opinions of judges Iredell and Chase, p. 44, 46, and 92.]

"§ 315. It is a written compact. Considered as a federal compact or alliance between the states, there is nothing new or singular in this circumstance, as all national compacts since the invention of letters, have probably been reduced to that form. But considered in the light of an original social compact, the American revolution seems to have given birth to this new political phenomenon. In every state a written constitution was framed, and adopted by the people both in their individual and sovereign capacity and character.(*n*)

"§ 316. It is a compact freely, voluntarily and solemnly entered into by the several states, and ratified by

when the thirteen states existed *constitutionally*, in the condition of thirteen *British colonies*, yet, *de facto*, *the people* of them exercised original, sovereign power in their institution in 1774, of the continental congress; and, especially, in June 1775, then vesting in it the great national powers, that will be described; scarcely any of which were resumed. The result will shew, that, on *revolutionary* principles, the general government was, by the *sovereign acts of this people*, first created *de novo*, and *de facto* instituted; and by the same acts, the people vested in it very extensive powers, which have ever remained in it modified and defined by the articles of confederation, and enlarged and arranged anew by the constitution of the United States—2d. that the state governments and states, as *free and independent states*, were, July 4th, 1776, created by the general government, empowered to do it by the people, acting on revolutionary principles, and in their *original, sovereign capacity;* and that all the state governments, *as such*, have been instituted during the existence of the general government, and in subordination to it, and two thirds of them since the constitution of the United States was *ordained and established* by all the people thereof; in that sovereign capacity. These *state* governments have been, by the people of each state, instituted under, and, expressly or impliedly, in subordination to the general government, which is expressly recognized by all to be supreme law; and as the power of the whole is, in the nature of things, superior to the power of a part, other things being equal; the power of a state, a part, is inferior to the power of all the states. Assertions that each of the twenty-four states is completely *sovereign*, that is, as *sovereign* as Russia, or France, of course as sovereign as all the states, and that this sovereignty is above judicial cognizance, merit special attention."

(*n*) 1 Tucker's Black. Comm. App. note D, p. 153.—There is an inaccuracy here; Connecticut did not form a constitution until 1818, and existed until that period under her colonial charter. Rhode Island still is without any constitution, and exercises the powers of government under her colonial charter.

the people thereof respectively; freely, there being neither external nor internal force or violence to influence, or promote the measure; the United States being at peace with all the world and in perfect tranquillity in each state; voluntarily, because the measure had its commencement in the spontaneous acts of the state legislatures, prompted by a due sense of the necessity of some change in the existing confederation; and solemnly, as having been discussed, not only in the general convention, which proposed and framed it; but afterwards in the legislatures of the several states; and finally in the conventions of all the states, by whom it was adopted and ratified.(*o*)

"§ 317. It is a compact by which the several states and the people thereof respectively have bound themselves to each other, and to the federal government. The constitution had its commencement with the body politic of the several states; and its final adoption and ratification was by the several legislatures referred to, and completed by conventions especially, called and appointed for that purpose in each state. The acceptance of the constitution was not only an act of the body politic of each state, but of the people thereof respectively in their sovereign character and capacity. The body politic was competent to bind itself, so far as the constitution of the state permitted.(*p*) But not having power to bind the people in cases beyond their constitutional authority, the assent of the people was indispensably necessary to the validity of the compact, by which the rights of the people might be diminished, or submitted to a new jurisdiction, or in any manner affected. From hence, not only the body politic of the several states, but every citizen thereof, may be considered as parties to the compact, and to have bound themselves reciprocally to each other for the due observance of it; and also to have bound themselves to the federal government, whose authority has been thereby created and established.(*q*)*

(*o*) 1 Tucker's Black. Comm. note D, p. 155, 156.
(*p*) Id. 169.
(*q*) Id. 170.

[* The *legislature* of a state can never of itself make a new constitution, since in so doing it must enlarge or limit its powers *other-*

"§ 318. Lastly. It is a compact, by which the federal government is bound to the several states, and to every citizen of the United States. Although the federal government can in no possible view be considered as a party to a compact made anterior to its existence, and by which it was in fact created; yet, as the creature of that compact, it must be bound by it to its creators, the several states in the Union, and the citizens thereof. Having no existence, but under the constitution, nor any rights but such as that instrument confers; and those very rights, being in fact duties, it can possess no legitimate power, but such as is absolutely necessary for the performance of a duty prescribed, and enjoined by the constitution.(*r*) Its duties then became the exact measure of its powers; and whenever it exerts a power for any other purpose, than the performance of a duty prescribed by the constitution, it transgresses its proper limits, and violates the public trust. Its duties being moreover imposed for the general benefit and security of the several states in their political character, and of the people, both in their sovereign and individual capacity, if these objects be not obtained, the government does not answer the end of its creation. It is, therefore, bound to the several states respectively, and to every citizen thereof, for the due execution of those duties, and the observance of this obligation is enforced under the solemn sanction of an oath from those, who administer the government.

"§ 319. Such is a summary of the reasoning of the learned author, by which he has undertaken to vindicate his views of the nature of the constitution. That reasoning has been quoted at large, and for the most part in his own words; not merely as his own, but as representing, in a general sense, the opinions of a large body of statesmen and jurists in different parts of the Union, avowed and acted upon in former times; and recently revived under

(*r*) 1 Tucker's Black. Comm. note D, p. 170.

wise than as prescribed by the constitution which gave it being. It can only refer the matter to the action of the people of *its own state* through a convention. And the action of such convention is *state* action, because the convention represents a separate and independent state. See Story, 330.]

circumstances, which have given them increased importance, if not a perilous influence.(*s*)

"§ 320. It is wholly beside our present purpose to engage in a critical commentary upon the different parts of this exposition. It will be sufficient for all the practical objects we have in view, to suggest the difficulties of main-

(*s*) Many traces of these opinions will be found in the public debates in the state legislatures and in congress at different periods. In the resolutions of Mr. Taylor, in the Virginia legislature in 1798, it was resolved, "that this assembly doth explicitly and peremptorily declare, that it views the powers of the federal government as resulting from the compact, *to which the states are parties.*"—See Dane's Apendix, p. 17. The original resolution had the word "*alone*" after "states," which was struck out upon the motion of the original mover, it having been asserted in the debate, that the *people* were parties also, and by some of the speakers, that the people were exclusively parties.

The Kentucky resolutions of 1797, (which were drafted by Mr. Jefferson,) declare "that to this compact [the federal constitution] each state acceded as a state, and is an integral party." North American Review, October 1830, p. 501, 545. In the resolutions of the senate of South Carolina, in November 1817, it is declared, "that the constitution of the United States is a compact between the people of the different states with each other, as separate and independent sovereignties." In November 1799, the Kentucky legislature passed a resolution, declaring, that the federal states had a right to judge of any infraction of the constitution, and, that a nullification by those sovereignties of all unauthorized acts done under colour of that instrument is the rightful remedy. North American Review, Id. 503. Mr. Madison, in the Virginia report of 1800, re-asserts the right of the states, as parties, to decide upon the unconstitutionality of any measure. Report, p. 6, 7, 8, 9. The Virginia legislature, in 1829, passed a resolution, declaring, that "the constitution of the United States being a federative compact between sovereign states, in construing which no common arbiter is known, each state has the right to construe the compact for itself."* Mr. vice president Calhoun's letter to governor Hamilton, of August 28, 1832, contains a very elaborate exposition of this among other doctrines.

Mr. Dane, in his Appendix, (§ 3, p. 11,) says, that for forty years one great party has received the constitution, as a federative compact among the states, and the other great party, not as such a compact, but in the main, national and popular. The grave debate in the senate of the United States, on Mr. Foot's resolution, in the winter of 1830, deserves to be read for its able exposition of the doctrines maintained on each side. Mr. Dane makes frequent references to it in his Appendix.—4 Elliot's Debates, 315 to 330.

*3 American Annual Register; Local History, 131.

taining its leading positions, to expound the objections, which have been urged against them, and to bring into notice those opinions, which rest on a very different basis of principles.

"§ 321. The obvious deductions,* which may be, and indeed have been, drawn from considering the constitution as a compact between the states, are, that it operates as a mere treaty, or convention between them, and has an obligatory force upon each state no longer, than suits its pleasure, or its consent continues; that each state has a right to judge for itself in relation to the nature, extent and obligations of the instrument, without being at all bound by the interpretation of the federal government, or by that of any other state; and that each retains the power to withdraw from the confederacy and to dissolve the connexion, when such shall be its choice; and may suspend the operations of the federal government, and nullify its acts within its own territorial limits, whenever, in its own opinion, the exigency of the case may require.(*t*) These con-

(*t*) Virginia, in the resolutions of her legislature on the tariff, in February 1829, declared, "that there is no common arbiter to construe the constitution; *being a federative compact between* sovereign states, each state has a right to construe the compact for itself." 9 Dane's Abridg. ch. 187, art. 20, § 14, p. 589. See also North American Review, October 1830, p. 488 to 528. The resolutions of Kentucky of 1798, contain a like declaration, that "to this compact [the constitution] each state acceded as a state, and is an integral party; that the government created by this compact was not made the exclusive, or final judge of the powers delegated to itself, &c.; but that, as in all other cases of compact among parties having no common judge, each party has an equal right to judge for itself, *as well of infractions, as of the mode and measure of redress.*" North American Review, October 1830, p. 501. The Kentucky resolutions of 1799, go further, and assert, "that the several states who formed that instrument, [the constitution,] being sovereign and independent, have the unquestionable right to judge of its infraction; and that a nullification by those sovereign-

[* How far these deductions are disavowed, and what principles are considered as legitimate, in reference to the right of a state to judge of infractions, and to determine for itself, the nature and extent of its obligations, will be hereafter shewn. It will then appear, that the author of these pages, is neither nullifier nor anarchist, and that however he differs from the learned commentator in his premises, he will not merit his reproaches for the conclusions to which he arrives.]

clusions may not always be avowed; but they flow naturally from the doctrines, which we have under consideration.(*u*) They go to the extent of reducing the government to a mere confederacy during pleasure; and of thus presenting the extraordinary spectacle of a nation existing only at the will of each of its constituent parts.

"§ 322. If this be the true interpretation of the instrument, it has wholly failed to express the intentions of its framers, and brings back, or at least may bring back, upon us all the evils of the old confederation, from which we were supposed to have had a safe deliverance. For the power to operate upon individuals, instead of operating merely on states, is of little consequence, though yielded by the constitution, if that power is to depend for its exercise upon the continual consent of all the members upon every emergency. We have already seen, that the framers of the instrument contemplated no such dependence. Even under the confederation it was deemed a gross heresy to maintain that a party to a compact has a right to revoke that compact; and the possibility of a question of this nature was deemed to prove the necessity of laying the foundations of our national government deeper, than in the mere sanction of delegated authority.(*v*) 'A compact between

ties of all unauthorized acts done under colour of that instrument is the rightful remedy." North American Review, Id. 503; 4 Elliot's Debates, 315, 322. In Mr. Madison's Report in the Virginia legislature, in January 1800, it is also affirmed that the states are parties to the constitution; but by *states* he here means (as the context explains) the people of the states. That report insists, that the states are in the last resort, the ultimate judges of the infractions of the constitution. p. 6, 7, 8, 9.

(*u*) I do not mean to assert, that all those, who held these doctrines, have adopted the conclusions drawn from them. There are eminent exceptions; and among them the learned commentator on Blackstone's Commentaries seems properly numbered. See 1 Tucker's Black. App. 170, 171, § 8. See the debates in the senate on Mr. Foot's resolution in 1830, and Mr. Dane's Appendix, and his Abridgment and Digest, 9th vol. ch. 187, art. 20, § 13 to 22, p. 588, et seq.; North American Review for October 1830, on the debates on the public lands, p. 481 to 486, 488 to 528; 4 Elliot's Debates, 315 to 330; Madison's Virginia Report, January 1800, p. 6, 7, 8, 9; 4 Jefferson's Correspondence, 415; vice president Calhoun's letter to governor Hamilton, August 28, 1832.

(*v*) The Federalist, No. 22; Id. No. 43; see also Mr. Patterson's opinion in the convention, 4 Elliot's Debates, 74, 75; and Yates's Minutes.

independent sovereigns, founded on acts of legislative authority, can pretend to no higher validity, than a league or treaty between the parties. It is an established doctrine on the subject of treaties, that all the articles are mutually conditions of each other; that a breach of any one article is a breach of the whole treaty; and that a breach committed by either of the parties absolves the others, and authorizes them, if they please, to pronounce the compact violated and void.'(*w*) Consequences like these, which place the dissolution of the government in the hands of a single state, and enable it at will to defeat, or suspend the operation of the laws of the Union, are too serious, not to require us to scrutinize with the utmost care and caution the principles, from which they flow, and by which they are attempted to be justified.*

"§ 350. In what light, then, is the constitution of the United States to be regarded?† Is it a mere compact, treaty, or confederation of the states composing the Union,

(*w*) The Federalist, No. 43.—Mr. Madison, in the Virginia Report of January 1800, asserts, (p. 6, 7,) that "the states being parties to the constitutional compact, and in their sovereign capacity, it follows of necessity, that there can be no tribunal above their authority to decide in the last resort, whether the compact made by them be violated; and consequently, that as the parties to it, they must themselves decide in the last resort such questions, as may be of sufficient magnitude to require their interposition." Id. p. 8, 9..

[* Such a heresy will not be found in these pages. While their author admits that every party to a compact has a right to judge of its infraction, and to refuse longer to be bound by it when broken, he contends on the other hand, that every other party has an equal right to judge, and that the recusant acts upon his own responsibility, in undertaking to decide and to act contrary to the prevailing opinion of the other parties to the contract.]

[† As a compact between the states, whereby they have ordained and established the constitution for the United States of America. The people of the thirteen distinct and separate political bodies or communities constituting states, agreed together in a general convention of delegates from them severally and respectively, to ordain and establish the constitution as a form of government for the United States. The constitution may therefore be looked upon rather as the *result* of the *agreement*, (see page 339,) than as the agreement itself. The *agreement* of the states is in the preamble, "We, the people of the United States, do ordain and establish this constitution for the United States of America."]

or of the people thereof, whereby each of the several states, and the people thereof, have respectively bound themselves to each other? Or is it a form of government, which, having been ratified by a majority of the people in all the states, is obligatory upon them, as the prescribed rule of conduct of the sovereign power, to the extent of its provisions?

"351. Let us consider, in the first place, whether it is to be deemed a compact. By this, we do not mean an act of solemn assent by the people to it, as a form of government, (of which there is no room for doubt,) but a contract imposing mutual obligations, and contemplating the permanent subsistence of parties having an independent right to construe, control, and judge of its obligations. If in this latter sense it is to be deemed a compact, it must be, either because it contains on its face stipulations to that effect, or because it is necessarily implied from the nature and objects of a frame of government.

"§ 352. There is nowhere found upon the face* of the constitution any clause, intimating it to be a compact, or in anywise providing for its interpretation, as such. On the contrary, the preamble emphatically speaks of it, as a solemn ordinance and establishment of government. The language is, 'We, the people of the United States, do *ordain* and *establish* this *constitution* for the United States of America.' *The people* do *ordain* and *establish*, not contract and stipulate with each other.(*x*) The people of the *United States*, not the distinct people of a *particular state*

(*x*) The words "ordain and establish" are also found in the 3d article of the constitution. "The judicial power shall be vested in one supreme court, and in such inferior courts, as the congress may from time to time *ordain* and *establish*." How is this to be done by congress? Plainly by a law; and when ordained and established, is such a law a contract or compact between the legislature and the people, or the court, or the different departments of the government? No. It is neither more nor less than a law, made by competent authority, upon an assent or agreement of minds. In *Martin* v. *Hunter*, (1 Wheat. R. 304, 324,) the supreme court said, "The constitution of the United States was ordained

[* The fallacy of this position, and of the greater part of those which follow in the extract from the Commentaries, cannot be fully exposed in a note. I shall therefore give, as we proceed, only a few short annotations, and hereafter take up and examine the residue of the passage in detail.]

with the people of the other states. The people ordain and establish a '*constitution*,' not a '*confederation*.' The distinction between a constitution and a confederation is well known and understood. The latter, or at least a pure confederation, is a mere treaty or league between independent states, and binds no longer, than during the good pleasure of each.(*y*) It rests forever in articles of compact, where each is, or may be the supreme judge of its own rights and duties. The former is a permanent form of government, where the powers, once given, are irrevocable, and cannot be resumed or withdrawn at pleasure. Whether formed by a single people, or by different societies of people, in their political capacity, a constitution, though originating in consent, becomes, when ratified, obligatory, as a fundamental ordinance or law.(*z*) The constitution of a confederated republic, that is, of a national republic formed of several states, is, or at least may be, not less an irrevocable form of goverment, than the constitution of a state formed and ratified by the aggregate of the several counties of the state.(*a*)*

"§ 353. If it had been the design of the framers of the constitution or of the people, who ratified it, to consider it a mere confederation, resting on treaty stipulations, it is difficult to conceive, that the appropriate terms should not have been found in it. The United States were no stran-

and established, not by the states in their sovereign capacities, but emphatically, as the preamble of the constitution declares, 'by the people of the United States.'" To the same effect is the reasoning of Mr. chief justice Marshall, in delivering the opinion of the court in *M'Culloch* v. *Maryland*, (4 Wheaton, 316, 402 to 405, already cited.)

(*y*) The Federalist, No. 9, 15, 17, 18, 33; Webster's Speeches, 1830; Dane's App. § 2, p. 11, § 14, p. 25, &c.; Id. § 10, p. 21; Mr. Martin's letter, 3 Elliot, 53; 1 Tucker's Black. Comm. App. 146.

(*z*) 1 Wilson's Lectures, 417.

(*a*) See The Federalist, No. 9; Id. No. 15, 16; Id. No. 33; Id. No. 39.

[* In this proposition I concur, with this modification, that though irrevocable by the ordinary forms of government, it may be revocable by the exercise of rights paramount to all constitutions; but the state which asserts these rights, does so on its own responsibility, since in matters between states, if one has a right to judge, others have also. The right of secession can only be revolutionary.]

gers to compacts of this nature.(*b*) They had subsisted to a limited extent before the revolution. The articles of confederation, though in some few respects national, were mainly of a pure federative character, and were treated as stipulations between states for many purposes independent and sovereign.(*c*) And yet (as has been already seen) it was deemed a political heresy to maintain, that under it any state had a right to withdraw from it at pleasure, and repeal its operation; and that a party to the compact had a right to revoke that compact.(*d*) The only places, where the terms, *confederation* or *compact*, are found in the constitution, apply to subjects of an entirely different nature, and manifestly in contradistinction to *constitution*. Thus, in the tenth section of the first article it is declared, that "no state shall enter into any treaty, alliance, or *confederation*;"—"no state shall, without the consent of congress, &c., enter into any agreement or *compact* with another state, or with a foreign power." Again, in the sixth article it is declared, that "all debts contracted, and engagements entered into, before the adoption of this constitution, shall be as valid against the United States under this *constitution*, as under the *confederation*." Again, in the tenth amendment it is declared, that "the powers not *delegated* by the constitution, nor prohibited by it to the states, are reserved to the states respectively, or to the people." A contract can in no just sense be called a delegation of powers.*

(*b*) New England Confederacy of 1643; 3 Kent. Comm. 190, 191, 192; Rawle on Const. Introduct. p. 24, 25. In the ordinance of 1787, for the government of the territory northwest of the Ohio, certain articles were expressly declared to be "articles of *compact* between the original states, [i. e. the United States,] and the people and states [states *in futuro*, for none were then in being] in the said territory." But to guard against any possible difficulty, it was declared, that these articles should "forever remain unalterable, unless by *common consent*." So, that though a compact, neither party was at liberty to withdraw from it at its pleasure, or to absolve itself from its obligations. Why was not the constitution of the United States declared to be articles of compact, if that was the intention of the framers?

(*c*) The Federalist, No. 15, 22, 39, 40, 43; *Ogden* v. *Gibbons*, 9 Wheaton's R. 1, 187.

(*d*) The Federalist, No. 22; Id. No. 43.

[* But why may there not be a compact amongst several *for* a delegation of powers?]

"354. But that, which would seem conclusive on the subject, (as has been already stated,) is the very language of the constitution itself, declaring it to be a supreme fundamental law, and to be of judicial obligation, and recognition in the administration of justice. 'This constitution,' says the sixth article, 'and the laws of the United States, which shall be made in pursuance thereof, and all treaties made, or which shall be made under the authority of the United States, *shall be the supreme law of the land;* and the *judges* in every state shall be bound thereby, *any thing in the constitution or laws* of any state to the contrary notwithstanding.' If it is the supreme law, how can the people of any state, either by any form of its own constitution, or laws, or other proceedings, repeal, or abrogate, or suspend it?

"§ 355. But, if the language of the constitution were less explicit and irresistible, no other inference could be correctly deduced from a view of the nature and objects of the instrument. The design is to establish a form of government. This, of itself, imports legal obligation, permanence, and uncontrollability by any, but the authorities authorized to alter, or abolish it. The object was to secure the blessings of liberty to the people, and to their posterity. The avowed intention was to supercede the old confederation, and substitute in its place a new form of government. We have seen, that the inefficiency of the old confederation forced the states to surrender the league then existing, and to establish a national constitution.(*e*) The convention also, which framed the constitution, declared this in the letter accompanying it. 'It is obviously impracticable in the federal government of these states,'

(*e*) The very first resolution adopted by the convention (six states to two states) was in the following words: "Resolved, that it is the opinion of this committee, that a national government ought to be established of a supreme legislative, judiciary, and executive;"* plainly shewing, that it was a national government, not a compact, which they were about to establish; a supreme legislative, judiciary, and executive, and not a mere treaty for the exercise of dependent powers during the good pleasure of all the contracting parties.†

* Journal of Convention, p. 83, 134, 139, 207; 4 Elliott's Debates, 49. See also 2 Pitkin's History, 232.

[† I earnestly protest against such strong inferences from a mere incipient proposition, which was never carried out in its spirit or principles.]

says that letter, 'to secure all rights of independent sovereignty to each, and yet provide for the interest and safety of all. Individuals entering into society must give up a share of liberty to preserve the rest.'(*f*)—'In all our deliberations on this subject, we kept steadily in our view that, which appeared to us the greatest interest of every true American, the *consolidation of our Union*, in which is involved our prosperity, felicity, safety, perhaps our national existence.' Could this be attained consistently with the notion of an existing treaty or confederacy, which each at its pleasure was at liberty to dissolve?(*g*)

"§ 356. It is also historically known, that one of the objections taken by the opponents of the constitution was, 'that it is not a *confederation* of the states but a *government* of individuals.'(*h*) It was, nevertheless, in the solemn instruments of ratification by the people of the several states, assented to, as a constitution.* The language of those instruments uniformly is, 'We, &c. do *assent* to, and *ratify* the said *constitution*.'(*i*) The forms of the convention of Massachusetts and New Hampshire, are somewhat peculiar in their language. 'The convention, &c. acknowledging, with grateful hearts, the goodness of the Supreme Ruler of the Universe in affording the people of the United States, in the course of his providence, an

(*f*) Journal of Convention, p. 367, 368.

(*g*) The language of the supreme court in *Gibbons* v. *Ogden*, (9 Wheat. R. 1, 187,) is very expressive on this subject:

"As preliminary to the very able discussions of the constitution which we have heard from the bar, and as having some influence on its construction, reference has been made to the political situation of these states, anterior to its formation. It has been said that they were sovereign, were completely independent, and were connected with each other only by a league. This is true. But when these allied sovereigns converted their league into a government, when they converted their congress of ambassadors, deputed to deliberate on their common concerns, and to recommend measures of general utility, into a legislature, empowered to enact laws on the most interesting subjects, the whole character, in which the states appear, underwent a change, the extent of which must be determined by a fair consideration of the instrument, by which that change was effected."

(*h*) The Federalist, No. 38, p. 247; Id. No. 39, p. 256.

(*i*) See the forms in the Journals of the Convention, &c. (1819), p. 390 to 465.

[* See *post*.]

opportunity, deliberately and peaceably, without force or surprise, of entering into an *explicit* and *solemn compact* with each other, *by assenting to and ratifying a new constitution*, &c. do assent to, and ratify the said constitution.'(*k*) And although many declarations of rights, many propositions of amendments, and many protestations of reserved powers are to be found accompanying the ratifications of the various conventions, sufficiently evincive of the extreme caution and jealousy of those bodies, and of the people at large, it is remarkable, that there is nowhere to be found the slightest allusion to the instrument, as a confederation or compact of states in their sovereign capacity, and no reservation of any right, on the part of any state, to dissolve its connexion, or to abrogate its assent, or to suspend the operations of the constitution, as to itself. On the contrary, that of Virginia, which speaks most pointedly to the topic, merely declares, 'that the powers granted under the constitution, *being derived from the people of the United States*, may be resumed by *them* [not by any one of the states] whenever the same shall be perverted to their injury or oppression.'(*l*)

"§ 357. So that there is very strong negative testimony against the notion of its being a compact or confederation, of the nature of which we have spoken, founded upon the known history of the times, and the acts of ratification, as well as upon the antecedent articles of confederation. The latter purported on their face to be a mere confederacy. The language of the third article was, 'The said states hereby severally enter into a firm *league* of friendship with each other for their common defence, &c. binding themselves to assist each other.' And the ratification was by delegates of the state legislatures, who solemnly plighted and engaged the *faith* of their respective constituents, that they should abide by the determination of the United States in congress assembled on all questions, which, by the said confederation, are submitted to them; and that the articles thereof should be inviolably observed by the states they respectively represented.(*m*)

(*k*) Journals of the Convention, &c. (1819), p. 401, 402, 412.

(*l*) Id. p. 416.—Of the right of a majority of the whole people to change their constitution, at will, there is no doubt. See 1 Wilson's Lectures, 418; 1 Tuck. Black. Comm. 165.

(*m*) Articles of Confederation, 1781, art. 13.

"§ 358. It is not unworthy of observation, that in the debates of the various conventions called to examine and ratify the constitution, this subject did not pass without discussion. The opponents, on many occasions, pressed the objection, that it was a consolidated government, and contrasted it with the confederation.(*n*) None of its advocates pretended to deny,* that its design was to establish a national government, as contradistinguished from a mere league or treaty, however they might oppose the suggestions, that it was a consolidation of the states.(*o*) In the North Carolina debates, one of the members laid it down, as a fundamental principle of every safe and free government, that 'a government is a compact between the rulers and the people.' This was most strenuously denied on the other side by gentlemen of great eminence. They said, 'A compact cannot be annulled, but by the consent of both parties. Therefore, unless the rulers are guilty of oppression, the people, on the principles of a compact, have no right to new-model their government. This is held to be the principle of some monarchical governments in Europe. Our government is founded on much nobler principles. The people are known with certainty to have originated it themselves. Those in power are their servants and agents. And the people without their consent, may new-model the government, whenever they think proper, not merely because it is oppressively exercised, but because

(*n*) I do not say, that the manner of stating the objection was just, but the fact abundantly appears in the printed debates. For instance, in the Virginia debates, (2 Elliot's Deb. 47,) Mr. Henry said, "That this is a consolidated government is demonstrably clear."—"The language [is] 'We, the people,' instead of 'We, the *states*.' *States* are the characteristics and soul of a confederation. If the states be not the agents of this compact, it must be one great consolidated national government of the people of all the states." The like suggestion will be found in various places in Mr. Elliot's Debates in other states. See 1 Elliot's Debates, 91, 92, 110. See also 3 Amer. Museum, 422; 2 Amer. Museum, 540, 546; Mr. Martin's letter, 4 Elliot's Debates, p. 53.

(*o*) 3 Elliot's Debates, 145, 257, 291; The Federalist, No. 32, 38, 39, 44, 45; 3 Amer. Museum, 422, 424.†

[* This is not correct. See *post*.]

[† The Federalist does not pretend to consider the government as consolidated, but the contrary. See the passages cited. See also 1 Story 334.]

they think another form will be more conducive to their welfare.'(*p*)

"359. Nor should it be omitted, that in the most elaborate expositions of the constitution by its friends, its character, as a permanent form of government, as a fundamental law, as a supreme rule, which no state was at liberty to disregard, suspend or annul, was constantly admitted, and insisted on, as one of the strongest reasons, why it should be adopted in lieu of the confederation.(*q*) It is matter of surprise, therefore, that a learned commentator should have admitted the right of any state, or of the people of any state, without the consent of the rest, to secede from the Union at its own pleasure.(*r*) The people of the United States have a right to abolish, or alter the constitution of the United States;* but that the people of a

(*p*) Mr. Iredell, 3 Elliot's Debates, 24, 25; Id. 200, Mr. M'Clure, Id. 25; Mr. Spencer, Id. 26, 27; Id. 139. See also 3 Elliot's Debates, 156. See also *Chisholm* v. *Georgia*, 3 Dall. 419; 2 Condensed Rep. 635, 667, 668. See also in Penn. Debates, Mr. Wilson's denial, that the constitution was a compact; 3 Elliot's Debates, 286, 287. See also *M'Culloch* v. *Maryland*, 4 Wheaton, 316, 404.

(*q*) The Federalist, No. 15 to 20, 38, 39, 44; North Amer. Review, Oct. 1827, p. 265, 266.

(*r*) Rawle on the Constitution, ch. 32, p, 295, 296, 297, 302, 305.

*[If we understand, as judge Story does, "the people of the United States" to mean the *people* considered as *one whole*, the proposition here laid down, is unhesitatingly denied. If all the people in six of the largest states were to concur, they would have no right to alter or abolish the constitution, though they would constitute a majority of the Union. For the compact can only be dissolved by the states, who made it, upon the clear principle, "*dissolvitur eo modo quolegatur*." Nor could it be dissolved by any one or more states, except upon the principles of revolution, which are above all law. It enters into no part of our system, that *because* the constitution is a compact, *any* party to it has a *right* to dissolve it, if it deems it to have been broken. This matter will be more fully developed hereafter.

We scarcely need to express our total dissent to the views of Mr. Dane, presented in this passage. We do not recognize him as *authority*, and still less do we defer to his very unsatisfactory reasoning. We prefer rather to adopt the remark of the Federalist, which judge Story (with what consistency I do not perceive) distinctly adopts: "that the constitution was the result of the *unanimous* assent of the *several states*, that are PARTIES TO IT."]

single state have such a right, is a proposition requiring some reasoning beyond the suggestion, that it is implied in the principles, on which our political systems are founded.(*n*) It seems, indeed, to have its origin in the notion of all governments being founded in *compact*, and therefore liable to be dissolved by the parties, or either of them; a notion, which it has been our purpose to question, at least in the sense, to which the objection applies.

"§ 360. To us the doctrine of Mr. Dane appears far better founded, that 'the constitution of the United States is not a compact or contract agreed to by two or more parties, to be construed by each for itself, and here to stop for the want of a common arbiter to revise the construction of each party or state. But that it is, as the people have named and called it, truly a constitution; and they properly said, 'We, the people of the United States, do ordain and establish this constitution,' and not, we, the people of each state.'(*o*) And this exposition has been sustained by opinions of some of our most eminent statesmen

(*n*) Dane's App. § 59, 60, p. 69, 71.

(*o*) Mr. (afterwards Mr. justice) Wilson, who was a member of the federal convention, uses, in the Pennsylvania Debates, the following language: "We were told, &c. that the convention no doubt thought they were forming a *compact* or contract of the greatest importance. It was matter of surprise to see the great leading principles of this system still so very much misunderstood. I cannot answer for what every member thought; but I believe it cannot be said, they thought they were making a contract, because I cannot discover the least trace of a compact in that system. *There can be no compact, unless there are more parties than one.* It is a new doctrine, that one can make a compact with himself. 'The convention were forming contracts? with whom? I know no bargains, that were there made; I am unable to conceive who the parties could be. The state governments make a bargain with each other. That is the doctrine, that is endeavoured to be established by gentlemen in the opposition; their state sovereignties wish to be represented. But far other were the ideas of the convention. *This is not a government founded upon compact. It is founded upon the power of the people.* They express in their name and their authority, we, the people, do ordain and establish,' &c. 3 Elliot's Debates, 286, 287. He adds, (Id. 288,) "This system is not a compact or contract. The system tells you, what it is; it is an ordinance and establishment of the people." 9 Dane's Abridg. ch. 187, art. 20, § 15, p. 589, 590; Dane's App. § 10, p. 21, § 59, p. 69.

and judges.(*p*) It was truly remarked by the Federalist,(*q*) that the constitution was the result neither from the decision of a majority of the people of the Union, nor from that of a majority of the states. It resulted from the unanimous assent of the several states that are parties to it, differing no otherwise from their ordinary assent, than its being expressed, not by the legislative authority but by that of the people themselves.

"§ 361. But if the constitution could in the sense, to which we have alluded, be deemed a compact, between whom is it to be deemed a contract? We have already seen, that the learned commentator on Blackstone, deems it a compact with several aspects, and first between the *states*, (as contradistinguished from the *people* of the states,) by which the several states have bound themselves to each other, and to the federal government.(*r*) The Virginia resolutions of 1798, assert, that 'Virginia views the powers of the federal government, as resulting from *the compact, to which the states are parties.*' This declaration was, at the time, matter of much debate and difference of opinion among the ablest representatives in the legislature. But when it was subsequently expounded by Mr. Madison in the celebrated report of January 1800, after admitting, that the term 'states' is used in different senses, and among others, that it sometimes means the *people* composing a political society in their highest sovereign capacity, he considers the resolution unobjectionable, at least in this last sense, because in that sense the constitution was submitted to the 'states;' in that sense the 'states' ratified it; and in that sense the states are consequently parties to the compact, from which the powers of the federal government result.(*s*) And that is the sense, in which he considers the states parties in his still later and more deliberate examinations.(*t*)

(*p*) See *Ware* v. *Hylton*, 3 Dall. 199; 1 Cond. Rep. 99, 112; *Chisholm* v. *Georgia*, 3 Dall. 419; 2 Cond. R. 668, 671; Elliot's Debates, 72; 2 Elliot's Debates, 47; Webster's Speeches, p. 410; The Federalist, No. 22, 33, 39; 2 Amer. Museum, 536, 546; Virginia Debates in 1798, on the Alien Laws, p. 111, 136, 138, 140; North Amer. Rev. Oct. 1830, p. 437, 444.

(*q*) No. 39.

(*r*) 1 Tuck. Black. Comm. 169; Hayne's speech in the senate, in 1830; 4 Elliot's Debates, 315, 316.

(*s*) Resolutions of 1800, p. 5, 6.

(*t*) North American Review, Oct. 1830, p. 537, 544.

"§ 362. This view of the subject is, however, wholly at variance* with that, on which we are commenting; and which, having no foundation in the words of the constitution, is altogether a gratuitous assumption, and therefore inadmissible. It is no more true, that a state is a party to the constitution, as such, because it was framed by delegates chosen by the states, and submitted by the legislatures thereof to the people of the states for ratification, and that the states are necessary agents to give effect to some of its provisions, than that for the same reasons the governor, or senate, or house of representatives, or judges, either of a state or of the United States, are parties thereto. No state, as such, that is, the body politic,† as it was

[* It is singular that the commentator does not advert to the obvious principle that it is not the legislature but the *people* of the state who constitute the states; and hence, that to constitute a compact between the *states*, the assent or act of the respective *legislatures* was not necessary, but the assent or act of the *people* themselves in the respective states, constituting distinct bodies politic from each other. The legislatures under our system could not have adopted the constitution. Acting under limited powers, *they* had no right to enter into any compact transferring part of their powers, and portions of the state sovereignty, to others. Such an act was not within the charter which created them. It was therefore necessary that the *people* of the state, who constitute the sovereignty, should ratify the instrument. *They* had that power, and when they exerted it, it was an exercise of state sovereignty; and so the ratification of the constitution by them, in their respective conventions, was an act of *state sovereignty*, by which each state contracted with every other to establish and maintain the stipulated form of government.]

[† Here the learned author clearly means the "*legislatures;*" and what he says of *their* want of power to form a constitution, is strictly true, and well expressed. But he admits that "the *people*, in their original, sovereign capacity, had a right to change their form of government." What people? Not the *people* of the whole confederacy, as ONE,—for there was none such; but the *people* of each of the confederate states, who were then, at least, sovereign and independent. Judge Story feels the force of the distinction, when he says in page 330, "And the states never, in fact, did in their *political capacity*, (*as contradistinguished from the people* THEREOF,) ratify the constitution." That is to say, the *legislatures* did not, though he admits the *people thereof* (that is, of each state) did. And this is all we contend for: believing that the ratification by the people of each state, in their conventions, was an act of separate state sovereignty, which made the constitution a compact between states, and not a national or consolidated government."]

actually organized, had any power to establish a contract for the establishment of any new government over the people thereof, or to delegate the powers of government in whole, or in part to any other sovereignty. The state governments were framed by the people to administer the state constitutions, such as they were, and not to transfer the administration thereof to any other persons, or sovereignty. They had no authority to enter into any compact or contract for such a purpose. It is no where given, or implied in the state constitutions; and consequently, if actually entered into, (as it was not,) would have had no obligatory force. The people, and the people only, in their original sovereign capacity, had a right to change their form of government, to enter into a compact, and to transfer any sovereignty to the national government.(*u*) And the states never, in fact, did in their political capacity, as contradistinguished from the people thereof, ratify the constitution. They were not called upon to do it by congress; and were not contemplated, as essential to give validity to it.(*v*)

(*u*) 4 Wheat. 404.

(*v*) The Federalist, No. 39.—In confirmation of this view, we may quote the reasoning of the supreme court in the case of *M'Culloch* v. *Maryland*, (4 Wheaton's R. 316,) in answer to the very argument. "The powers of the general government, it has been said, are delegated by the states, who alone are truly sovereign; and must be exercised in subordination to the states, who alone possess supreme dominion.

"It would be difficult to sustain this proposition. The convention, which framed the constitution, was indeed elected by the state legislatures. But the instrument, when it came from their hands, was a mere proposal, without obligation, or pretensions to it. It was reported to the then existing congress of the United States, with a request, that it might 'be submitted to a convention of delegates, chosen in each state by the people thereof, under the recommendation of its legislature, for their assent and ratification.' This mode of proceeding was adopted; and by the convention, by congress, and by the state legislatures, the instrument was submitted to the people. They acted upon it in the only manner in which they can act safely, effectively, and wisely, on such a subject, by assembling in convention. It is true, they assembled in their several states—and where else should they have assembled ?*

[*This is an evasion unworthy of the chief justice. The argument of his adversaries did not rest upon the *place where* the conventions met, but upon the convention of each state representing its own state alone as a *sovereign state*, and not as a fragment of the aggregate nation.]

"§ 363. The doctrine, then, that the states are parties is a gratuitous assumption. In the language of a most dis-

No political dreamer was ever wild enough to think of breaking down the lines, which separate the states, and of compounding the American people into one common mass.* Of consequence, when they act, they act in their states. But the measures they adopt do not, on that account, cease to be the measures of the people themselves, or become the measures of the state governments.

"From these conventions the constitution derives its whole authority. The government proceeds directly from the people;† is 'ordained and established' in the name of the people; and is declared to be ordained, 'in order to form a more perfect union, establish justice, ensure domestic tranquillity, and secure the blessings of liberty to themselves and to their posterity.' The assent of the states, in their sovereign capacity,‡ is implied in calling a convention, and thus submitting that instrument to the people. But the people were at perfect liberty to accept or reject it; and their act was final. It required not the affirmance, and could not be negatived by the state governments. The constitution, when thus adopted, was of complete obligation, and bound the state sovereignties.

"It has been said, that the people had already surrendered all their powers to the state sovereignties, and had nothing more to give. But surely, the question, whether they may resume and modify the powers granted to government, does not remain to be settled in this country. Much more might the legitimacy of the general government be doubted, had it been created by the states.§ The powers delegated to the state sovereignties were to be exercised by themselves, not by a distinct and independent sovereignty, created by themselves. To the formation of a league, such as was the confederation, the state sovereignties were certainly competent. But when, 'in order to form a more perfect union,' it was deemed necessary to change this alliance into an effective government, possessing great and sovereign powers, and acting directly on the people, the necessity of referring it to the people, and of deriving its powers directly from them, was felt and acknowledged by all.

[* What would the chief justice have thought of the dreams of judge Story, Mr. Webster, and Mr. Dane, whose favourite hypothesis is "the compounding the American people into one common mass." See § 363.]

[† What people? The people of the *separate*, free and independent states of the confederacy; each acting for *itself*: each having a power of absolute rejection whether ratified by others or not.]

[‡ The calling the conventions was an act of the *legislatures* and not the act of the states in their *sovereign* capacity as to this matter. The *conventions, quoad hoc*, represented the state sovereignties. Throughout this whole passage, the chief justice speaks of the *legislatures* as the state sovereigns, whereas, in truth, they had no power to bind the people by their assent, for the reasons so forcibly given by judge Story in § 362.]

[§ If not created by the states (I do not mean the *legislatures* of the states) why on the question of acceptance were not the votes of all the states aggregated to ascertain the majority? Why could each state reject? Why was little Delaware made equal with Virginia?

tinguished statesman,(*w*) 'the constitution itself in its very front refutes that. It declares that it is ordained and established *by the* PEOPLE *of the United States.* So far from saying that it is established by the governments of the several states, it does not even say, that it is established *by the people of the several states.* But it pronounces that it is established by the people of the United States in the aggregate.* Doubtless the people of the several states, taken collectively, constitute the people of the United States. But it is in this their collective capacity, it is as all the people of the United States, that they establish the constitution.'(*x*)

"§ 364. But if it were admitted, that the constitution is a compact between the states, 'the inferences deduced from it,' as has been justly observed by the same states-

"The government of the Union, then, (whatever may be the influence of this fact on the case,) is, emphatically, and truly, a government of the people. In form and in substance it emanates from them. Its powers are granted by them, and are to be exercised directly on them, and for their benefit.

"This government is acknowledged by all to be one of enumerated powers. The principle, that it can exercise only the powers granted to it, would seem too apparent to have required to be enforced by all those arguments, which its enlightened friends, while it was depending before the people, found it necessary to urge. That principle is now universally admitted. But the question respecting the extent of the powers actually granted, is perpetually arising, and will probably continue to arise, as long as our system shall exist."

(*w*) Webster's Speeches, 1830, p. 431; 4 Elliot's Debates, 326.

(*x*) Mr. Dane reasons to the same effect, though it is obvious, that he could not, at the time, have had any knowledge of the views of Mr. Webster.* He adds, "If a contract, when and how did the Union become a party to it? If a compact, why is it never so denominated, but often and invariably in the instrument itself, and in its amendments, styled, '*this* constitution? And if a contract, why did the framers and people call it the supreme law?'† In *Martin* v. *Hunter*, (1 Wheat. R. 304, 324,) the supreme court expressly declared, that "the constitution was ordained and established," not by the states in their sovereign capacity, but emphatically, as the preamble of the constitution declares, "by the people of the United States."

[* Can we suppress our wonder at the *distinct* avowal of such an opinion by such a man!!! This is the *wild political dream* which the chief justice himself conceived to be impossible. It compounds the American people *into one common mass.*]

* 9 Dane's Abridg. ch. 189, art. 20, § 15, p. 589, 590; Dane's App. 40, 41, 42.
† 9 Dane's Abridg. 590.

man,(y) are warranted by no just reason. Because, if the constitution be a compact between the states, still that constitution or that compact has established a government with certain powers; and whether it be one of these powers, that it shall construe and interpret for itself the terms of the compact in doubtful cases, can only be decided by looking to the compact, and enquiring, what provisions it contains on that point. Without any inconsistency with natural reason, the government even thus created might be trusted with this power of construction. The extent of its powers must, therefore, be sought in the instrument itself.' 'If the constitution were the mere creation of the state governments, it might be modified, interpreted, or construed according to their pleasure. But even in that case, it would be necessary, that they should agree. One alone could not interpret it conclusively. One alone could not construe it. One alone could not modify it.'—'If all the states are parties to it, one alone can have no right to fix upon it her own peculiar construction.'(z)*

"§ 365. Then, is it a compact between the people of the several states, each contracting with all the people of the other states?(a) It may be admitted, as was the early

(y) Webster's Speeches, 429; 4 Elliot's Debates, 324.

(z) Even under the confederation, which was confessedly, in many respects, a mere league or treaty, though in other respects national, congress unanimously resolved, that it was not within the competency of any state to pass acts for interpreting, explaining, or construing a national treaty, or any part or clause of it. Yet in that instrument there was no express judicial powers given to the general government to construe it. It was, however, deemed an irresistible and exclusive authority in the general government, from the very nature of the other powers given to them; and especially from the power to make war and peace, and to form treaties. Journals of Congress, April 13, 1787, p. 32, &c.; Rawle on Const. App. 2, p. 316, 320.

(a) In the resolutions passed by the senate of South Carolina, in December 1827, it was declared, that "the constitution of the United States is a compact between the people of the different states with each other, as separate and independent sovereignties." Mr. Grimke filed a protest founded on different views of it. See Grimke's Address and Resolutions in 1828, (edition, 1829, at Charleston,) where his exposition of the constitution is given at large, and maintained in a very able speech.

[* In this remark I cordially concur. My views upon this portion of our subject will be given, however, hereafter, somewhat at large.]

exposition of its advocates, 'that the constitution is founded on the assent and ratification of the people of America, given by deputies elected for the special purpose; but that this assent and ratification is to be given by the whole people, not as individuals, composing one entire nation, but as composing the distinct and independent states, to which they respectively belong. It is to be the assent and ratification of the several states, derived from the supreme authority in each state, the authority of the people themselves. The act, therefore, establishing the constitution will not be [is not to be] a national, but a federal act.'(*b*) 'It may also be admitted,' in the language of one of its most enlightened commentators, that 'it was formed, not by the governments of the component states, as the federal government, for which it was substituted, was formed. Nor was it formed by a majority of the people of the United States, as a single community, in the manner of a consolidated government. It was formed by the states, that is, by the people in each of the states acting in their highest sovereign capacity; and formed, consequently, by the same authority, which formed the state constitutions.'(*c*) But this would not necessarily draw after it the conclusion, that it was to be deemed a compact, (in the sense, to which we have so often alluded,) by which each state was still, after the ratification, to act upon it, as a league or treaty, and to withdraw from it at pleasure. A government may originate in the voluntary compact or assent of the people of several states, or of a people never before united, and yet when adopted and ratified by them, be no longer a matter resting in compact; but become an executed government or constitution, a fundamental law, and not a mere league. But the difficulty in asserting it to be a compact between the people of each state, and all the people of the other states is, that the constitution itself contains no such expression, and no such designation of parties.(*d*) We, 'the people of the United States, &c. do *ordain*, and *establish* this *constitution*,' is the language; and not we, the

(*b*) The Federalist, No. 39; see *Sturgis* v. *Crowninshield*, 4 Wheat. R. 122, 193.

(*c*) Mr. Madison's letter in North American Review, October 1830, p. 537, 538.

(*d*) See Dane's App. § 32, 33, p. 41, 42, 43.

people of each state, do establish this *compact* between ourselves, and the people of all the other states.* We are obliged to depart from the words of the instrument, to sustain the other interpretation; an interpretation, which can serve no better purpose, than to confuse the mind in relation to a subject otherwise clear. It is for this reason, that we should prefer an adherence to the words of the constitution, and to the judicial exposition of these words according to their plain and common import.(*e*)

"§ 366. But supposing, that it were to be deemed such a compact among the people of the several states, let us see what the enlightened statesman, who vindicates that opinion, holds as the appropriate deduction from it. 'Being thus derived (says he) from the same source, as the constitutions of the states, it has, within each state, the same authority as the constitution of the state; and is as much a constitution within the strict sense of the term, within its prescribed sphere, as the constitutions of the states are, within their respective spheres. But with this obvious and essential difference, that being a compact among the states in their highest sovereign capacity, and *constituting the people thereof one people for certain* purposes, it cannot be altered, or annulled at the will of the states individually, as the constitution of a state may be at its individual will.'(*f*)

(*e*) *Chisholm* v. *Georgia*, 2 Dall. 419; 2 Cond. Rep. 668, 671; *Martin* v. *Hunter*, 1 Wheat. R. 304, 324; Dane's App. p. 22, 24, 29, 30, 37, 39, 40, 41, 42, 43, 51.

(*f*) Mr. Madison's letter, North American Review, October 1830, p. 538. Mr. Paterson (afterwards Mr. justice Paterson) in the convention which framed the constitution, held the doctrine, that under the confederation no state had a right to withdraw from the Union without the consent of all. "The confederation (said he)

[* The constitution of the United States is a compact between the people of the different states with each other as separate and independent sovereignties, whereby they *ordained* and *established* a government for the conduct of their national concerns. Its first clause is the act of all the states *agreeing* with each other to establish that constitution. The national *government* is the *result* of this agreement. There are, moreover, other clauses in the constitution which may be regarded as express engagement of each state with the other states on certain specified points. Such are some of those in art. 1, § 10, as to entering into treaties, alliances, &c., coining money, laying duties, keeping troops, &c.]

"§ 367. The other branch of the proposition, we have been considering, is, that it is not only a compact between the several states, and the people thereof, but also a compact between the states and the *federal government;* and *e converso* between the *federal government*, and the several states, and every citizen of the United States.(*g*). This seems to be a doctrine far more involved, and extraordinary, and incomprehensible, than any part of the preceding. The difficulties have not escaped the observation of those, by whom it has been advanced. 'Although (says the learned commentator) the federal government can, in no *possible view*, be considered as a party to a compact made anterior to its existence; yet, as the creature of that compact, it must be bound by it to its creators, the several states in the Union, and the citizens thereof.'(*h*) If by this, no more were meant than to state, that the federal government cannot lawfully exercise any powers, except those conferred on it by the constitution, its truth could not admit of dispute. But it is plain, that something more was in the author's mind. At the same time, that he admits, that the federal government could not be a party to the compact of the constitution, 'in any possible view,' he still seems to insist upon it, as a compact, by which the

is in the nature of a compact; and can any state, unless by the consent of the whole, either in politics or law, withdraw their powers? Let it be said by Pennsylvania and the other large states, that they, for the sake of peace, assented to the confederation; can she now resume her original right without the consent of the donee?"* Mr. Dane unequivocally holds the same language in respect to the constitution. "It is clear (says he) the people of any *one* state alone, never can take, or withdraw power from the United States, which was granted to it by all, as the people of *all* the states can do rightfully in a justifiable revolution, or as the people can do in the manner their constitution prescribes." Dane's App. § 10, p. 21.

The ordinance of 1787, for the government of the western territory, contains (as we have seen) certain articles declared to be "articles of *compact;*" but they are are also declared to "remain forever unalterable, except by *common consent*." So that there may be a compact, and yet by the stipulations neither party may be at liberty to withdraw from it, or absolve itself from its obligations. Ante, p. 269.

(*g*) 1 Tucker's Black. Comm. 169, 170.

(*h*) 1 Tucker's Black. Comm. 170.

* Yates's Debates, 4 Elliot's Debates, 75.

federal government is bound to the several states, and to every citizen; that is, that it has entered into a contract with them for the due execution of its duties.

"§ 368. And a doctrine of a like nature, viz: that the federal government is a party to the compact, seems to have been gravely entertained on other solemn occasions.(*i*) The difficulty of maintaining it, however, seems absolutely insuperable. The federal government is the result of the constitution, or (if the phrase is deemed by any person more appropriate) the creature of the compact.* How, then, can it be a party to that compact, to which it owes its own existence?(*k*) How can it be said, that it has entered into a contract, when at the time it had no capacity to contract; and was not even *in esse?* If any provision was made for the general government's becoming a party, and entering into a compact, after it was brought into existence, where is that provision to be found? It is not to be found in the constitution itself. Are we at liberty to *imply* such a provision, attaching to no power given in the constitution. This would be to push the doctrine of im-

(*i*) Debate in the senate, in 1830, on Mr. Foot's resolution, 4 Elliot's Debates, 315 to 331.

(*k*) Webster's Speeches, 429; 4 Elliot's Debates, 324.

[* Most true. It was the result of that compact or agreement between the several states, by which it was ordained and constituted. The *government* is not the *party* to the contract. It is, indeed, the creature of it. It is but the servant or agent of the contracting parties. If this servant violates its authority, its aberrations are corrected by various means provided by the instrument. First, the judiciary may pronounce its acts void. Secondly, the people may change their representatives, the states their senators, and the nation its executive. These are the remedies provided by the constitution itself. But it may happen that the wrongs *originate* with the constituency. One part of the Union persists in what the other thinks oppression. If this be actually so, then are the oppressed driven back to their original rights and the law of self-preservation. But this is *revolution;* and though the right of revolution is undeniable, it is justified only by extreme cases and serious oppression. It is always an evil, and is an alternative never to be lightly adopted. It is better to "bide our time" and wait for the correction (in the natural course of things) of evils that are not intolerable, than to upturn the fabric of society for trifles. If the complaining party has a right to judge, so has the party complained of, and while it holds the mastery, there is no remedy except revolution, or submission to the will of the majority until they can be made to "kick the beam," in their turn.]

plication to an extent truly alarming; to draw inferences, not from what is, but from what is not, stated in the instrument. But, if any such implication could exist, when did the general government signify its assent to become such a party? When did the people authorize it to do so?(*l*) Could the government do so, without the express authority of the people? These are questions, which are more easily asked, than answered.

"§ 369. In short, the difficulties attendant upon all the various theories under consideration, which treat the constitution of the United States, as a compact, either between the several states, or between the people of the several states, or between the whole people of the United States, and the people of the several states, or between each citizen of all the states, and all other citizens, are, if not absolutely insuperable, so serious, and so wholly founded upon mere implication, that it is matter of surprise, that they should have been so extensively adopted, and so zealously propagated. These theories, too, seem mainly urged with a view to draw conclusions, which are at war with the known powers, and reasonable objects of the constitution; and which, if successful, would reduce the government to a mere confederation. They are objectionable, then, in every way; first, because they are not justified by the language of the constitution; secondly, because they have a tendency to impair, and indeed to destroy, its express powers and objects; and thirdly, because they involve consequences, which, at the will of a single state, may overthrow the constitution itself. One of the fundamental rules in the exposition of every instrument is, so to construe its terms, if possible, as not to make them the source of their own destruction, or to make them utterly void, and nugatory. And if this be generally true, with how much more force does the rule apply to a constitution of government, framed for the general good, and designed for perpetuity? Surely, if any implications are to be made beyond its terms, they are implications to preserve, and not to destroy it.(*m*)

(*l*) Dane's App. § 32, p. 41; Id. § 38, p. 46.

(*m*) The following strong language is extracted from instructions given to some representatives of the state of Virginia by their constituents in 1787, with reference to the confederation: "Govern-

"§ 370. The cardinal conclusion, for which this doctrine of a compact has been, with so muoh ingenuity and ability, forced into the language of the constitution, (for the language no where alludes to it,) is avowedly to establish, that in construing the constitution, there is no common umpire; but that each state, nay each department of the government of each state, is the supreme judge for itself, of the powers, and rights, and duties, arising under that instrument.(*n*)* Thus, it has been solemnly asserted on more than one occasion, by some of the state legislatures, that there is no common arbiter, or tribunal, authorized to decide in the last resort, upon the powers and the interpretation of the constitution. And the doctrine has been recently revived with extraordinary zeal, and vindicated with uncommon vigour.(*o*) A majority of the states,

ment without coercion is a proposition at once so absurd and self-contradictory, that the idea creates a confusion of the understanding. It is form without substance; at best a body without a soul. If men would act right, governments of all kinds would be useless. If states or nations, who are but assemblages of men, would do right, there would be no wars or disorders in the universe. Bad as individuals are, states are worse. Clothe men with public authority, and almost universally they consider themselves, as liberated from the obligations of moral rectitude, because they are no longer amenable to justice." 1 Amer. Mus. 290.

(*n*) Madison's Virginia Report, January 1800, p. 6, 7, 8, 9; Webster's Speeches, 407 to 409, 410, 411, 419 to 421.

(*o*) The legislature of Virginia in 1829, resolved that there is no common arbiter to construe the constitution of the United States; the constitution being a federative compact between sovereign states, each state has a right to construe the compact for itself." Georgia and South Carolina have recently maintained the same doctrine; and it has been asserted in the senate of the United States, with an uncommon display of eloquence and pertinacity.* It is not a little remarkable, that in 1810, the legislature of Virginia thought very differently, and then deemed the supreme court a fit and impartial tribunal.† Pennsylvania at the same time, though she did not deny the court to be, under the constitution, the appro-

[* It will be seen in the sequel that we contend for no such *unqualified* proposition, but deny as earnestly as our author, the whole notion of nullification. It is not necessary to enter upon the subject here.]

* 9 Dane's Abridg. ch. 187, art. 20, § 13, p. 589, &c. 591; Dane's App. 52 to 59, 67 to 72; 3 American Annual Register, Local Hist. 131.

† North American Review, October 1830, p. 509, 512; 6 Wheat. R. 358.

however, have never assented to this doctrine; and it has been, at different times, resisted by the legislatures of several of the states, in the most formal declarations.(*p*)

"§ 371. But if it were admitted that the constitution is a compact, the conclusion, that there is no common arbiter, would neither be a necessary, nor natural conclusion from that fact standing alone. To decide upon the point, it would still behove us to examine the very terms of the constitution, and the delegation of powers under it. It would be perfectly competent even for confederated states to agree upon, and delegate authority to construe the compact to a common arbiter. The people of the United States had an unquestionable right to confide this power to the government of the United States, or to any department thereof, if they chose so to do. The question is, whether they have done it. If they have, it becomes obligatory and binding upon all the states.

priate tribunal, was desirous of substituting some other arbiter.* The recent resolutions of her own legislature (in March 1831) shew, that she now approves of the supreme court, as the true and common arbiter. One of the expositions of the doctrine is, that if a single state denies a power to exist under the constitution, that power is to be deemed defunct, unless three fourths of the states shall afterwards reinstate that power by an amendment to the constitution.† What, then, is to be done, where ten states resolve, that a power exists, and one, that it does not exist? See Mr. vice-president Calhoun's letter of 28th August 1832, to Gov. Hamilton.

(*p*) Massachusetts openly opposed it in the resolutions of her legislature of the 12th of February 1799, and declared, "that the decision of all cases in law and equity arising under the constitution of the United States, and the construction of all laws made in pursuance thereof, are exclusively vested by the people, in the judicial courts of the United States."‡ Six other states, at that time, seem to have come to the same result.§ And on other occasions, a larger number have concurred on the same point.‖ Similar resolutions have been passed by the legislatures of Delaware and Connecticut in 1831, and by some other states. How is it possible, for a moment, to reconcile the notion, that each state is the supreme judge for itself of the construction of the constitution, with the very first resolution of the convention, which formed the constitution: "Resolved, &c. that a *national government* ought to be established, consisting of a *supreme* legislative, judiciary and executive?"¶

* North American Review, id. 507, 508.
† 4 Elliot's Debates, 320, 321.
‡ Dane's App. 58.
§ North American Review, October 1830, p. 500.
‖ Dane's App. 67; id. 52 to 59.
¶ Journals of Convention, 83; 4 Elliot's Deb. 49.

"§ 372. It is not, then, by artificial reasoning founded upon theory, but upon a careful survey of the language of the constitution itself, that we are to interpret its powers, and its obligations. We are to treat it, as it purports on its face to be, as a CONSTITUTION of government; and we are to reject all other appellations, and definitions of it, such, as that it is a compact, especially as they may mislead us into false constructions and glosses, and can have no tendency to instruct us in its real objects."

LECTURE VI.

Having thus presented at length judge Story's views of the nature of the constitution of the United States, I shall now proceed to a critical examination of some of his positions. The principal foundation upon which they rest, is the assumption that the *states* are not parties to the constitution; that it is the act of the people of the United States as a nation; that it is therefore not a compact, and that our institutions are national not federative. My first duty, therefore, shall be to shew, that these assumptions are not warranted by the history of the transaction. I shall contend

1. That the formation of the constitution was in its origination, its progress, and its final ratification, the act of the states as free and independent sovereignties, and not of the whole people of America as one people.(*a*)

2. That if the sovereignty of the states be admitted, no constitution could have been made without the assent of those sovereignties.

3. That if it be the act of the *states*, it is a compact; a compact to establish a particular form of government or system of polity for the conduct of the external relations of the states, and for some other specified purposes.

And first, it was the act of the states as sovereignties, and not of the whole people of America as one people.

This proposition affirms, in the first place, that when the constitution of the United States was formed and adopted, the several states of the Union were sovereign and inde-

(*a*) In the case of *Martin* v. *Hunter*, judge Story, for the supreme court, said, that "the constitution of the United States was ordained and established, *not by the states* in their sovereign capacity, but, emphatically, as the preamble of the constitution declares, by the people of the United States." I offer as a set-off to this, the remark of the venerable judge Pendleton, in 2 W. 298, "that though the different states of America form a *confederated* government, yet the several states retain their individual sovereignties, and with respect to their municipal laws are to each other foreign." If their original sovereignties are retained, how could the constitution be formed but by their act as a federal compact?

pendent. The *truth* of the proposition is abundantly manifest. Whatever may be our *speculations* on the subject of the relation of the colonies towards each other before or after the declaration of independence, the articles of confederation leave no doubt of the character of its members subsequent to *its* adoption. In the second section, it is formally declared that each state retains its sovereignty, freedom and independence, so that the clause in effect has the operation of an assertion by each, and an acknowledgment by all, of their respective pretensions to the character of sovereign and independent states.

Such being their condition when the articles of confederation were adopted, the confederation itself was nothing but a league between sovereign powers, in which, no power not expressly delegated, was possessed by the league, but every power, jurisdiction and right, not expressly delegated, was retained by the states.

The league was declared to be perpetual and unalterable, except by the consent of every state: and it was ratified and signed by the delegates of the several states who "solemnly plighted and engaged the faith of their *respective* constituents (*the states*) for its observance."

The league thus made, having been declared to be perpetual, could only have been properly dissolved by those who made it; i. e. by the *states*, as *sovereignties*, by whose authority it had been adopted. Accordingly, when in 1786, as we have already seen, the difficulties and embarrassments of the existing state of things, suggested the absolute necessity of a change, certain commissioners were appointed by the *legislature* of the state of Virginia, one of the sovereign parties to the confederacy, to meet other commissioners from the other states, for the purpose of proposing *amendments to the confederation*. These commissioners were agents and representatives of the respective state sovereignties, and acted as such; each delegation acting for itself, voting for itself, and the majority of each giving the vote of its state.(*b*) The representatives of the five states who assembled, recommended to *congress*, the appointment (with the assent of the states) of a convention to meet at Philadelphia. What was congress? It

(*b*) See 1 L. U. S. 55.

was an assembly of *states*, by their separate and distinct delegations, without a single trait of national government. *Their* action was of course *state action.* They did recommend the appointment of delegates by the *states* to a general convention of the states in Philadelphia. The states accordingly,—aye, the very legislatures themselves, representing the state sovereignty,—appointed delegates with separate commissions and instructions. The people had no agency in this, except through their legislatures. Thus far, then, all is clearly *state action.* The convention met. Of whom was it composed? Of delegates *representing the states* through *the state legislatures.* Having thus met as delegates of state sovereignties, could they put off that character and assume that of representatives of the people, as forming one nation or people? They *could* not, neither did they attempt it. On the contrary, they acted throughout as the representatives of separate state sovereignties. They voted throughout by states. The delegates from each state voted together, and the majority of the delegation gave the vote of the state. Nor was this all. Every measure was decided by the majority of *states,* not of individual votes. Every state had an equal weight in this great council of sovereigns. The dwarf and the giant were upon an equality. Delaware and Pennsylvania, Georgia and New York—all were equal, for all were sovereigns; and in the estimate of the law of nations, every sovereign has equal rights with others. In all these proceedings, we see not a single feature of nationality, but every distinctive characteristic of *state action.* The delegates had been appointed *for states,* they acted accordingly *for states*, and they voted *by states.* Even *by states* they *voted* upon the final adoption of the constitution. In what character, then, was the act done by them? In what character *only* could it have been done? Could it have been done in any other character than as representatives of the states? Could they *lawfully* put off the character given them and throw up their commissions, and yet continue to act, and to act in another character? Could they not only put off the character they held, but also *assume* the character of representatives of the *people*, by whom they were *not appointed*, and even of the whole people of the Union, with a large portion of whom they had no sort of communion. It would have been rank usurpation, and the act would have been void, as totally destitute of authority. Of this they did not dream. They signed the draft of the constitution as an act of the STATES. The attestation is, "*Done in convention by the unanimous consent of the* STATES *present*," and each delegation signed separately and apart from the others. What then becomes of the pretence, that "We the people of the United States," means the people nationally, as one whole, and not the people of each state with the people of the other states? What justifies the assertion, that "the constitution was ordained and established "*not by the states in their sovereign* capacities," but emphatically as the preamble of the constitution declares, "by the people of the United States?" If this was the meaning of the words "We the people of the United States," in the constitution, then, as I have already said, the whole act was an usurpation, since the delegates were not empowered to act but for the states in their sovereign capacities. Shall we, then, by a forced construction, attribute to the delegates an action in a character which they did *not* possess, and which in no other part of their proceedings they appear to have arrogated? Shall we gratuitously attribute to them usurpation, when the language used by them, is as fairly applicable to the character they really filled? Shall we suppose that the whole convention *nem. con.* with one consent, but without any formal proposition to that effect, agreed to put off the character that really belonged to them, and to usurp one that did not, and that at the head of these was the patriot *Washington*, the president of the convention, and deputy from Virginia? *Credat judæus appella, non ego!*

It is of no little importance in the consideration of the import of these words, to remark upon the received meaning of the words *United States*, at the time of the adoption of the constitution. Did those words, in common acceptation, or, according to technical use or philological accuracy, mean one people or thirteen sovereignties? There is little reason to doubt that, in common parlance, "United States" implied the several political bodies which had united for common defence. Such is its true meaning philologically, for when we speak of things united, we imply a previous separation of the parts. But what is conclusive, the words are used in the articles of confederation itself, not as indicating oneness or nationality, but as applying to thirteen distinct sovereignties. The first article declares that "The style of the confederacy shall be THE UNITED STATES of America," while in the very next, the separate sovereignty of each state is anxiously secured. "United States," therefore, does not mean one people, but *several peoples united*, and in this sense must the delegates appointed under that confederation have used the language. For where known words are used, to which a distinct meaning has attached, the accustomed interpretation of them must be followed; and, as under the confederation, the words "United States" could not imply one whole, because the parts were kept distinct, so the same words cannot, in the constitution, mean one whole, but the several parts. "We, the people of the United States," therefore, means "We, the people of the several states composing this confederacy," and not "We, the people of the United States constituting one people." In the former sense it was natural that it should be used by delegates representing distinct states, for when they used those words they were acting under the confederacy, and used them as used in the articles themselves; but it is altogether unnatural, that in speaking of an act *done while the confederacy still subsisted*, they should use expressions which implied its obliteration at the moment of their use. They could not, with truth, speak of the people as one whole in the act of forming the constitution; for they were then thirteen distinct states under the confederation, and even if they *became one*, by the *adoption* of the constitution, they were *not one* in the *act of its formation*.

Let us proceed. After the adoption of the plan of the constitution by the convention, that body again met; "present, THE STATES of New Hampshire," &c. (enumerating them,) and resolved that the constitution should be laid before congress, and afterwards submitted to a *convention* of delegates, chosen in EACH STATE by the people thereof, under the recommendation of *its legislature*, for their assent. Here then we see that there was, in the *ratification*, to be a *separate* action of *each* state, under the recommendation of its regularly constituted organ. And the reason why it was referred to the people for adoption, and not to the legislatures, was that before given, and strongly stated by judge Story himself, vol. 1, p. 330. The ordinary legislatures having been empowered merely to administer the state constitutions, such as they were, had no power to enlarge or limit their own powers by transferring them to another, and still less to give away the powers of the state without its authority.

But what were the conventions thus formed? They came directly from, and did, beyond question, represent the *people*. But what people? The people of the state as a sovereign state, or a part of the people of the United States, considered as one whole? Undoubtedly the former, for the ratification was to be by states. Each state convention met separately, acted separately, adopted separately. The whole action of the conventions, then, was state action. It could not be otherwise. The states were still sovereign. They were still in the bonds of the confederacy. These could only be thrown off, as I have already said, by *state action*, since the states themselves had imposed them. All this is rendered beyond question, by the ratifications of the respective conventions. These ratifications, in almost every instance, distinctly evince *state action* on the part of the conventions. They are too important to the question before us to be entirely omitted. Short extracts follow:

Delaware. We, the deputies of the *people* of *Delaware state*, &c., &c., in virtue of the power and authority to us given, for and *in behalf of ourselves and our constituents*, do ratify and confirm, &c.

Pennsylvania. We, the delegates of the *people* of the commonwealth of Pennsylvania do, *in the name and by the authority of the same people*, ratify, &c.

New Jersey. We, the delegates of the *state* of New Jersey, do hereby, *for and on behalf of the people of the said state*, agree to, &c.

Connecticut. *In the name of the people of the state* of Connecticut. We, the delegates of the *people of the said state*, have, &c.

Massachusetts. The convention having impartially discussed, &c., *do, in the name and in behalf of the commonwealth of Massachusetts*, assent to and ratify the said constitution, &c.

Georgia. We, the delegates of the *people of the state of Georgia,* have assented to, &c., in virtue of the powers and authority given to us by the *people of the said state.*

Maryland. We, the *delegates of the people of Maryland,* having, &c., do, for ourselves, and *in the name and on the behalf of the people of this state,* ratify, &c.

South Carolina. In convention of the people of South Carolina, by their representatives; the convention, &c., &c., do, *in the name and behalf of the people of this state,* assent to, &c.

New Hampshire. In convention *of the delegates of the people of the state of New Hampshire.* The convention do, *in the name and behalf of the people of New Hampshire,* &c. ratify, &c.

Virginia. We, the delegates of the people of Virginia, do, *in the name and behalf of the people of Virginia,* assent to, &c.

New York. We, the delegates of the people of the state of New York, in the *name and behalf of the people of New York,* do, &c.

North Carolina. Resolved that this convention, *in behalf of the freemen, citizens and inhabitants of North Carolina,* do adopt, &c.

Rhode Island. We the delegates of the people of the state of Rhode Island, in the *name and behalf of the people of the said state,* &c.

Thus, with all deference to the learned commentator, it appears to me that in the origin, progress and adoption of the constitution of the United States, the states, free, sovereign and independent, were the actors, and emphatically the parties. The ratifications evince, beyond question, that in the adoption of the constitution, each convention represented its own state only, and assented to the plan of government in the *name* and *behalf* of *the people thereof.* It can never be too much regretted that the able commentator, whose work is destined to be so much the manual of our youth, should, in *his* account of the ratifications by the states, have omitted this important fact, which takes away the whole force of the argument so much insisted on as to the first words of the constitution. It is contended, that, as the convention has used the language "We the people of the United States," the act was in the name and behalf of the whole people, and not "of the people of the respective states;" whereas all the ratifications being, in fact, in the *name* and *behalf* of the *respective states*, the last *clinching* act done by conventions, acting distinctly for the people of each state alone, establishes, beyond question, that the constitution is the act of the states as such, and *not of the people of the whole United States as one people.*

Nothing then is wanting to refute the positions that the constitution "was not ordained and established by the states in their sovereign capacities," and "that the states were not the parties to the instrument." For if the states had not ratified it, the projet would have been defeated; and as it was ratified by *states* or conventions, in the name and in behalf of states who were then at least sovereign, it must derive its whole vigour, force and effect from the action of those sovereign states themselves.

The considerations which go to establish this view of the matter are abounding. Among others, we ought not to omit some provisions on the face of the constitution itself. Thus it is provided, that the *legislatures* of the states may propose amendments, and that amendments, when proposed, shall be adopted by *legislatures* or *conventions* of three fourths of the states—not three fourths of the *whole population* of the *United States;* thus distinctly shewing that the sovereignties are looked to as the parties, and their rights respected as such upon the principles of national law. On what other principle could we justify the election of a president by the house of representatives—

> " that great Procrustes bed,
> The acknowledged work of huckstering compromise;
> On which the sov'reign states are prostrate laid
> And stretched or clipped to the same common size:
> Where the leviathan with all its pride,
> Shrinks to a minnow; or the pigmy fay
> Grown to a giant, with important stride,
> And new born power struts its hour away,
> Then shrinks again its humbler part to play."

Again, how is it, if this was a national government, and one "not ordained by the states," that only those states were bound who ratified? Why, as in all national governments, did not the majority prevail and bind the rest? Why, as in all federal compacts, were none bound but those who ratified? Why, but because it was a government of federative character?

New states formed out of old states, or parts of old states, may be admitted into the union. In what character? And in what character do they come under the obligations of the constitution? As states. Could a portion of the *people*, who had *not formed* a government, and erected themselves into a state, enter the union? Assuredly not; for they could have no representative in the senate, as they would have no legislature to elect one. Thus, so far from not being a government of states, it is a government which can only subsist by states and to which states alone are parties.

A person charged with *treason* against any state, and fleeing from justice, shall be delivered up. Treason, then, the *crimen læsæ majistatis*, can be committed against a state; it is, therefore, conceded by the constitution itself to be sovereign; and if sovereign, it can only be bound by its own act and consent. It must then be a party to the constitution, or the constitution has no existence.

The inhibitions upon the exercise of powers by states, in art. 1, § 10, are all admissions of state sovereignty. That section restrains the exercise of sovereign powers which did belong to the states, but which they have consented to forego for the public good.

The citizens of each state are secured the privileges of citizens in every other. Evidences might be further multiplied, derived from the "face of the constitution" itself, of the admitted sovereignty of the states, and of the fact that they were the contracting parties in the formation of the government. It was ordained and established by the people, indeed, but by the people of the several communities constituting separate and distinct states. It was the work of thirteen lesser sovereignties, and not of one great sovereignty. The thirteen states have never yet been fused into one common mass. There is no act by which the *people of them respectively* have put off their separate sovereignty, and been melted into one whole. They still retain that sovereignty, and are, and have ever been in the actual exercise of it, except so far as they disrobed *themselves*, by the grant of certain powers to the government of the United States. All other powers are *reserved* to the states *respectively*, or to the people; a significant expression, denoting a continued distinctness of the several sovereignties composing this great confederacy.

I have not thought it necessary in this examination of the character of the government to array the arguments of the authors of the Federalist on the subject, demonstrating that the constitution of the United States is partly national and partly federal; since they have been so recently the subject of your studies, as to be fresh in your recollections. But it would be improper not to advert to the letter of the convention to congress, in which it is declared "to be obviously impracticable in the federal government of *these states*" (still recognizing their political character) "to secure ALL RIGHTS of *independent sovereignty* to each, and yet provide for the interest and safety of all. Individuals entering into society must give up a share of liberty to preserve the rest." And so it was necessary to give up a part of the rights of independent sovereignty to secure the residue. But it is obvious, from the whole letter, that the convention looked upon their act as the act of the states, and not of individuals. "The constitution," says the Federalist, "is founded indeed, on the assent and ratification of the people of America, given by delegates elected for the special purpose: but this assent and ratification is to be given by the whole people, not as *individuals* composing one entire nation, but as composing the distinct and independent states, to which they respectively belong. It is to be the assent and ratification of the *several states*, derived from the *supreme authority in each state*, THE PEOPLE THEMSELVES. The act, therefore, establishing the constitution will NOT BE A NATIONAL, BUT A FEDERAL ACT." Such is the language of the Federalist,(*c*) written pending the controversies respecting the constitution, to reconcile the people to the plan of government, and to remove among others, the vital objection, that it was national, and not federal in its character. In like manner, one of the authors of those papers, at a later date, tells us that the constitution of the United States "was not formed by a majority of the people of the United States, *as a single community*, in the manner of a consolidated government. It was formed

(*c*) No. 39.

by the *states*, that is, by the *people in each* of the states, acting in their *highest sovereign capacity*, and formed consequently by the same authority which formed the state constitutions."(*d*)

With these prominent evidences before him, it is truly remarkable that judge Story should have ventured on the assertion,(*e*) that although the opponents of the constitution, on many occasions, pressed the objection that it was a consolidated government, and contrasted it with a confederative, yet *none of its advocates pretended to deny* that its design was to establish a *national government*, as contradistinguished from a mere league or treaty, however they might oppose the suggestion that "it was a consolidation of the states." The passage already quoted from the Federalist proves that those papers alleged it "*not to be a national* but a *federal* act." And Mr. Madison, an advocate for the constitution in the Virginia convention,(*f*) obviously using the word "consolidated" as "national," observes, "I conceive, myself, the government is of a mixed nature. In some respects it is of a federal nature, in others it is of a consolidated nature. Who are parties to it? The people; but *not the people as composing one great body*, but the people *as composing* thirteen sovereignties." And if this be so, how can the government be otherwise than the act of the states as distinct sovereignties? "If," he continues, "it were a consolidated" [i. e. national] "government, the assent of a majority of the people would be sufficient for its establishment,(*g*) and as a *majority* [of the whole people of the United States] have adopted it already, the remaining states would be bound by the act of that majority, even if they unanimously reprobated it, and it would be now binding on this state without its having had the privilege of deliberation on it: but as it is, no

(*d*) Mr. Madison's letter, quoted 1 Story 334.

(*e*) Pa. 325.

(*f*) Debates '76.

(*g*) And so now for its abolition. But who will admit this power in the majority of the people of the Union, to abrogate by their voices this constitution, ordained and established by STATES? Who will admit that the unanimous vote of three fourths of the population of the whole United States, can abrogate, or even alter the constitution, without the assent of three fourths of the states themselves in their political capacity?

state is bound by it, without its own consent. Should all the states adopt it, it will then be a government *established by the thirteen states* of America, not through the intervention of the legislatures, but by the people at large."

2. I proceed now to my second proposition, that if the states were sovereign at the time of the adoption of the constitution of the United States, no constitution could have been made (without the assent of those sovereignties).(*h*) They are consequently parties to it.

And here it may be necessary to refer to the well known distinction between the ordinary legislature, and the sovereignty in each state. The *legislature* is not the sovereign power, though it represents it in the matters committed to its authority. The *people* of *each state* is the sovereign power of that state; and the proposition therefore means that no constitution for the Union could have been adopted without the assent of the *people of each* state, as distinct and independent sovereignties. Such they were under the confederation, which recognized and declared the fact, if it could have been reasonably doubted before. But they would not have been sovereign, if the people of the rest of the Union could have bound them without their own assent. Now, if *their* assent was necessary; if the constitution could not have been ordained without it, the constitution is the result of state action; it is the creature of the states, and the states are consequently the parties to it.

3. If the constitution be the result of state action, and if the STATES are parties to it, the constitution is a compact. And this seems sufficiently obvious, since the only method by which joint action between several states can take place, is compact or agreement.

What then was the compact or agreement between the thirteen states in the adoption of the constitution? I have already intimated the opinion, that the form or system of government was rather the result of the compact, than the compact itself. The *compact* is to be found in the first clause, by which it was *agreed* between the states to *establish a particular form of government.* This was a compact between the states with each other, and not between

(*h*) See Upshur's Review, 58. There is no power to change a government except the power which formed it.

them and their *servants*, appointed by them to administer the proposed government. These are but their agents, and *their* illegal acts are to be corrected by the remedies prescribed by the constitution. An attention to this distinction will relieve us from much difficulty hereafter in considering some interesting questions.

After this tedious examination, I shall close these remarks on this part of our subject, with a further extract from judge Upshur's masterly discussion of it:

"The third division of the work commences with a history of the adoption of the constitution. This, also, is given in an abridged form; but it omits nothing which can be considered material to the enquiry. Perhaps the author has fallen into one error, an unimportant one, certainly, in stating that, 'at the time and place appointed, the representatives of twelve states assembled.' When the deputies first met in Philadelphia, in May 1787, the representatives of only *nine* states appeared; they were, soon after, joined by those of three others. The author next proceeds to state the various objections which were urged against the constitution, with the replies thereto; to examine the nature of that instrument; to ascertain whether it be a compact or not; to enquire who is the final judge or interpreter in constitutional controversies; to lay down rules of interpretation; and, finally, to examine the constitution in its several departments and separate clauses. In the execution of this part of his task, he has displayed great research, laborious industry, and extensive judicial learning. The brief summary which he has given of the arguments by which the constitution was assailed on the one hand, and defended on the other, is not only interesting as matter of history, but affords great aid in understanding that instrument. We should be careful, however, not to attach to these discussions an undue importance. All the members of the various conventions, did not engage in the debates, and, of course, we have no means of determining by what process of reasoning they were led to their conclusions. And we cannot reasonably suppose, that the debaters always expressed their deliberate and well weighed opinions in all the arguments, direct and collateral, by which they sought to achieve a single great purpose. We are not, therefore, to consider the constitution as the one thing or the other, merely because some of the framers, or some of the adopters of it, chose so to characterize it in their debates. Their arguments are valuable as guides to our judgments, but not as authority to bind them.

"In the interpretation of the constitution, the author founds himself, whenever he can, upon the authority of the supreme court. This was to be expected; for, in so doing, he has, in most cases, only reiterated his own judicial decisions. We could not suppose that one, whose opinions are not lightly adopted, would advance, as a commentator, a principle which he rejected as a judge. In most cases, too, no higher authority in the interpretation of the constitution is known in our systems, and none *better* could be desired. It is only in questions of *political power*, involving the rights of the states in reference to the federal government, that any class of politicians are disposed to deny the authority of the judgments of the supreme court. We shall have occasion to examine this subject more at large, in a subsequent part of this review.

"In discussing the various clauses of the constitution, the author displays great research, and a thorough acquaintance with the history of that instrument. It is not perceived, however, that he has presented any new views of it, or offered any new arguments in support of the constructions which it has heretofore received. As a compendium of what others have said and done upon the subject, his work is very valuable. It facilitates investigation, whilst, at the same time, it is so full of matter, as to render little farther investigation necessary. Even in this view of the subject, however, it would have been much more valuable, if it had contained references to the authorities on which its various positions are founded, instead of merely extracting their substance. The reader who, with this book as his guide, undertakes to acquaint himself with the constitution of the United States, must take the authority of the author as conclusive, in most cases; or else he will often find himself perplexed to discover the sources from which he derives his information. This is a great defect in a work of this sort, and is the less excusable, because it might have been easily avoided. A writer who undertakes to furnish a treatise upon a frame of government, in relation to which great and contested political questions have arisen, owes it alike to his reader and to himself, to name the sources whence he draws whatever information he ventures to impart, and the authorities upon which he founds whatever opinions he ventures to inculcate. The reader requires this for the satisfaction of his own judgment; and the writer ought to desire it as affording the best evidence of his own truth and candour.

"In this division of the work, the author pursues the idea cautiously hinted in the first division, and more plainly announced in the second; and he now carries it boldly out in its results. Having informed us that, as colonies, we were 'for many purposes one people,' and that the declaration of independence made us 'a nation *de facto*,' he now assumes the broad ground that this 'one people,' or nation *de facto*, formed the constitution under which we live. The consequences of this position are very apparent throughout the remainder of the work. The inferences fairly deduced from it, impart to the constitution its distinctive character, as the author understands it; and, of course, if this fundamental position be wrong, that instrument is not, in many of its provisions, what he represents it to be. The reader, therefore, should settle this question for himself in the outset; because, if he differ from the author upon this point, he will be compelled to reject by far the most important part of the third and principal division of these commentaries.

"The opinion, that the constitution was formed by 'the people of the United States,' as contradistinguished from the people of the several states, that is, as contradistinguished from the states as such, is founded exclusively on the particular terms of the preamble. The language is, 'We, the people of the United States, do ordain and establish this constitution for the United States of America.' 'The people do ordain and establish, not contract and stipulate with each other. *The people of the United States*, not the distinct people of a particular state, with the people of the other states.' In thus relying on the language of the preamble, the author rejects the lights of history altogether. I will endeavour in the first place to meet him on his own ground.

"It is an admitted rule, that the preamble of a statute may be resorted to in the construction of it; and it may, of course, be used to the same extent in the construction of a constitution, which is a supreme law. But the only purpose for which it can be used is to aid in the discovery of the true object and intention of the law, where these would otherwise be doubtful. The preamble can, in no case, be allowed to *contradict* the law, or to vary the meaning of its plain language. Still less can it be used *to change the true character of the law-making power*. If the preamble of the constitution had declared that it was made by the people of France or England, it might, indeed, have been received as evidence of that fact, in the absence of all proof to the contrary; but surely it would not be so received against the plain testimony of the instrument itself, and the authentic history of the transaction. If the convention which formed the constitution was not, in point of fact, a convention of the people of the United States, it had no right to give itself that title; nor had it any right to act in that character, if it was appointed by a different power. And if the constitution, when formed, was adopted by the several states, acting through their separate conventions, it is historically untrue that it was adopted by the aggregate people of the United States. The preamble, therefore, is of no sort of value in settling this question; and it is matter of just surprise that it should be so often referred to, and so pertinaciously relied on, for that purpose. History alone can settle all difficulties upon this subject.

"The history of the preamble itself ought to have convinced our author, that the inference which he draws from it could not be allowed. On the 6th of August 1787, the committee appointed for that purpose, reported the first draft of a constitution. The preamble was in these words: 'We, the people of the states of New Hampshire, Massachusetts, Rhode Island and Providence Plantations, Connecticut, New York, New Jersey, Pennsylvania, Delaware, Maryland, Virginia, North Carolina, South Carolina and Georgia, do ordain, declare and establish the following constitution, for the government of ourselves and our posterity.' (1 Elliot's Debates, 255.) On the very next day this preamble was unanimously adopted; and the reader will at once perceive, that it carefully preserves the distinct sovereignty of the states, and discountenances all idea of consolidation. (*Ib.* 263.) The draft of the constitution thus submitted was discussed, and various alterations and amendments adopted, (but without any change in the preamble,) until the 8th of September 1787, when the following resolution was passed: 'It was moved and seconded to appoint a committee of five, to revise the style of, and arrange the articles agreed to, by the house; which passed in the affirmative.' (*Ib.* 324.) It is manifest that this committee had no power to change the *meaning* of any thing which had been adopted, but were authorized merely to 'revise the style,' and arrange the matter in proper order. On the 12th of the same month they made their report. The preamble, as they reported it, is in the following words: 'We, *the people of the United States*, in order to form a more perfect union, to establish justice, insure domestic tranquillity, provide for the common defence, promote the general welfare, and secure the blessings of liberty to ourselves and our posterity, do ordain and establish this constitution for the United States of America.' (*Ib.* 326.) It does not appear that any attempt was made to change this phraseology in any material point, or to reinstate the original. The presumption is, therefore, that the two were considered as substantially the same, particularly as the committee had no authority to make any change, except in the style. The difference in the mere phraseology of the two was certainly not overlooked; for on the 13th September 1787, 'it was moved and seconded to proceed to the comparing of the report from the committee of revision, with the articles which were agreed to by the house, and to them referred for arrangement; which passed in the affirmative. And the same was read by paragraphs, compared, and, in some places, corrected and amended.' (*Ib.* 338.) In what particulars these corrections and amendments were made, we are not very distinctly informed. The only change which was made in the preamble was by striking out the word 'to,' before the words 'establish justice;' and the probability is, that no other change was made in any of the articles, except such as would make 'the report of the committee of revision'—'correspond with the articles agreed to by the house." The inference, therefore, is irresistible, that the convention considered the preamble reported by the committee of revision, as substantially corresponding with the original draft, as unanimously 'agreed to by the house.'

"There is, however, another and a perfectly conclusive reason for the change of phraseology, from the states by name, to the more general expression 'the United States;' and this, too, without supposing that it was intended thereby to convey a different idea as to the parties to the constitution. The revised draft contained a proviso, that the constitution should go into operation when adopted and ratified by *nine* states. It was, of course, uncertain whether more than nine would adopt it, or not; and if they should not, it would be altogether improper to name them as parties to that instrument. As to one of them, Rhode Island, she was not even represented in the convention, and, consequently, the others had no sort of right to insert her as a party. Hence it became necessary to adopt a form of expression which would apply to those who should ratify the constitution, and not to those who should refuse to do so. The expression actually adopted answers that purpose fully. It means simply, 'We, the people of those states who have united for that purpose, do ordain,' &c. This construction corresponds with the historical fact, and reconciles the language employed with the circumstances of the case. Indeed, similar language was not unusual, through the whole course of the revolution. 'The people of his majesty's colonies,'—'the people of the United Colonies,'—'the people of the United States,' are forms of expression which frequently occur, without intending to convey any other idea than that of the people of the *several* colonies or states.

"It is, perhaps, not altogether unworthy of remark, in reference to this enquiry, that the word 'people' has no plural termination in our language. If it had, the probability is that the expression would have been 'we, the peoples,' conveying, distinctly, the idea of the people of the several states. But, as no such plural termination is known in our language, the least that we can say is, that the *want of it* affords no argument in favour of the author's position.

"This brief history of the preamble, collected from the Journals of the Convention, will be sufficient to shew that the author has allowed it an undue influence in his construction of the constitution. It is not from such vague and uncertain premises, that conclusions, so important and controlling, can be wisely drawn. The author, however, is perfectly consistent with himself in the two characters in which he appears before us; the *commentator* takes no ground which the *judge* does not furnish. It is remarkable that although this question was directly presented in the case of *Martin* v. *Hunter's lessees*, and although the fact, that the constitution of the United States 'was ordained and established, not by the states in their sovereign capacities, but emphatically by the people of the United States,' is made the foundation of the judgment of the supreme court in that case; yet, judge Story, in delivering the opinion of the court, rests that position upon the preamble alone, and offers no other argument whatever to support it. And this too, although, in his own opinion, upon the right decision of that case rested 'some of the most solid principles which have hitherto been supposed to sustain and protect the constitution of the United States.' It is much to be regretted, that principles so important should be advanced as mere dogmas, either by our judges, or by the instructers of our youth.

"In this case, as in others, however, we ought not to be satisfied with simply proving that the author's conclusions are not warranted by the facts and arguments from which he derives them. Justice to the subject requires a much more full and detailed examination of this important and fundamental question.

"I have endeavoured to shew, in the preceding part of this review, that the people of the several states, while in a colonial condition, were not 'one people' in any political sense of the terms; that they did not become so by the declaration of independence, but that each state became a complete and perfect sovereignty within its own limits; that the revolutionary government, prior to the establishment of the confederation, was, emphatically, a government of the states as such, through congress, as their common agent and representative, and that, by the articles of confederation, each state expressly reserved its entire sovereignty and independence. In no one of the various conditions, through which we have hitherto traced them, do we perceive any feature of consolidation; but their character as distinct and sovereign states is always carefully and jealously preserved. We are, then, to contemplate them as sovereign states, when the first movements towards the formation of the present constitution were made.

"Our author has given a correct history of the preparatory steps towards the call of a convention. It was one of those remarkable events, (of which the history of the world affords many examples,) which have exerted the most important influence upon the destiny of mankind, and yet have sprung from causes which did not originally look to any such results. It is true, the defects of the confederation, and its total inadequacy to the purposes of an effective government, were generally acknowledged; but I am not aware that any decisive step was taken in any of the states, for the formation of a better system, prior to the year 1786. In that year, the difficulties and embarrassments under which our trade suffered, in consequence of the conflicting and often hostile commercial regulations of the several states, suggested to the legislature of Virginia the necessity of forming among all the states a general system, calculated to advance and protect the trade of all of them. They accordingly appointed commissioners, to meet, at Annapolis, commissioners from such of the other states as should approve of the proceeding, for the purpose of preparing a uniform plan of commercial regulations, which was to be submitted to all the states, and, if by them ratified and adopted, to be executed by congress. Such of the commissioners as met, however, soon discovered that the execution of the particular trust with which they were clothed, involved other subjects not within their commission, and which could not be properly adjusted without a great enlargement of their powers. They therefore simply reported this fact, and recommended to *their respective legislatures* to appoint delegates to meet in general convention in Philadelphia, for the purpose not merely of forming a uniform system of commercial regulations, but of reforming the government in any and every particular in which the interests of the states might require it. This report was also transmitted to congress, who approved of the recommendation it contained, and on the 21st of February 1787, resolved, 'that in the opinion of congress it is expedient that on the second Monday in May next, a convention of delegates, who shall *have been appointed by the several states*, be held at Philadelphia, for the sole and express purpose of revising the articles of confederation, and reporting to congress and the *several legislatures*, such alterations and provisions therein, as shall, when agreed to in congress, and *confirmed by the states*, render the federal constitution, adequate to the exigencies of government, and the preservation of the union.' (1 Elliot's Debates, 155.)

"Such was the origin of the convention of 1787. It is apparent that the delegates to that body were to be 'appointed by the several states,' and not by 'the people of the United States;' that they were to report their proceedings to 'congress and the several legislatures,' and not to 'the people of the United States;' and that their proceedings were to be part of the constitution, only when 'agreed to in congress and confirmed by the states,' and not when confirmed by 'the people of the United States.' Accordingly, delegates were, in point of fact, appointed by the states; those delegates did, in point of fact, report to congress and the states; and congress did, in point of fact, approve, and the states did, in point of fact, adopt, ratify and confirm the constitution which they formed. No other agency than that of the states as such, and of congress, which was strictly the representative of the states, is to be discerned in any part of this whole proceeding. We may well ask, therefore, from what unknown source our author derives the idea, that the constitution was formed by 'the people of the United States,' since the history of the transaction, even as he has himself detailed it, proves that 'the people of the United States,' did not appoint delegates to the convention, were not represented in that body, and did not adopt and confirm its act as their own!

"Even, however, if the question now before us be not, merely and exclusively, a question of historical fact, there are other views of it scarcely less decisive against our author's position. In the first place, I have to remark, that *there were no such people* as 'the people of the United States,' in the sense in which he uses those terms. The articles of confederation formed, at that time, the only government of the United States; and, of course, we are to collect from them alone the true nature of the connexion of the states with one another. Without deeming it necessary to enumerate all the powers which they conferred on congress, it is sufficient to remark that they were all exercised in the name of the states, as free, sovereign and independent states. Congress was, in the strictest sense, the representative of the states. The members were appointed by the states, in whatever mode each state might choose, without reference either to congress or the other states. They could, at their own will and pleasure, recall their representatives, and send others in their places, precisely as any sovereign may recall his minister at a foreign court. The members voted in congress by states, each state having one vote, whatever might be the number of its representatives. There was no president, or other common executive head. The states alone, as to all the more important operations of the government, were relied on to execute the resolves of congress. In all this, and in other features of the confederation, which it is unnecessary to enumerate, we recognize a league between independent sovereignties, and not one nation composed of all of them together. It would seem to follow, as a necessary consequence, that if the states, thus united together by league, did not form one nation, there could not be a citizen or subject of that nation. Indeed, congress had *no power to make such citizen, either by naturalization or otherwise.* It is true, the citizens of every state were entitled, with certain exceptions, such as paupers, vagabonds, &c. to all the privileges of citizens of every other state, when within the territories thereof; but this was by express compact in the articles of confederation, and did not otherwise result from the nature of their political connexion. It was only by virtue of citizenship in some particular state, that its citizens could enjoy within any other state the rights of citizens thereof. They were not known as *citizens of the United States*, in the legislation either of congress or of the several states. He who ceased to be a citizen of some particular state, without becoming a citizen of some other particular state, forfeited all the rights of a citizen in each and all of the states. There was no one right which the citizen could exercise, and no one duty which he could be called on to perform, except as a citizen of some particular state. In that character alone could he own real estate, vote at elections, sue or be sued; and in that character alone could he be called on to bear arms, or to pay taxes.

"What, then, was this citizenship of the United States, which involved no allegiance, conferred no right, and subjected to no duty? Who were 'the people of the United States?' Where was their domicil, and what were the political relations, which they bore to another? What was their sovereignty, and what was the nature of the allegiance which it claimed? Whenever these questions shall be satisfactorily answered without designating *the people of the several states distinctively as such*, I shall feel myself in possession of new and unexpected lights upon the subject.

"Even, however, if we concede that there was such a people as 'the people of the United States,' our author's position is still untenable. I admit that the people of any country may, if they choose, alter, amend or abrogate their form of government, or establish a new one, without invoking the aid of their constituted authorities. They *may* do this, simply because they have the physical power to do it, and not because such a proceeding would be either wise, just, or expedient. It would be *revolution* in the strictest sense of the term. Be this as it may, no one ever supposed that this course was pursued in the case under consideration. Every measure, both for the calling of the convention, and for the ratification of the constitution, was adopted in strict conformity with the recommendations, resolutions and laws of congress and the state legislatures. And as 'the people of the United States' *did not*, in point of fact, take the subject into their own hands, independent of the constituted authorities, they *could not* do it by any agency of those authorities. So far as the federal government was concerned, the articles of confederation, from which alone it derived its power, contained no provision by which 'the people of the United States' could express authoritatively a joint and common purpose to change their government. A law of congress authorizing them to do so would have been void, for want of right in that body to pass it. No mode, which congress might have prescribed for ascertaining the will of the people upon the subject, could have had that sanction of legal authority, which would have been absolutely necessary to give it force and effect. It is equally clear that there was no right or power reserved to the states themselves, by virtue of which, any such authoritative expression of the common will and purpose of the people of *all* the states could have been made. The power and jurisdiction of each state were limited to its own territory; it had no power to legislate for the people of any other state. No single state, therefore, could have effected such an object; and if they had all concurred in it, each acting, as it was only authorized to act, *for itself*, that would have been strictly the action of the *states as such*, and as contradistinguished from the action of the mass of the people of *all* the states. If 'the people of the United States' could not, by any aid to be derived from their common government, have effected such a change in their constitution, that government itself was equally destitute of all power to do so. The only clause in the articles of confederation, touching this subject, is in the following words: 'And the articles of this confederation shall be inviolably observed by every state, and the union shall be perpetual; nor shall any alteration, at any time hereafter, be made in any of them, unless such alteration be agreed to in the congress of the United States, and *be afterwards confirmed by the legislature of every state*.' Even if this power had been given to congress alone, without subjecting the exercise of it to the negative of the states, it would still have been the power of the states in their separate and independent capacities, and not the power of the people of the United States, as contradistinguished from them. For congress was, as we have already remarked, strictly the representative of the states; and each state, being entitled to one vote, and one only, was precisely equal, in the deliberations of that body, to each other state. Nothing less, therefore, than *a majority of the states*, could have carried the measure in question, even in congress. But, surely there can be no doubt that the power to change their common government was reserved to the states alone, when we see it expressly provided that nothing less than their *unanimous consent, as states*, should be sufficient to effect that object.

"There is yet another view of this subject. It results from the nature of all government, freely and voluntarily established, that there is no power to *change*, except the power which *formed* it. It will scarcely be denied by any one, that the confederation was a government strictly of the states, formed by them as such, and deriving all its powers from their consent and agreement. What authority was there, *superior* to the states, which could undo their work? What power was there, other than that of the states themselves, which was authorized to declare that their solemn league and agreement should be abrogated? Could a majority of the people of all the states have done it? If so, whence did they derive that right? Certainly not from any agreement among the states, or the people of all the states; and it could not be legitimately derived from any other source. If, therefore, they had exercised such a power, it would have been a plain act of usurpation and violence. Besides, if we may judge from the apportionment of representation as proposed in the convention, a majority of the people of all the states were to be found in the four states of Massachusetts, New York, Pennsylvania and Virginia; so that, upon this idea, the people of less than one third of all the states could change the articles of confederation, although those articles expressly provided that they should not be changed without the consent of *all the states!* There was, then, no power superior to the power of the states; and consequently, there was no power which could alter or abolish the government which they had established. If the constitution has superceded the articles of confederation, it is because the parties to those articles have agreed that it should be so. If they have not so agreed, there is no such constitution, and the articles of confederation are still the only political tie among the states. We need not, however, look beyond the attestation of the constitution itself, for full evidence upon this point. It professes to have been 'done by the unanimous consent of the states present,' &c., and not in the name or by the authority of 'the people of the United States.'

"But it is not the mere *framing* of a constitution which gives it authority as such. It becomes obligatory only by its *adoption and ratification*; and surely that act, I speak of free and voluntary government, makes it the constitution of those only who do adopt it. Let us ascertian then, from the authentic history of the times, by whom our constitution was adopted and ratified.

"The resolution of congress already quoted, contemplates a convention 'for the sole and express purpose of revising the articles of confederation,' and reporting suitable 'alterations and provisions therein.' The proceedings of the convention were to be reported to congress and the several legislatures, and were to become obligatory, only when 'agreed to in congress and confirmed by the states.' This is precisely the course of proceeding prescribed in the articles of confederation. Accordingly, the new constitution was submitted to congress; was by them approved and agreed to, and was afterwards, in pursuance of the recommendation of the convention, laid before conventions of the several states, and by them ratified and adopted. In this proceeding, each state acted for itself, without reference to any other state. They ratified at different periods; some of them unconditionally, and others with provisoes and propositions for amendment. This was certainly *state action*, in as distinct a form as can well be imagined. Indeed, it may well be doubted whether any other form of ratification, than by the states themselves, would have been valid. At all events, none other was contemplated, since the constitution itself provides, that it shall become obligatory, when ratified by 'nine states,' between the states ratifying the same. 'The people of the United States,' as an aggregate mass, are no where appealed to, for authority and sanction to that instrument. Even if they could have made it their constitution, by adopting it, they could not, being as they were separate and distinct political communities, have united themselves into one mass for that purpose, without previously overthrowing their own municipal governments; and, even then, the new constitution would have been obligatory only on those who agreed to and adopted it, and not on the rest.

"The distinction between the people of the several states and the people of the United States, as it is to be understood in reference to the present subject, is perfectly plain. I have already explained the terms, 'a people,' when used in a political sense. The distinction of which I speak may be illustrated by a single example. If the constitution had been made by 'the people of the United States,' a certain portion of those people would have had authority to adopt it. In the absence of all express provision to the contrary, we may concede that a *majority* would, *prima facie*, have had that right. Did that majority, in fact, adopt it? Was it ever ascertained whether a majority of the *whole people* were in favour of it or not? Was there any provision, either of law or constitution, by which it was possible to ascertain that fact? It is perfectly well known that there was no such provision; that no such majority was ever ascertained, or even contemplated. Let us suppose that the people of the states of Massachusetts, New York, Pennsylvania and Virginia, containing, as we have seen they probably did, a majority of the whole people, had been unanimous against the constitution, and that a bare majority of the people in each of the other nine states, acting in their separate character as states, had adopted and ratified it. There can be no doubt, that it would have become the constitution of the United States; and that, too, by the suffrages of a decided minority, probably not exceeding one fourth of the aggregate people of all the states. This single example shews, conclusively, that the people of the United States, as contradistinguished from the people of the several states, had nothing to do, and could not have had any thing to do with the matter.

"This brief history of the formation and adoption of the constitution, which is familiar to the mind of every one who has attended to the subject at all, ought, as it seems to me, to be perfectly satisfactory and conclusive; and should silence forever, all those arguments in favour of consolidation, which are founded on the preamble to that instrument. I do not perceive with what propriety it can be said, that the 'people of the United States,' formed the constitution, since they neither appointed the convention, nor ratified their act, nor otherwise adopted it as obligatory upon them. Even if the preamble be entitled to all the influence which has been allowed to it, our author's construction of its language is not, as has already been remarked, the only one of which it is susceptible. 'We, the people of the United States,' may, without any violence to the rules of fair construction, mean 'we, the people of the states united.' In this acceptation, its terms conform to the history of the preamble itself, to that of the whole constitution, and those who made it. In any other acceptation, they are either without meaning, or else they affirm what history proves to be false.

"It would not, perhaps, have been deemed necessary to bestow quite so much attention on this part of the work, if it were not evident that the author himself considered it of great consequence, not as matter of history, but as warranting and controlling his construction of the constitution, in some of its most important provisions. The argument is not yet exhausted, and I am aware that much of what I have said is trite, and that little, perhaps no part of it, is new. Indeed, the subject has been so often and so ably discussed, particularly in parliamentary debates, that it admits very few new views, and still fewer new arguments in support of old views. It is still, however, an open question, and there is nothing in the present condition of public opinion, to deprive it of any portion of its original importance. The idea that the people of these states were, while colonists, and, consequently, are now, 'one people,' in some sense which has never been explained, and to some extent which has never been defined, is constantly inculcated by those who are anxious to consolidate all the powers of the states in the federal government. It is remarkable, however, that scarcely one systematic argument, and very few attempts of any sort, have yet been made to *prove* this important position. Even the vast and clear mind of the late chief justice of the United States, which never failed to disembarrass and elucidate the most obscure and intricate subject, appears to have shrunk from this. In all his judicial opinions in which the question has been presented, the unity or identity of the people of the United States has been taken as a postulatum, without one serious attempt to prove it. The continued repetition of this idea, and the boldness with which it is advanced, have, I am induced to think, given it an undue credit with the public. Few men, far too few, enquire narrowly into the subject, and even those who do, are not in general sceptical enough to doubt what is so often and so peremptorily asserted; and asserted, too, with that sort of hardy confidence which seems to say, that all argument to prove it true would be supererogatory and useless. It is not, therefore, out of place, nor out of time, to refresh the memory of the reader, in regard to those well established historical facts, which are sufficient in themselves, to prove that the foundation on which the consolidationists build their theory is unsubstantial and fallacious.

"I would not be understood as contending, in what I have already said, that the constitution is *necessarily* federative, *merely* because it was made by the states as such, and not by the aggregate people of the United States. I readily admit, that although the previous system was strictly federative, and *could* not have been changed except by the states who made it, yet there was nothing to prevent the states from surrendering, in the provisions of the new system which they adopted, all their power, and even their separate existence, if they chose to do so. The true enquiry is, therefore, whether they have in fact done so, or not; or, in other words, what is the true character, in this respect, of the present constitution. In this enquiry the history of their previous condition, and of the constitution itself, is highly influential and important."

"It is worthy of remark, that of the states, New Hampshire and the author's own state of Massachusetts, expressly call the constitution a compact, in their acts of ratification; and no other state indicates a different view of it. This tends to prove that public opinion at the time had not drawn the nice distinction which is now insisted on, between a government and a compact; and that those who for eight years had been living under a compact, and forming treaties with foreign powers by virtue of its provisions, had never for a moment imagined that it was not a government.

"But little importance, however, ought to be attached to reasoning of this kind. Those who contend that our constitution is a compact, very properly place their principles upon much higher ground. They say that the constitution is a compact, *because it was made by sovereign states, and because that is the only mode in which sovereign states treat with one another.* The conclusion follows irresistibly from the premises; and those who would deny the one, are bound to disprove the other. Our adversaries *begin* to reason at the very point at which reasoning becomes no longer necessary. Instead of disproving our premises, they *assume* that they are wrong, and then triumphantly deny our conclusion also. If we establish that the constitution was made by the states, and that they were, at the time, distinct, independent and perfect sovereignties, it follows that they could not treat with one another, even with *a view* to the formation of a new common government, except in their several and sovereign characters. They must have maintained the same character, when they entered upon that work, and throughout the whole progress of it. Whatever the government may be, therefore, in its essential character, whether a federative or a consolidative government, it is still a compact, or the result of a compact, because those who made it *could not* make it in any other way. In determining its essential character, therefore, we are bound to regard it as a compact, and to give it such a construction as is consistent with that idea. We are not to *presume* that the parties to it designed to change the character in which they negotiated with one another. Every fair and legitimate inference is otherwise. Its sovereignty is the very last thing which a nation is willing to surrender; and nothing short of the clearest proof can warrant us in concluding that it has surrendered it. In all cases, therefore, where the language and spirit of the constitution are doubtful, and even where their most natural construction would be in favour of consolidation, (if there be any such case,) we should still incline against it, and in favour of the rights of the states, unless no other construction can be admitted.

"Having disposed of this preliminary question, we now approach the constitution itself. I affirm that it is, in its structure, a federative and not a consolidated government; that it is so, in all its departments, and in all its leading and distinguishing provisions; and, of course, that it is to be so interpreted, *by the force of its own terms*, apart from any influence to be derived from that rule of construction which has just been laid down. We will first examine it in the structure of its several departments.

"*The Legislature.*—This consists of two houses. The senate is composed of two members from each state, chosen by its own legislature, whatever be its size or population, and is universally admitted to be strictly federative in its structure. The house of representatives consists of members chosen in each state, and is regulated in its numbers, according to a prescribed ratio of representation. The number to which each state is entitled is proportioned to its own population, and not to the population of the United States; and if there happen to be a surplus in any state less than the established ratio, that surplus is not added to the surplus or population of any other state, in order to make up the requisite number for a representative, but is wholly unrepresented. In the choice of representatives, each state votes by itself, and for its own representatives, and not in connexion with any other state, nor for the representatives of any other state. Each state prescribes the qualifications of its own voters, the constitution only providing that they shall have the qualifications which such state may have prescribed for the voters for the most numerous branch of its own legislature. And, as the *right* to vote is prescribed by the state, the *duty* of doing so cannot be enforced, except by the authority of the state. No one can be elected to represent any state, except a citizen thereof. Vacancies in the representation of any state, are to be supplied under writs of election, issued by the executive of such state. In all this, there is not one feature of nationality. The whole arrangement has reference to the states as such, and is carried into effect solely by their authority. The federal government has no agency in the choice of representatives, except only that it may prescribe the 'times, places and manner, of holding elections.' It can neither prescribe the qualifications of the electors, nor impose any penalty upon them, for refusing to elect. The states alone can do these things; and, of course, the very existence of the house of representatives depends, as much as does that of the senate, upon the action of the states. A state may withdraw its representation altogether, and congress has no power to prevent it, nor to supply the vacancy thus created. If the house of representatives were national, in any practical sense of the term, the 'nation' would have authority to provide for the appointment of its members, to prescribe the qualifications of voters, and to enforce the performance of that duty. All these things the state legislatures can do, within their respective states, and it is obvious that they are strictly national. In order to make the house of representatives equally so, the people of the United States must be so consolidated that the federal government may distribute them, without regard to state boundaries, into numbers according to the prescribed ratio; so that *all* the people may be represented, and no unrepresented surplus be left in any state. If these things could be done under the federal constitution, there would then be a strict analogy between the popular branches of the federal and state legislatures, and the former might, with propriety, be considered 'national.' But it is difficult to imagine a national legislature which does not exist under the authority of the nation, and over the very appointment of which the nation, as such, can exert no effective control.

"There are only two reasons which I have ever heard assigned for the opinion that the house of representatives is national, and not federative. The first is, that its measures are carried by the votes of a majority of the *whole number*, and not by those of a majority of the states. It would be easy to demonstrate that this fact does not warrant such a conclusion; but all reasoning is unnecessary, since the conclusion is disproved by the example of the other branch of the federal legislature. The senate, which is strictly federative, votes in the same way. The argument, therefore, proves nothing, because it proves too much.

"The second argument is, that the states are not *equally* represented, but each one has a representation proportioned to its population. There is no reason, apparent to me, why a league may not be formed among independent sovereignties, giving to each an influence in the management of their common concerns, proportioned to its strength, its wealth, or the interest which it has at stake. This is but simple justice, and the rule ought to prevail in all cases, except where higher considerations disallow it. History abounds with examples of such confederations, one of which I will cite. The states general of the United Provinces were strictly a federal body. The council of state had almost exclusively the management and control of all their military and financial concerns; and in that body, Holland and some other provinces had three votes each, whilst some had two, and others only one vote each. Yet it never was supposed that for this reason the United Provinces were a consolidated nation. A single example of this sort affords a full illustration of the subject, and renders all farther argument superfluous.

"It is not, however, from the apportionment of its powers, nor from the modes in which those powers are exercised, that we can determine the true character of a legislative body, in the particular now under consideration. The true rule of decision is found in the manner in which the body is constituted, and that we have already seen, is, in the case before us, federative, and not national.

"We may safely admit, however, that the house of representatives is not federative, and yet contend, with perfect security, that *the legislative department* is so. Congress consists of the house of representatives and senate. Neither is a complete legislature, in itself, and neither can pass any law without the concurrence of the other. And, as the senate is the peculiar representative of the states, no act of legislation whatever can be performed, without the consent of the states. They hold, therefore, a complete check and control over the powers of the people in this respect, even admitting that those powers are truly and strictly represented in the other branch. It is true that the check is mutual; but if the legislative department were national, there would be no federative feature in it. It cannot be replied, with equal propriety, that, if it were federative, there would be no national feature in it. The question is, whether or not the states have preserved their distinct sovereign characters, in this feature of the constitution. If they have done so, in any part of it, the whole must be considered federative; because national legislation implies a *unity*, which is absolutely inconsistent with all idea of a confederation; whereas, there is nothing to prevent the members of a confederation from exerting their several powers, in any form of *joint action* which may seem to them proper.

"But there is one other provision of the constitution which appears to me to be altogether decisive upon this point. Each state, whatever be its population, is entitled to at least one representative. It may so happen that the unrepresented surplus, in some one state, may be greater than the whole population of some other state; and yet such latter state would be entitled to a representative. Upon what principle is this? Surely, if the house of representatives were national, something like *equality* would be found in the constitution of it. Large surpluses would not be arbitrarily rejected in some places, and smaller numbers, not equal to the general ratio, be represented in others. There can be but one reason for this: As the constitution was made by the states, the true principles of the confederation could not be preserved, without giving to each party to the compact a place and influence in each branch of the common legislature. This was due to their perfect *equality* as sovereign states.

"*The Executive.*—In the election of the president and vice president, the exclusive agency of the states, as such, is preserved with equal distinctness. These officers are chosen by electors, who are themselves chosen by the people of each state, acting by and for itself, and in such mode as itself may prescribe. The number of electors to which each state is entitled is equal to the whole number of its representatives *and senators.* This provision is even more federative than that which apportions representation in the house of representatives; because it adds two to the electors of each state, and, so far, places them upon an equality, whatever be their comparative population. The people of each state vote *within* the state, and not elsewhere; and for their own electors, and for no others. Each state prescribes the qualifications of its own electors, and can alone compel them to vote. The electors, when chosen, give their votes within their respective states, and at such times and places as the states may respectively prescribe.

"There is not the least trace of national agency, in any part of this proceeding. The federal government can exercise no rightful power in the choice of its own executive. 'The people of the United States' are equally unseen in that important measure. Neither a majority, nor the whole of them together, can choose a president, except in their character of citizens of the several states. Nay, a president may be constitutionally elected, *with a decided majority of the people against him.* For example, New York has forty-two votes, Pennsylvania thirty, Virginia twenty-three, Ohio twenty-one, North Carolina fifteen, Kentucky fourteen, and South Carolina fifteen. These seven states can give a majority of all the votes, and each may elect its own electors by a majority of only one vote. If we add their minorities to the votes of the other states, (supposing those states to be unanimous against the candidate,) we may have a president constitutionally elected, with less than half—perhaps with little more than a fourth—of the people in his favour. It is true that he may also be constitutionally elected, with a majority of the *states*, as such, against him, as the above example shews; because the states may, as before remarked, properly agree, by the provisions of their compact, that they shall possess influence, in this respect, proportioned to their population. But there is no mode, consistent with the true principles of free, representative government, by which a minority of those to whom, *en masse*, the elective franchise is confided, can countervail the concurrent and opposing action of the majority. If the president could be chosen by the people of 'the United States' in the aggregate, instead of by the states, it is difficult to imagine a case in which a majority of those people, concurring in the same vote, could be overbalanced by a minority.

"All doubt upon this point however, is removed by another provision of the constitution touching this subject. If no candidate should receive a majority of votes in the electoral colleges, the house of representatives elects the president, from the three candidates who have received the largest electoral vote. In doing this two thirds of the states must be present by their representatives, or one of them, and then *they vote by states, all the members from each state giving one vote, and a majority of all the states being necessary to a choice.* This is precisely the rule which prevailed in the ordinary legislation of that body, under the articles of confederation, and which proved its federative character, as strongly as any other provision of those articles. Why, then, should this federative principle be preserved, in the election of the president by the house of representatives, if it was designed to abandon it, in the election of the same officer by the electoral colleges? No good reason for it has yet been assigned, so far as I am informed. On the contrary, there is every just reason to suppose, that those who considered the principle safe and necessary in one form of election, would adhere to it as equally safe and necessary in every other, with respect to the same public trust. And this is still farther proved by the provision of the constitution relating to the election of the *vice* president. In case of the death or constitutional disability of the president, every executive trust devolves on him; and, of course, the same general principle should be applied, in the election of both of them. This is done in express terms, so far as the action of the electoral colleges is contemplated. But if those colleges should fail to elect a vice president, that trust devolves on the *senate*, who are to choose from the two highest candidates. Here the federative principle is distinctly seen; for the senate is the representative of the states.

"This view of the subject is still farther confirmed by the clause of the constitution relating to impeachments. The power to try the president is vested in the senate alone, that is, in the representatives of the states. There is a strict fitness and propriety in this; for those only, whose officer the president is, should be entrusted with the power to remove him.

"It is believed to be neither a forced nor an unreasonable conclusion from all this, that the executive department is, in its structure, strictly federative.

"*The Judiciary.*—The judges are nominated by the president, and approved by the senate. Thus the nominations are made by a federative officer, and the approval and confirmation of them depend on those who are the exclusive representatives of the states. This agency is manifestly federative, and 'the people of the United States' cannot mingle in it, in any form whatever.

"As the constitution is federative in the structure of all three of its great departments, it is equally so *in the power of amendment.*

"Congress may *propose* amendments, 'whenever two thirds of both houses shall deem it necessary.' This secures the states against any action upon the subject, by the people at large. In like manner, congress may call a convention for proposing amendments, 'on the application of the legislatures of two thirds of the several states.' It is remarkable that, whether congress or the states act upon the subject, the *same proportion* is required; not less than two thirds of either being authorized to act. From this it is not unreasonable to conclude, that the convention considered that the *same power* would act in both cases; to wit, the power of the states, who might effect their object either by their separate action as states, or by the action of congress, their common federative agent; but, whether they adopted the one mode or the other, not less than two thirds of them should be authorized to act efficiently.

"The amendments thus proposed 'shall be valid to all intents and purposes, as part of this constitution, *when ratified by the legislatures of three fourths of the several states, or by conventions in three fourths thereof*, as the one or the other mode of ratification may be proposed by congress.' It is the act of adoption or ratification alone which makes a constitution. In the case before us, the states alone can perform that act. The language of the constitution admits of no doubt, and gives no pretext for double construction. It is not the people of the United States in the aggregate, merely *acting* in their several states, who can ratify amendments. *Three fourths of the several states* can alone do this. The idea of separate and independent political corporations could not be more distinctly conveyed, by any form of words. If the people of the United States, as one people, but acting in their several states, could ratify amendments, then the very language of the constitution requires that *three fourths of them* shall concur therein. Is it not, then, truly wonderful, that no mode has yet been prescribed to ascertain whether three fourths of them do concur or not? By what power can the necessary arrangement upon this point be effected? In point of fact, amendments have already been made, in strict conformity with this provision of the constitution. We ask our author, whether three fourths of the people of the United States concurred in those amendments or not; and if they did, whence does he derive the proof of it?

"If our author, and the politicians of his school, be correct in the idea, that the constitution was formed by 'the people of the United States,' and not by the states, as such, this clause relating to amendments presents a singular anomaly in politics. Their idea is, that the state sovereignties were merged, to a certain extent, in that act, and that the government established was emphatically the government of the people of the United States. And yet, those same people can neither alter nor amend that government! In order to perform this essential function, it is necessary to call again into life and action those very state sovereignties which were supposed to be merged and dead, by the very act of *creating* the instrument which they are required to amend! To alter or amend a government requires the same extent of power which is required to *form* one; for every alteration or amendment is, as to so much, a new government. And, of all political acts, the formation of a constitution of government is that which admits and implies, the most distinctly and to the fullest extent, the existence of absolute, unqualified, unconditional and unlimited sovereignty. So long, therefore, as the power of amending the constitution rests exclusively with the states, it is idle to contend that they are less sovereign now than they were before the adoption of that instrument.

"The idea which I am endeavouring to enforce, of the federative character of the constitution, is still farther confirmed by that clause of the article under consideration, which provides that no amendment shall be made to deprive any state of its equal suffrage in the senate, without its own consent. So strongly were the states attached to that perfect equality which their perfect sovereignty implied, and so jealous were they of every attack upon it, that they guarded it, by an express provision of the constitution, against the possibility of overthrow. All other rights they confided to that power of amendment which they reposed in three fourths of all the states; but *this* they refused to entrust, except to the separate, independent and sovereign will of each state; giving to each, in its own case, an absolute negative upon all the rest.(*i*)

"The object of the preceding pages has been to shew that the constitution is federative, in the power which framed it; federative in the power which adopted and ratified it; federative in the power which sustains and keeps it alive; federative in the power by which alone it can be altered or amended; and federative in the structure of all its departments. In what respect, then, can it justly be

(*i*) So absolutely is the federal government dependent on the states for its existence at all times, that it may be absolutely dissolved, without the least violence, by the simple refusal of a part of the states to act. If, for example, a few states, having a majority of electoral votes, should refuse to appoint electors of president and vice-president, there would be no constitutional executive, and the whole machinery of the government would stop.

called a consolidated or national government? Certainly the mere fact that, in particular cases, it is authorized to act directly on the people, does not disprove its federative character, since that very sovereignty in the states, which a confederation implies, includes within it the right of the state to subject its own citizens to the action of the common authority of the confederated states, in any form which may seem proper to itself. Neither is our constitution to be deemed the less federative, because it was the object of those who formed it to establish 'a government,' and one effective for all the legitimate purposes of government. Much emphasis has been laid upon this word, and it has even been thought, by one distinguished statesman of judge Story's school, that ours is '*a government proper*,' which I presume implies that it is a government in a peculiarly emphatic sense. I confess that I do not very clearly discern the difference between a government and a government proper. Nothing is a government which is not *properly* so, and whatever is properly a government, is a government proper. But whether ours is a 'government proper,' or only a simple government, does not prove that it is not a confederation, unless it be true that a confederation cannot be a government. For myself, I am unable to discover why states, absolutely sovereign, may not create for themselves, by compact, a common government, with powers as extensive and supreme as any sovereign people can confer on a government established by themselves. In what other particular ours is a consolidated or national government, I leave it to the advocates of that doctrine to shew."

LECTURE VII.

Having thus established, I trust, beyond all reasonable doubt, that the constitution of the United States is the creature of the sovereign states, that it was agreed to by them in that character, and that it is of consequence a compact between them, whereby they have ordained and established a form of government for the management of their affairs, we are brought next to the natural enquiry, "What are the consequences of those principles, and in what respect do the two great parties of the nation differ in relation to those consequences?"

That portion of the statesmen and politicians in our country who deny that the constitution was established by the states themselves, in their sovereign character, and insist that it was ordained and "established by the people of the United States in the aggregate, as one people,"(*a*) very consistenly, perhaps, deny, that there is any power in the *states* to call in question the constitutionality of laws made by the general government.(*b*) Such were the opinions of Massachusetts and five other states in the year 1799, and such seem distinctly to be the views of the commentator on the constitution. On the other hand, it is contended by those who look upon the states as parties to the constitution, that that character, upon ordinarily received principles, invests them with a right to judge of its infractions, and of the nature, extent and obligations of the instrument.(*c*) These views are very fully presented,

(*a*) Webster's speech, cited and approved 1 Story 332.

(*b*) Resolutions of Delaware, Rhode Island, Massachusetts, New York, New Hampshire and Vermont.

(*c*) The difference must always be borne in mind between the mere declaration or manifesto of a state denouncing an infraction of the constitution, and calling the attention of its own people, and of the other members of the confederacy to its violation, and the act of resistance or nullification of a law regularly passed by the constituted authorities. The former is without objection, as it is the exercise of the ordinary right of canvassing and arraigning the acts of the servants of the people. The latter is without jus-

not only in the extracts made by judge Story from the work of judge Tucker, but also in the able report of Mr. Madison in 1799, which forms a part of the manual of the student.

It is certainly not altogether clear, even upon the principles of those who look upon the constitution as the act of the people, in their collective capacity as one people, that the states constituting organized bodies, to whom all rights not granted are reserved, except what may be reserved to the people, have no right to look into the acts of the general government, to canvass them freely, and to enquire whether they have passed those limits, which the people, the common masters of both governments, have laid down between them. Considering the legislatures as representing the residuary sovereignty of the states, one might imagine that as servants and trusted agents of the people, it was their *duty* to sound the alarm when their rights were transcended. If the right of the people peaceably to assemble in *irregular* assemblies, and to petition the government for redress of grievances, was worthy of being secured, it would seem *a fortiori* that their legislatures representing their will and their sovereignty should be untrammelled in the free expression of their opinions as to the constitutionality of the measures pursued by the general government. To what extent they may go will be presently considered. But there seems to be no good reason to deny, as was done by the eastern states already referred to, that the legislatures "have the right," or "are competent," or "are proper tribunals to decide on the constitutionality of," or "to supervise the acts of the general government." Nor did some of the states in question hesitate for a moment, at a subsequent period, to exercise the right, which at a former period they had questioned. For the embargo and the declaration of war, certainly called forth from some of them, not only a free examination of the measures themselves, but the most angry denunciations also of the course of the general government. The true point of

tification, and partakes of a revolutionary character: for there is no constitutional provision for such a proceeding, and whatever is out of, or subversive of, the subsisting and established order of things, is revolutionary in its tendencies and effects.

difference, therefore, probably is, not as to the existence of the *right* to interfere, but as to the extent of interference only. On this point, it is believed, that the opinions of those, belonging to what is familiarly called the states rights party, were at one time seriously divided; though there may be reason to hope that the advocates of some of the extravagant positions attributed by judge Story to all the party, are no longer urgent in pressing these questionable pretensions. The learned commentator thus states "the deductions, which, he says, may be, and indeed have been drawn, from considering the constitution as a compact between the states."—"They are, that it operates as a mere treaty or convention between them, and has an obligatory force upon each no longer than it suits its pleasure, or its consent continues; that each state has a right to judge for itself in relation to the nature, extent and obligations of the instrument, without being at all bound by the interpretation of the federal government, or by that of any other state: *and that each retains the power to withdraw from the confederacy and to dissolve the connexion when such shall be its choice;* and *may suspend the operations of the federal government and* NULLIFY *its acts within its own territorial limits, whenever, in its own opinion, the exigency of the case may require.*" The part in *italics* embraces the much talked of doctrines of *secession* and *nullification*, which must not be passed without remark.

The doctrine of *nullification*, which is thus presented as flowing naturally from the position, that the constitution is a compact between the states, is not fairly to be attributed to the report and resolutions of the state of Virginia. They only declare "that in case of a deliberate, palpable and dangerous exercise of powers not granted by the compact, the *states*, who are parties thereto, have the right, and are in duty bound, to *interpose for arresting the progress of the evil*, and for maintaining within their respective limits, the authorities, rights and liberties appertaining to them."(*d*)

When the resolutions of 1798, of which this was a part, were introduced by John Taylor of Caroline, it was de-

(*d*) Taylor's resolutions of 1798. The REPORT of 1799 reviews and sustains them.

clared by one of them, that the alien and sedition laws were "unconstitutional and *not law, but utterly* NULL, *void, and of no force or effect:*" but these words were stricken out upon motion, without opposition; the general assembly thus not only disavowing every attempt to *nullify*, but even disclaiming the declaration that the law was a nullity. This was indeed going farther than was necessary, since their resolution had not the effect of a law, and could not even in their own courts, have had any influence or force; and they certainly had the right as men, as citizens, and as a legislative body, to express their mere opinion of the unconstitutionality and consequent invalidity of the obnoxious laws.

Virginia, then, has never by her public acts avowed *the doctrine of nullification;* which is understood to mean "the right of a state to continue to be a member of the Union, to receive its benefits, to exercise its authority, to unite in its legislation by its senators and representatives, and in the election of the president by the votes of its people, and at the same time to pass laws arresting the execution of laws of congress, and nullifying those laws throughout its limits by its own legislation or authority." Such a pretension has, I think, been very justly deemed, by a large portion of our statesmen and politicians, inconsistent, mischievous and inadmissible; leading inevitably to inequality, disorder and civil war, or to a severance of the Union, with its innumerable attendant evils. That it is inconsistent is apparent in this; that the opposing state may stand alone in its opinions, and while it resists the unanimous sentiment of all the rest, claims and receives the benefits of the Union. It may thus be said to claim to be in and out of the Union at the same time. It is moreover mischievous and unequal because it arrogates to a single state the right to throw from its shoulders, a burden which it thinks, or affects to think, unconstitutional, while it falls on twenty-five other acquiescing states; and thus renders unequal those contributions for the common defence and general welfare, which justice and the constitution require to be uniform. Thus, if a direct tax of ten millions were laid, and one state, whose quota was half a million, should nullify the law, while others complied with it as just and lawful, the effect would be, that it would enjoy all the benefits of the government without the payment of a cent, and the taxes must be increased on others to supply its deficit. Could other states be expected patiently to submit to such an inequality? Is it not obvious that collision between the general government and the state would be unavoidable, and that the only result must be compulsion, or expulsion from the Union? How long could a state expect her senators or representatives to be admitted to seats upon the floor of congress, while her legislature at home was engaged in hostile acts in contempt of the unanimous opinion of her sister states? Or how could she expect her five and twenty confederates to surrender *their* concurrent views to the harsh negative of her discordant voice? Or how could she look to an exemption from the exertion of that power which is vested in the general government, to "call forth the militia to execute the laws of the Union," backed by regular forces, raised under the express provisions of the constitution? Or if the strong sentiment of brotherly love, which the bond of fifty years standing has rendered, I trust, all-powerful, should prompt to milder measures, what less could be said to the discontented and rebellious member, than as Abram said unto Lot, "Do thou take to the right hand, and I will take to the left, so that there may be no dispute between thine and mine. If you will not yield to the unanimous judgment of twenty-five against one, all of whom have equal right to decide with yourself, *secede;* withdraw from the Union, for which you are not fit, since you are unwilling to submit to the decision of a majority, however overwhelming." Thus it is clear, that the least evil resulting from *nullification* is *disunion;* while the history of the world but too forcibly demonstrates how much more probable may be the remedy of the sword.

But let us examine this question a little more closely. The pretensions of nullification are very distinctly stated by Mr. Madison, in his letter to Everett of August 1830, in which he says; "this brings us to the expedient lately advanced, which claims for a single state a right of appeal, (against an exercise of power by the government of the United States, decided by the state to be unconstitutional,) to the parties to the constitutional compact; the decision of the state to have the effect of nullifying the act of the government of the United States, unless the decision of the state be reversed by three fourths of the parties. [States.] If the doctrine were to be understood as requiring the three fourths to *sustain*, instead of that proportion to *reverse*, the *decision* of the appealing state, the *decision* to be without effect during the appeal, it would be sufficient to remark, that this extra-constitutional course might well give way to that marked out by the constitution, which authorizes two thirds of the states to institute, and three fourths to effectuate, an amendment to the constitution, establishing a permanent rule of the highest authority, in place of an irregular precedent of construction only. But it is understood, that the nullifying doctrine imports, that the decision of the state is to be presumed to be valid, and that it overrules the law of the United States, unless it be itself overruled by three fourths of the states," and suspends the law until the state decision be so overruled.

Now the first question which here presents itself is in relation to this appeal of a single state to the parties to the constitution. Has the state *legislature* a right to make this appeal, or are their powers confined to the authorizing a convention who may make it? Again, can the legislatures of other states *respond* to this appeal, or must not they act also through the agency of conventions, who alone represent the people of the respective states on these momentous occasions. It would seem clear from what has already been said in the course of these lectures, that though the constitution is a compact between the people of the respective states, as sovereign and independent, it was a compact entered into between them, not through the medium of the ordinary legislatures, whose powers embraced no authority to ordain and establish a federative government, but through the medium of conventions in the several states, representing their respective sovereignties in the great act of accepting, ratifying and establishing the constitution. The state legislatures were constituted by the state constitutions to exercise certain functions entrusted to them, but there is nothing in any of these instruments to authorize the legislatures to enter into a contract for the states for the establishment of another government, and giving to it sovereign powers, which they were no where authorized to give. Conventions, therefore, were properly resorted to, and the people of the states became parties through conventions. The states then can only properly make or answer appeals through conventions. Accordingly a convention was in the sequel of her proceedings, called together by South Carolina, in *her* appeal to her sister states, when she was strenuously maintaining her doctrines of nullification.(*e*) With this preliminary remark let us now see what would be the consequences of this doctrine.

In the first place, no effectual appeal can be made, except through the call of a convention, by the dissatisfied state, and thus the heavy burdens of an extra deliberate body must be incurred whenever the discontented are sufficiently numerous at home to succeed in such a measure.

Secondly; if this call is to be responded to, it can only be answered by the deliberation and decision of five and twenty other state conventions called together for that purpose: And as there are already six and twenty states, there must thus be, upon every factious or fretful appeal made by any one of the whole number, the heavy burden of six and twenty conventions throughout the Union, which, in addition to their expenses, would keep the public mind in a state of perpetual ferment and excitement. Yet upon the principles contended for, the *uncomplaining* states must acquiesce in appointing conventions, since "the law is to be *suspended* until the decision of the appealing state" has been reversed by three fourths of the parties!

Thirdly; it must be observed that as there is no provision in the constitution for any such proceeding, and as in each case there must be, to the people, a direct appeal, the whole must be *above* the constitution, not under it. It must be then, of course, subversive of the subsisting order of things: And what is this but revolution upon every petty cavil as to the character of a law enacted by the representatives, both of the people and the states, sustained by the signature of the president, and stamped with validity by the seal of the judiciary?

(*e*) Where powers are reserved to the states, and they are invaded by congress, the state, of course, will proceed to exercise its powers in the ordinary mode, and in the event of collision, the judiciary (the umpire appointed to decide all cases arising under the constitution) must decide.

Fourthly; let us proceed a step farther. The appeal and responses, if proceeding from conventions, or even from legislative bodies, must be tardy and protracted, and the consequences of a suspension of vital laws, until the decision is promulgated as to their supposed validity, must be dangerous and sometimes fatal. If an embargo is laid(*f*) on the eve of war, which Massachusetts thinks unconstitutional, the law must be suspended at her instance, and our ports thrown open, until three fourths of the states shall overrule her objections. If the requisitions of militia service, *flagrante bello,* are deemed unconstitutional,(*g*) if a border state refuses to permit its militia to cross the Canada line to consummate a victory already half won, they must be halted till three fourths of the states shall silence their scruples. If direct taxes are laid(*h*) to carry on a war for liberty and existence, the collection must be suspended till all the states are heard from. If a fort is to be erected, we may be compelled by one state to wait till all the rest shall respond to some technical and quibbling objection, and if the surrender of our runaway slaves, or of the negro stealers, who carry them off is evaded, against the plain words of the constitution, we must wait for redress until three fourths of the states shall decide that the act of our northern brethren is not justified by the compact. And when may that be expected? *Ad Græcas Calendas!* Never! Never, at least, if the spirit of abolition and fanaticism are not checked in their rapid and alarming growth. Until then we must wait for a declaration, by the states, that the recent laws of Pennsylvania and New York, on the subject of the trial of the master's rights before a jury, are unconstitutional and void! Fortunately for the south, a shorter and a surer remedy was afforded by the decision of the supreme court of the United States in the case of *Prigg* v. *State of Pennsylvania,* in which the laws for the protection of fugitive slaves, and giving to them a jury trial when demanded by their masters, was declared unconstitutional and void. But what is to be the effect, (even upon this decision,) of the resistance of Pennsylvania, if the principles of nullification are

(*f*) Case of embargo during late war.
(*g*) Case during last war.
(*h*) E. g. the carriage tax.

brought to bear upon it? It will be annulled and held for nought, until it be sustained by *three fourths* of the states.

Nor can it escape observation that by the adoption of such a principle, those salutary and sacred provisions in the constitution, which were the result of compromise, may be put in jeopardy. The northern interest, it is well known, were greatly opposed to the principle, which, in the estimate of our slaves on the question of representation, treated them in some degree as persons, whereby we gained many representatives in the south; whereas in the assessment of taxes, they were not all looked upon as property, and we were thus saved no small portion of the burden of taxation. We have representatives for three fifths of the slaves, and in the estimate of taxes, two fifths are excluded.(*i*) If this important provision had not been secured at the formation of the constitution of the United States, what prospect would there be of obtaining it now? And plain as it is, if on any pretext it could be resisted, resistance would amount to repeal, since the northern states never would assent to it as an independent provision in behalf of the southern states.

There is, indeed, no point of view in which this gratuitous notion of nullification—this notion, which finds no place in the constitution, and was never among the dreams of the most visionary in our conventions,—this notion, which is the mere figment of the brain of politicians teeming with new conceptions generated by the heat of party feuds, there is no point of view in which it can be considered, in which its mischievous and incongruous operation is not most wofully conspicuous. Let us imagine to ourselves half a dozen dissatisfied states, each having its own peculiar grievance, appealing, with all the exacerbation of party feeling, against particular laws of the general government. Let us then fairly estimate the influence of such a combination of circumstances upon the peace, the happiness and fraternity of the Union. Let us, moreover, call

(*i*) Considering them as property, they ought to have given us no additional representatives; considering them as persons, they ought to have been estimated in the population in laying direct taxes. Yet three fifths are estimated in the representation, and two fifths are excluded in the apportionment of taxes. They are persons when it avails us, and property when it does not.

to mind the time that must be required to carry out the discussions, and to come to a conclusion in six and twenty states, spread over this extensive continent. Let us then, moreover, duly estimate the changing opinions of men, and still more of political bodies, in the short space of one revolving year. A legislature in 1842, remonstrates and appeals against a law. Before a response to its appeal, a new election changes the political phase of the body, and what was before abhorred as unconstitutional, is now approved by acclamation. Such things have well nigh been. In 1808, a Virginia house of delegates proposed an amendment to the constitution of the United States, providing for the removal of the judges upon the vote of the two houses of congress. Had the measure passed, Virginia in two years afterwards would have strained every nerve for its repeal. Before her sister states would all have passed upon it, she would have been the earnest opponent of her own proposition. These considerations furnish the most abundant reasons against too hasty and ill considered amendments, and they are yet more weighty, when applied to maiming and crippling the constitution, by the innumerable wounds, and ingenious devices of modern nullification.

Nor is the notion of a power in the state governments to nullify the laws of the Union, more mischievous than the application of the same principle to the decisions of the judiciary. We are told by the very able and ingenious author of the review of judge Story's commentaries(*k*) that "if in a controversy between the United States and a citizen,(*l*) the decision is against the citizen in the supreme court of the United States, there is no relief for him in any other *judicial* proceeding." In this we must all concur. But he goes on to observe, that "*his only relief* is by an *appeal to his own state*," a position as novel and alarming as it is believed to be in utter subversion of the

(*k*) Pa. 87.

(*l*) I do not understand judge Upshur's *reasoning* as being confined to a case between the *United States* and a citizen. It goes the full length of shewing that where the citizen is in *any* case aggrieved by the enforcement of a law "*which the state did not consent that congress should pass*," he may appeal to the state for its decision on the question. I shall therefore treat the matter without reference to the party *by* whom the aggrieved citizen is sued.

very first principles of legitimate government. Let us present, however, the whole passage in justice to the author.

"He" (the citizen) he continues, "is under no obligation to submit to federal decisions at all, except so far only as his own state has commanded him to do so; and he has, therefore, a perfect right to ask his state whether her commands extend to the particular case or not. He does not ask whether the federal court has *interpreted the law* correctly or not, but whether or not she *ever consented that congress should pass the law.* If congress had such power, he has no relief, for the decision of the highest federal court is final; if congress had not such power, then he is oppressed by the action of a usurped authority, and has a right to look to his own state for redress. His state may interpose in his favour or not, as she may think proper. If she does not, then there is an end of the matter; if she does, then it is no longer a judicial question. The question is then between new parties, who are not bound by the former decision; between a sovereign state and its own agent; between a state and the United States. As between these parties the federal tribunals have no jurisdiction, there is no longer a common umpire to whom the controversy can be referred. The state must of necessity judge for itself, by virtue of that inherent, sovereign power and authority, which, as to this matter, it has never surrendered to any other tribunal. Its decision, whatever it may be, is binding upon itself and upon its own people, and no farther."

Again, in page 90, our author observes, "that ordinarily, the judiciary are the proper interpreters of the powers of government, *but they interpret in subordination to the power which created them.*" How are we to understand this remark? Is it that the judiciary of the United States must conform their decisions to the rescripts of the state, and bow with submission to the constitutional interpretation of a political body, pronouncing upon its own rights, swayed by its peculiar interests, and animated by its political prejudices and views of state policy. Had the learned judge, once himself a luminary of the bench, forgotten the object and the character of the judiciary, and what is mainly looked for in the character of a judge. Had he forgotten the terms of that oath, in which the state, addressing the judicial functionary, gives him this solemn injunction:

"You shall faithfully and impartially discharge your duty as a judge, by doing equal justice to all men, high and low, rich and poor, without fear, favour, affection or partiality. You shall deny justice to none, by reason of any letter of request or solicitation from any, but you shall, in all things, do right, according to law, according to the best of your skill, ability and judgment, so help you God." These are the commands of the sovereign people to this important servant. These are its only commands. Beyond these, the judge is the servant of no man; he is the slave of no man's will. His only guide is his conscience; his only light, the law and the intelligence it has pleased God to give him. The object of his creation is perfect independence. He is the only officer who holds his place for life in this government of responsibility. He is the only officer who holds a salary by a certain tenure. It cannot be diminished during his continuance in office. He is the only officer, therefore, who is altogether independent, even of his masters, so long as he behaves himself honestly and faithfully. *They* have made him so—*they* intended to make him so, and justly, too, for he who is to ascend the seat of justice and pronounce between the state and her subjects, ought to be placed in circumstances to defy her frowns. It is thus, only, that he can be the barrier between innocence and its persecutor. It is thus, only, that he can be elevated to the high character of being deaf as an adder and insensible as a stoic to the threats of a tyrant or the terrors of the crowd.

Justum et tenarum &c.

The construction of the judicial branch of the government, both in England and America, is indeed one of the greatest discoveries of modern times. The judge is designed to be, as far as may be, an impossible being, an intellectual essence, elevated above the storms and contentions of political parties; unswayed by feeling, unmoved by passion, disenthralled from prejudice, uninfluenced by power, either of government or people; a being without fear and without reproach; dauntless and intrepid in the discharge of his duties, calm and elevated in their performance; the follower of no man's opinions, but pursuing the unbiassed dictates of his own honest and upright judgment, with the devotion of a worshipper at the throne of eternal justice. He feels his independence, and is conscious that it was given to make him an *impartial* umpire in the controversies of states, not less than in the petty squabbles of village warfare. Such a man would spurn the idea of holding his opinions in subordination to any one—even to a state.

I cannot, therefore, think that more is here meant by the writer than the restoration of the notion, presented in a former page, of the right of the citizen to appeal to his state, to appeal from this permanent tribunal, placed as far as possible, above all the pernicious influences of prejudice, interest and passion, to one which is but the child of a day, which owes its very creation wholly to the ferment of party, which is appointed but to serve its ends, and is the slave of its will, which lives but in its warmth, and whose brief existence expires when it has fulfilled the behests which called it into being. Heaven protect my rights from such a judiciary! Such an one will the legislature or convention of Pennsylvania be, when it is called upon to decide in the case of ***Prigg*** v. ***The State.*** Yet its decision is to supersede the judgment of the supreme court, until that judgment shall be affirmed by three fourths of the states; an event which 'tis obvious the spirit of abolition never will permit.

The whole error of the able and learned author, indeed, may be traced, I conceive, to the unfounded notion, that the constitution has appointed no common umpire to settle questions of constitutional power between the states and the United States, (page 87.) Such an umpire is appointed in the establishment of the supreme court, with powers extending to "all cases arising under the constitution." Every judiciary is an umpire! Every judiciary is invested with power to pronounce upon the rights of the parties, not under the influence of party passions or political feelings, or even with a view to national interest, but according to the laws of the land and the immutable and eternal principles of justice. In relation to every question submitted to them by this constitution, and by the sovereignties who are parties to it, they are as clearly umpires as the king of Holland was in the recent controversy respecting the northern boundary. The umpire between sovereigns is not necessarily a sovereign; for the monarch may be a dolt, who finds it necessary to call in his ministers to his aid, who are then the real umpires. The umpire of states, by their own consent, may be the wise and good among their own people. Such are the commissioners very frequently appointed by states to adjust disputed points, and settle details, to which the sovereigns may of themselves be incompetent. And such are a wise and pure and independent judiciary, selected for their sagacity, distinguished for their purity, and marked out by their matchless firmness and integrity. Such are the proper, the best umpires between confederated states! Such are ours!

What, then, is their duty, and how far does their power extend? Their duty is to decide according to the right! According to the right as dictated by a sound and unbiassed judgment! Their power extends to the settlement of the controversy. Good faith demands *obedience*, even from those who created them, to the award of their referees. Is this a novel doctrine in our land? Is it the introduction of a principle hitherto unknown to our laws? Far from it! In some, perhaps in many of the states, the right of a citizen to sue the state before her own tribunals is admitted. In all, suits are prosecuted by the states against individuals, and in all, the state, as well as the individual, bows submissive to the award of the judges acting under their warrant. So under the constitution. The states have appointed these elevated dignitaries, and raised them as far as possible, above fear and above temptation, for the purpose of ministering in the great temple of justice. They are bound then by their decisions; they have no power to gainsay their award; there is *no appeal* from their authoritative judgments. This is confessedly so, where the states are parties on the record. The judicial power by the express compact of the confederate sovereigns, extends to all controversies between two or more states. Whatever the decision of the court, whether upon a constitutional question, or upon any other point, the losing party must acquiesce, for she cannot appeal to herself in her own case. She has then no appeal. No *constitutional* appeal being provided, the faith of the sovereign is plighted to obey. And if the state itself is absolutely bound, how happens it, that her people, whose cases are equally submitted to this tribunal, can have a right of appeal? Such a pretension is pregnant with difficulties which, I cannot think, have presented themselves to the mind of the learned reviewer.

In the first place, let us enquire to what tribunal is this appeal to be taken. We are told, indeed, he is to appeal to his state. But to what department of the state government is he to carry his complaints? Is it to be to a political, or to a judicial body? If it be a political body pronouncing upon the question as one of the parties to the compact, then, as we have elsewhere seen, the legislative body which did not represent the sovereignty in the formation of the constitution, is not the proper authority, but a *convention* must be called to decide the great political question brought up by appeal for its decision. And thus, whenever the party to any controversy in a federal court, can raise a question as to the exercise of jurisdiction, or the validity of a law of congress, and brings it before the legislature, they must call a convention to settle it. Verily this "medicine of the constitution would soon become our daily bread!"

Another and another difficulty presents itself. How is it that the question which is judicial in its character, is to be brought and decided before so ephemeral a tribunal as a convention of the state? How is it that what has been decided by the calm and sublimated tribunal erected by the states, is now to be re-examined before a political body under all the excitement so natural to their creation, without a hearing of the adversary party, without provision for superseding the judgment and enforcing its own decision, and without the means of getting the opinions of other states upon the political question in which all are equally interested? It is clear enough that this bungling contrivance is not under the constitution. If the constitution had contemplated an appeal from the supreme court to the state authorities, whether judicial, legislative, or conventional, it would have made the necessary provisions for conducting it. It would have prescribed the tribunal; it would have provided for the parties being heard; it would have prescribed the effect of the appellate decision, and the manner of enforcing it, and it would have contrived some mode of reconciling the conflicting opinions of contending states. For if, as would commonly happen, the plaintiff should be of one state, and the defendant of another, and the *losing* party should appeal to his state and reverse the decision, the other party would then be aggrieved, and would in turn appeal to his state for redress. Thus "with two authorities up—neither supreme," the direst mischiefs would result, unless adequate remedies had been provided by the constitution. This was not done, because nothing like it was in contemplation. The measure then, of appeal, is not *under* the constitution, but *beside* it, or *above* it. It is a resort to original rights and the law of self-preservation. It is therefore revolutionary, as every such resort must be. I do not question the right of revolution when either the government through all the branches, or the members of the confederacy itself, shall concur in gross and intolerable oppression and usurpation. When that is the case, the "remedy is one never provided by human institutions. It is by a resort to the ultimate right of all human beings in *extreme* cases to resist oppression, and to apply *force* against ruinous injustice."(*m*) Such resort however is upon the responsibility of the party asserting it;—and a heavy responsibility that is, which rests upon those who break up the foundations of society, who reduce government to its elements, and expose a suffering people to all the horrors of that elemental war. No! the right of resistance against oppression is the most holy of rights; but nothing is more mischievous than to make every petty grievance an occasion for its exercise!

It must further be remarked, that the great object for which this right of appeal is asserted, is to protect the respective members of the confederacy from the operation of unconstitutional laws, or unconstitutional adjudications. But in these questions, *one* state is not alone interested. All are interested; and one may be as willing to *enforce*, as another to *arrest* a statute or decision. If one has a right to decide, others have the same right; and thus we have twenty-six courts of appeal, each of which is to have the final right, as far as its own people are concerned, to decide on the constitutional question.(*n*) Suppose twenty-five decide in favour of the law or decision of the supreme

(*m*) 1 Story 374-5.
(*n*) Review 88.

court. Shall they, and their people, be subject to its burdens and requirements, while one is exempt? Is this the equality of our system? Or is the decision of one to be overruled by the decision of twenty-five? If so, provision ought certainly to be made for procuring, collating and comparing the various adjudications. Or are we to follow the rule before spoken of, that the judgment of the supreme court is to be arrested until three fourths of the states confirm it? Taking this to be rule, let us see how it would work.

A citizen of Pennsylvania sues a Virginian in the federal court of this state in a case in which the constitutional question of the right to sue is involved. Judgment is rendered against the Virginian. He appeals to his state for redress. Virginia decides that the law or judgment is unconstitutional, and that there was no right to sue. The judgment then must be suspended till three fourths approve it. With this state of things the Pennsylvanian is dissatisfied. He appeals to his state, which decides that there was a right to sue. He then demands an enforcement of the judgment until three fourths of the states pronounce it wrong. Thus Virginia denies that there is any right to sue unless three fourths of the states determine otherwise. On the other hand, Pennsylvania, with equal rights, insists that there is a right to sue until three fourths of the states determine otherwise.

Both cannot be. For one or the other must be overruled by one more than *one* fourth. Which shall it be? A casuist even would be puzzled to decide.

It is earnestly contended, indeed, that the right of the states to determine, for themselves, every question of constitutional law, and to decide whether the compact is broken, is inseparable from its sovereignty. This is, indeed, most true, where no umpire is appointed to decide the question. But where parties standing in antagonist relations appoint an umpire, they cannot question or renounce his decision. *Bona fides* demands their compliance with it. Now, as will be presently shewn, the judiciary have been appointed by the states to decide all questions arising under the constitution. They do therefore constitute the umpire between the states and the United States, and between the several states of the confederacy and their citizens, and both parties are conclusively bound by its decisions. Nor can there be danger in such an umpirage. Selected for their virtues and ability, and lifted above all fear or favour or affection, they merit confidence from all; but as they are citizens of the states and attached peculiarly to them, the *states* have surely little reason for distrust: And if we could suspect them of any leaning which does not spring from honest conviction, we should surely apprehend a leaning to the states.

Let us see then in whom are the judicial powers of the government vested by the constitution. The third article, section 1st, declares that they "shall be vested in ONE *supreme court*, and in such inferior courts as congress may from time to time ordain and establish." And in the 2d section it provides, that the judicial power shall extend to ALL *cases arising under the constitution*," so that the decision of ALL *cases arising under the constitution*, is vested in the SUPREME COURT, and such inferior courts, &c. But if the constitution of the United States vests the power to *decide* a question arising under the constitution in the supreme court, there can be no constitutional appeal from its decision; for if there could, it would no longer be supreme. For the power to *decide* (which is the judicial power), is a power to determine a question or dispute;(*o*) and the vesting that power in one supreme court, is a negative of the power of any other body to controvert its determination. For if the judgment of the supreme court may be controverted by another court, then it is clear that the court is not supreme, and that its judgment has not *determined* [or put an end to] the question, although, the power to determine it is given by the constitution. The judgments then of the supreme court, "in cases arising under the constitution," must be final and conclusive. This, indeed, seems to be admitted as to all other tribunals;(*p*) and I think I have shewn there can be no other appeal, except that which consists in a rejection of the "cancelled obligations of the violated compact, and a resort to original rights, and the law of self-preservation."

What then are "cases arising under the constitution?" Are questions of constitutional law, and questions of the

(*o*) Walker's Dictionary.
(*p*) Review p. 80, para. 2.

jurisdiction of the supreme court such cases? If so, they are comprehended by the judicial power which is vested in the supreme court, and its decisions thereupon are final and conclusive.

Now, it would not seem to admit of doubt that all questions of constitutional law, whether respecting the true meaning and intention of the instrument, or the extent and character of the several powers granted to the federal government, or any department thereof, are *questions* arising under the constitution; and all cases *between proper parties*, which *depend* upon such questions, are, therefore, CASES arising under the constitution. To all such cases it is declared that the jurisdiction shall extend. When, therefore, the court is in possession of such a case, the determination of which depends upon a constitutional question, it must of necessity determine that *question*, if it determines the *case;* and that determination, we have endeavoured to shew, must be final and conclusive. This is emphatically the case as to the subject of jurisdiction,(*q*) and, therefore, the judgment of the supreme court, on a question of jurisdiction, however erroneous it may seem, is final and conclusive, and cannot be controverted by any other court or organ of the government. The supreme court itself, indeed, may, in a subsequent case, reconsider the question and overrule the precedent; but until they do so, it must be held to be final and conclusive, and can in no wise be lawfully resisted. The states may, indeed, amend the constitution, but until amended there seems to be no mode of getting rid of an obnoxious precedent, but by the act of the court itself in overruling it.

(*q*) "It is admitted," says the reviewer very truly, "that every court must necessarily determine every question of jurisdiction before it, and, so far, it must of course be the judge of its own powers. If it be a court of the last resort, its decision is necessarily final, so far as those authorities are concerned which belong to the same system of government with itself."

LECTURE VIII.

There are cases however, arising under the constitution, which never can be brought before the judiciary for its decision. "As to these cases," says the reviewer, "each state must, of necessity, be its own final judge or interpreter." Very true! but in these cases of controversy between the states and the United States as to the extent of the powers of the latter, if any one state has the power of judging or interpreting for itself, all the other five and twenty have an equal power; and if they persist(*a*) in maintaining and upholding what the single state resists, it must either by reason and its remonstrances bring about a change of opinion, or it must finally yield its objections and submit to the interpretation of the constitution by its sister states until it can procure an amendment in conformity with its own views. Until then the obnoxious measure will be carried out, not, indeed, by action upon the state itself, through its several organs, but upon the individuals composing the state, according to the true theory and principles of the constitution.

It sometimes, indeed, may happen that the federal government will have no power to enforce the states to do their duty. Thus, if a state refuses to elect senators, or to appoint electors, there is no remedy, and thus, it is true, by combination among the states, the government may be destroyed. On the other hand, in some cases of collision between the states and general government, where the latter can act on individuals, it may do so and carry out its laws in spite of the resistance of the states. It proceeds to execute the law, and if resisted, the offender is sub-

(*a*) If they or a majority of congress do not, then the obvious remedy is a repeal of the obnoxious law. If the majority of congress approve it, and the judiciary pronounce it valid, no state can have a *constitutional* right to resist it. Its only remedy is above the constitution. In other words it must be by revolution, or secession, which is revolution; and as all the states have equal right to judge, secession must always be upon the responsibility of the seceding state.

jected to the laws of the Union. It will be no justification to him in its forum that he acted under a conflicting state law. So, if the governor of a state were to issue an order to the militia while in the actual service of the United States during war, the executive of the Union could not act, indeed, upon the *governor*, but a court martial would act upon the *individual who should foolishly obey his orders.* So as to the legislative bodies. Congress cannot act directly on the legislatures, however gross their violations of the constitution. The legislature of one sovereign cannot act upon the legislature of another unless by express compact; and hence congress cannot compel the state legislatures to pass, or forbid them from passing any law. If they pass unconstitutional laws, which *can* come under judicial cognizance in the federal courts, those courts arrest their operation by action on individuals. If the law can in no wise be brought within the judicial sphere, the federal legislature acts without regarding it, though no political dreamer has ever thought of compulsive repeal, or instructions to proceed according to its mandate.(*b*)

With these views of my own on the interesting topics of nullification, and the powers of the supreme court, I shall present to the student the striking observations of several distinguished statesmen and politicians. It cannot but have been remarked, that in these constitutional questions, I occupy an isthmus that divides two great contending parties in the nation. I have endeavoured to maintain a middle course between dangerous extremes. On the one hand is nullification, and upon the other centralization; the rocks of Scylla and the engulphing whirlpool of Charybdis. In shunning both, I have followed, I am sure, the track of the wisest and most virtuous of our statesmen; and I feel the sincerest gratification in being able to sustain myself on both points, by the authority of one who shared in the adoption of the constitution, and who has always maintained its federative character, while he has resisted with the force of truth the disorganizing doctrines falsely deduced from it. I shall first, however, avail myself of judge Story's able disquisitions, which will be found

(*b*) The late apportionment bill is charged with this absurdity. I have not yet seen it.

to repel with great force of argument the unfounded and mischievous pretensions of the advocates of nullification. At the conclusion of them will be found Mr. Madison's views as presented in his letter to Everett in August 1830:

"§ 373. The consideration of the question, whether the constitution has made provision for any common arbiter to construe its powers and obligations, would properly find a place in the analysis of the different clauses of that instrument. But, as it is immediately connected with the subject before us, it seems expedient in this place to give it a deliberate attention.(*c*)

"§ 374. In order to clear the question of all minor points, which might embarrass us in the discussion, it is necessary to suggest a few preliminary remarks. The con-

(*c*) The point was very strongly argued, and much considered, in the case of *Cohens* v. *Virginia*, in the supreme court, in 1821, (6 Wheat. R. 264.) The whole argument, as well as the judgment, deserves an attentive reading. The result, to which the argument against the existence of a common arbiter leads, is presented in a very forcible manner by Mr. chief justice Marshall, in pages 376, 377:

"The questions presented to the court by the two first points made at the bar are of great magnitude, and may be truly said vitally to affect the Union. They exclude the enquiry, whether the constitution and laws of the United States have been violated by the judgment, which the plaintiffs in error seek to review; and maintain, that, admitting such violation, it is not in the power of the government to apply a corrective. They maintain, that the nation does not possess a department capable of restraining peaceably, and by authority of law, any attempts, which may be made by a part against the legitimate powers of the whole; and that the government is reduced to the alternative of submitting to such attempts, or of resisting them by force. They maintain, that the constitution of the United States has provided no tribunal for the final construction of itself, or of the laws or treaties of the nation; but that this power may be exercised in the last resort by the courts of every state in the Union. That the constitution, laws and treaties, may receive as many constructions, as there are states; and that this is not a mischief, or, if a mischief, is irremediable. These abstract propositions are to be determined; for he, who demands decision without permitting enquiry, affirms, that the decision he asks does not depend on enquiry.

"If such be the constitution, it is the duty of this court to bow with respectful submission to its provisions. If such be not the constitution, it is equally the duty of this court to say so; and to perform that task, which the American people have assigned to the judicial department."

stitution, contemplating the grant of limited powers, and distributing them among various functionaries, and the state governments, and their functionaries, being also clothed with limited powers, subordinate to those granted to the general government, whenever any question arises as to the exercise of any power by any of these functionaries under the state, or federal government, it is of necessity, that such functionaries must, in the first instance, decide upon the constitutionality of the exercise of such power.(*d*) It may arise in the course of the discharge of the functions of any one, or of all, of the great departments of government, the executive, the legislative, and the judicial. The officers of each of these departments are equally bound by their oaths of office to support the constitution of the United States, and are therefore conscientiously bound to abstain from all acts, which are inconsistent with it. Whenever, therefore, they are required to act in a case, not hitherto settled by any proper authority, these functionaries must, in the first instance decide, each for himself, whether, consistently with the constitution, the act can be done. If, for instance, the president is required to do any act, he is not only authorized, but required, to decide for himself, whether, consistently with his constitutional duties, he can do the act.(*e*) So, if a proposition be before congress, every member of the legislative body is bound to examine, and decide for himself, whether the bill or resolution is within the constitutional reach of the legislative powers confided to congress. And

(*d*) See the Federalist, No. 33.

(*e*) Mr. Jefferson carries his doctrine much farther, and holds, that each department of government has an exclusive right, independent of the judiciary, to decide for itself, as to the true construction of the constitution. "My construction," says he, "is very different from that, you quote. It is, that each department of the government is truly independent of the others, and has an equal right to decide for itself, what is the meaning of the constitution in the laws submitted to its action, and especially when it is to act ultimately and without appeal." And he proceeds to give examples, in which he disregarded, when president, the decisions of the judiciary, and refers to the alien and sedition laws, and the case of *Marbury* v. *Madison*, (1 Cranch 137.) 4 Jefferson's Corresp. 316, 317. See also 4 Jefferson's Corresp. 27; Id. 75; Id. 372, 374.

in many cases, the decisions of the executive and legislative departments, thus made, become final and conclusive, being from their very nature and character incapable of revision. Thus, in measures exclusively of a political, legislative, or executive character, it is plain, that as the supreme authority, as to these questions, belongs to the legislative and executive departments, they cannot be re-examined elsewhere. Thus, congress having the power to declare war, to levy taxes, to appropriate money, to regulate intercourse and commerce with foreign nations, their mode of executing these powers can never become the subject of re-examination in any other tribunal. So the power to make treaties being confided to the president and senate, when a treaty is properly ratified, it becomes the law of the land, and no other tribunal can gainsay its stipulations. Yet cases may readily be imagined, in which a tax may be laid, or a treaty made, upon motives and grounds wholly beside the intention of the constitution.(*f*) The remedy, however, in such cases, is solely by an appeal to the people at the elections; or by the salutary power of amendment, provided by the constitution itself.(*g*)

"§ 375. But, where the question is of a different nature, and capable of judicial enquiry and decision, there it admits of a very different consideration. The decision then made, whether in favour, or against the constitutionality of the act, by the state, or by the national authority, by the legislature, or by the executive, being capable, in its own nature, of being brought to the test of the constitution, is subject to judicial revision. It is in such cases, as we conceive, that there is a final and common arbiter provided by the constitution itself, to whose decisions all

(*f*) See 4 Elliot's Debates, 315 to 320.

(*g*) The Federalist, No. 44.—Mr. Madison, in the Virginia Report of January 1800, has gone into a consideration of this point, and very properly suggested, that there may be infractions of the constitution not within the reach of the judicial power, or capable of remedial redress through the instrumentality of courts of law. But we cannot agree with him, that in such cases, each state may take the construction of the constitution into its own hands, and decide for itself in the last resort; much less, that in a case of judicial cognizance, the decision is not binding on the states. See Report, p. 6, 7, 8, 9.

others are subordinate; and that arbiter is the supreme judicial authority of the courts of the Union.(*h*)

"§ 376. Let us examine the grounds on which this doctrine is maintained. The constitution declares, (art. 6,) that '*This constitution*, and the *laws* of the United States, which shall be made in pursuance thereof, and all *treaties*, &c. shall be the *supreme law* of the land.' It also declares, (art. 3,) that 'The judicial power shall extend to all cases in law and equity, arising under this constitution, the laws of the United States, and treaties made, and which shall be made under their authority.' It further declares, (art. 3,) that the judicial power of the United States 'shall be vested in one supreme court, and in such inferior courts, as the congress may, from time to time, ordain and establish.' Here, then, we have express, and determinate provisions upon the very subject. Nothing is imperfect, and nothing is left to implication. The constitution is the supreme law; the judicial power extends to all cases arising in law and equity under it; and the courts of the United States are, and, in the last resort, the supreme court of the United States is, to be vested with this judicial power. No man can doubt or deny, that the power to construe the constitution is a judicial power.(*i*) The power to construe a treaty is clearly so, when the case arises in judgment in a controversy between individuals.(*k*)

(*h*) Dane's App. § 44, 45, p. 52 to 59.—It affords me very sincere gratification to quote the following passage from the learned commentaries of Mr. chancellor Kent, than whom very few judges in our country are more profoundly versed in constitutional law. After enumerating the judicial powers in the constitution, he proceeds to observe: "The propriety and fitness of these judicial powers seem to result, as a necessary consequence, from the union of these states in one national government, and they may be considered as requisite to its existence. The judicial power in every government must be co-extensive with the power of legislation. Were there no power to interpret, pronounce, and execute the law, the government would either perish through its own imbecility, as was the case with the old confederation, or other powers must be assumed by the legislative body to the destruction of liberty." 1 Kent's Comm. (2d edi. p. 296,) Lect. 14, 277.

(*i*) 4 Dane's Abridg. ch. 187, art. 20, § 15, p. 590; Dane's App. § 42, p. 49, 50; § 44, p. 52, 53; 1 Wilson's Lectures, 461, 462, 463.

(*k*) See Address of Congress, Feb. 1787; Journals of Congress, p. 33; Rawle on the Constitution, App. 2, p. 316.

The like principle must apply where the meaning of the constitution arises in a judicial controversy; for it is an appropriate function of the judiciary to construe laws.(*l*) If, then, a case under the constitution does arise, if it is capable of judicial examination and decision, we see, that the very tribunal is appointed to make the decision. The only point left open for controversy is, whether such decision, when made, is conclusive and binding upon the states, and the people of the states. The reasons, why it should be so deemed, will now be submitted.

"§ 377. In the first place, the judicial power of the United States rightfully extending to all such cases, its judgment becomes *ipso facto* conclusive between the parties before it, in respect to the points decided, unless some mode be pointed out by the constitution, in which that judgment may be revised. No such mode is pointed out. Congress is vested with ample authority to provide for the exercise by the supreme court of appellate jurisdiction from the decisions of all inferior tribunals, whether state or national, in cases within the purview of the judicial power of the United States; but no mode is provided by which any superior tribunal can re-examine, what the supreme court has itself decided. Ours is emphatically a government of laws, and not of men; and judicial decisions of the highest tribunal, by the known course of the common law, are considered, as establishing the true construction of the laws, which are brought into controversy before it. The case is not alone considered as decided and settled; but the principles of the decision are held, as precedents and authority, to bind future cases of the same nature. This is the constant practice under our whole system of jurisprudence. Our ancestors brought it with them, when they first emigrated to this country; and it is, and always has been considered, as the great security of our rights, our liberties, and our property. It is on this account, that our law is justly deemed certain, and founded in permanent principles, and not dependent upon the caprice, or will of particular judges. A more alarming doctrine could not be promulgated by any American court, than that it was at liberty to disregard all former rules and

(*l*) Bacon's Abridgment, statute H.

decisions, and to decide for itself, without reference to the settled course of antecedent principles.

"§ 378. This known course of proceeding, this settled habit of thinking, this conclusive effect of judicial adjudications, was in the full view of the framers of the constitution. It was required, and enforced in every state in the Union; and a departure from it would have been justly deemed an approach to tyranny and arbitrary power, to the exercise of mere discretion, and to the abandonment of all the just checks upon judicial authority. It would seem impossible, then, to presume, if the people intended to introduce a new rule in respect to the decisions of the supreme court, and to limit the nature and operations of their judgments in a manner wholly unknown to the common law, and to our existing jurisprudence, that some indication of that intention should not be apparent on the face of the constitution. We find, (art. 4,) that the constitution has declared, that full faith and credit shall be given in each state to the judicial proceedings of every other state. But no like provision has been made in respect to the judgments of the courts of the United States, because they were plainly supposed to be of paramount and absolute obligation throughout all the states. If the judgments of the supreme court upon constitutional questions are conclusive and binding upon the citizens at large, must they not be equally conclusive upon the states? If the states are parties to that instrument, are not the people of the states also parties?

"§ 379. It has been said, 'that however true it may be, that the judicial department is, in all questions submitted to it by the forms of the constitution, to decide in the last resort, this resort must necessarily be deemed the last, *in relation to the other departments of the government, not in relation to the rights of the parties to the constitutional compact*, from which the judicial, as well as the other departments hold their delegated trusts. On any other hypothesis, the delegation of judicial power would annul the authority delegating it; and the concurrence of this department with the others in usurped powers might subvert for ever, and beyond the possible reach of any rightful remedy, the very constitution, which all were instituted to preserve.'(*m*) Now, it is certainly possible, that all the de-

(*m*) Madison's Virginia Report, Jan. 1800, p. 8, 9.

partments of a government may conspire to subvert the constitution of that government, by which they are created. But if they should so conspire, there would still remain an adequate remedy to redress the evil. In the first place, the people, by the exercise of the elective franchise, can easily check and remedy any dangerous, palpable and deliberate infraction of the constitution in two of the great departments of government; and, in the third department, they can remove the judges, by impeachment, for any corrupt conspiracies. Besides these ordinary remedies, there is a still more extensive one, embodied in the form of the constitution, by the power of amending it, which is always in the power of three fourths of the states. It is a supposition not to be endured for a moment, that three fourths of the states would conspire in any deliberate, dangerous, and palpable breach of the constitution. And if the judicial department alone should attempt any usurpation, congress, in its legislative capacity, has full power to abrogate the injurious effects of such a decision. Practically speaking, therefore, there can be very little danger of any such usurpation or deliberate breach.

"§ 380. But it is always a doubtful mode of reasoning to argue from the possible abuse of powers, that they do not exist.(*n*) Let us look for a moment at the consequences, which flow from the doctrine on the other side. There are now twenty-four states in the Union, and each has, in its sovereign capacity, a right to decide for itself in the last resort, what is the true construction of the constitution; what are its powers; and what are the obligations founded on it. We may, then, have, in the free exercise of that right, twenty-four honest, but different expositions of every power in that constitution, and of every obligation involved in it. What one state may deny, another may assert; what one may assert at one time, it may deny at another time. This is not mere supposition. It has, in point of fact, taken place. There never has been a single constitutional question agitated, where different states, if they have expressed any opinion, have not expressed different opinions; and there have been, and, from the fluctuating nature of legislative bodies, it may be supposed,

(*n*) See *Anderson* v. *Dunn*, 6 Wheaton's R. 204, 232.

that there will continue to be, cases, in which the same state will at different times hold different opinions on the same question. Massachusetts at one time thought the embargo of 1807 unconstitutional; at another a majority, from the change of parties, was as decidedly the other way. Virginia, in 1810, thought that the supreme court was the common arbiter; in 1829 she thought differently;(*o*) what, then, is to become of the constitution, if its powers are thus perpetually to be the subject of debate and controversy? What exposition is to be allowed to be of authority? Is the exposition of one state to be of authority there, and the reverse to be of authority in a neighbouring state, entertaining an opposite exposition? Then, there would be at no time in the United States the same constitution in operation over the whole people. Is a power, which is doubted, or denied by a single state, to be suspended either wholly, or in that state? Then, the constitution is practically gone, as a uniform system, or indeed, as any system at all, at the pleasure of any state. If the power to nullify the constitution exists in a single state, it may rightfully exercise it at its pleasure. Would not this be a far more dangerous and mischievous power, than a power granted by all the states to the judiciary to construe the constitution? Would not a tribunal, appointed under the authority of all, be more safe, than twenty-four tribunals acting at their own pleasure, and upon no common principles and co-operation? Suppose congress should declare war; shall one state have power to suspend it? Suppose congress should make peace; shall one state have power to involve the whole country in war? Suppose the president and senate should make a treaty; shall one state declare it a nullity, or subject the whole country to reprisals for refusing to obey it? Yet, if every state may for itself judge of its obligations under the constitution, it may disobey a particular law or treaty, because it may deem it an unconstitutional exercise of power, although every other state shall concur in a contrary opinion. Suppose congress should lay a tax upon imports burthensome to a particular state, or for purposes, which such state

(*o*) Dane's App. § 44, 45, p. 52 to 59; § 54, p. 66; 4 Elliot's Debates, 338, 339.

deems unconstitutional, and yet all the other states are in its favour; is the law laying the tax to become a nullity? That would be to allow one state to withdraw a power from the Union, which was given by the people of all the states. That would be to make the general government the servant of twenty-four masters, of different wills and different purposes, and yet bound to obey them all.(*p*)

"§ 381. The argument, therefore, arising from a possibility of an abuse of power, is, to say the least of it, quite as strong the other way. The constitution is in quite as perilous a state from the power of overthrowing it lodged in every state in the Union, as it can be by being lodged in any department of the federal government. There is this difference, however, in the cases, that if there be federal usurpation, it may be checked by the people of all the states in a constitutional way. If there be usurpation by a single state, it is upon the theory we are considering, irremediable. Other difficulties, however, attend the reasoning we are considering. When it is said, that the decision of the supreme court in the last resort is obligatory, and final 'in relation to the authorities of the other departments of the government,' is it meant of the federal government only, or of the states also? If of the former only, then the constitution is no longer the supreme law of the land, although all the state functionaries are bound by an oath to support it. If of the latter also, then it is obligatory upon the state legislatures, executives and judiciaries. It binds them; and yet it does not bind the people of the states, or the states in their sovereign capacity. The states may maintain one construction of it, and the functionaries of the state are bound by another. If, on the other hand, the state functionaries are to follow the construction of the state, in opposition to the construction of the supreme court, then the constitution, as actually administered by the different functionaries, is different; and the duties required of them may be opposite, and in collision with each other. If such a state of things is the just result of the reasoning, may it not justly be suspected, that the reasoning itself is unsound?

(*p*) Webster's Speeches, 420; 4 Elliot's Debates, 339.

"§ 382. Again; it is a part of this argument, that the judicial interpretation is not binding 'in relation to the rights of the parties to the constitutional compact.'—'On any other hypothesis the delegation of judicial power would annul the authority delegating it.' Who then are the parties to this contract? Who did delegate the judicial power? Let the instrument answer for itself. The people of the United States are the parties to the constitution. The people of the United States delegated the judicial power. It was not a delegation by the people of one state, but by the people of all the states. Why then is not a judicial decision binding in each state, until all, who delegated the power, in some constitutional manner concur in annulling or overruling the decision? Where shall we find the clause, which gives the power to each state to construe the constitution for all; and thus of itself to supersede in its own favour the construction of all the rest? Would not this be justly deemed a delegation of judicial power, which would annul the authority delegating it?(q) Since the whole people of the United States have concurred in establishing the constitution, it would seem most consonant with reason to presume, in the absence of all contrary stipulations, that they did not mean, that its obligatory force should depend upon the dictate or opinion of any single state. Even under the confederation, (as has been already stated,) it was unanimously resolved by congress, that 'as state legislatures are not competent to the making of such compacts or treaties, [with foreign states,] *so neither are they competent in that capacity authoritatively to decide on*, or ascertain the construction and sense of them.' And the reasoning, by which this opinion is supported, seems absolutely unanswerable.(r) If this was true under such an instrument, and that construction was avowed before the whole American people, and brought home to the knowledge of the state legislatures, how can

(q) There is vast force in the reasoning of Mr. Webster on this subject, in his great speech on Mr. Foot's resolutions in the senate, in 1830, which well deserves the attention of every statesman and jurist. See 4 Elliot's Debates, 338, 339, 343, 344, and Webster's Speeches, p. 407, 408, 418, 419, 420; Id. 430, 431, 432.

(r) Journals of Congress, April 13, 1787, p. 32, &c. Rawle on the Constitution, App. 2, p. 316, &c.

we avoid the inference, that under the constitution, where an express judicial power in cases arising under the constitution was provided for, the people must have understood and intended, that the states should have no right to question, or control such judicial interpretation?

"§ 383. In the next place, as the judicial power extends to all cases arising under the constitution, and that constitution is declared to be the supreme law, that supremacy would naturally be construed to extend, not only over the citizens, but over the states.(*s*) This, however, is not left to implication, for it is declared to be the supreme law of the land, 'any thing in the constitution or laws of any state to the contrary notwithstanding.' The people of any state cannot, then, by any alteration of their state constitution, destroy or impair that supremacy. How, then, can they do it in any other less direct manner? Now, it is the proper function of the judicial department to interpret laws, and by the very terms of the constitution to interpret the supreme law. Its interpretation, then, becomes obligatory and conclusive upon all the departments of the federal government, and upon the whole people, so far as their rights and duties are derived from, or affected by that constitution. If then all the departments of the national government may rightfully exercise all the powers, which the judicial department has, by its interpretation, declared to be granted by the constitution; and are prohibited from exercising those, which are thus declared not to be granted by it, would it not be a solecism to hold, notwithstanding, that such rightful exercise should not be deemed the supreme law of the land, and such prohibited powers should still be deemed granted? It would seem repugnant to the first notions of justice, that in respect to the same instrument of government, different powers, and duties, and obligations should arise, and different rules should prevail, at the same time among the governed, from a right of interpreting the same words (manifestly used in one sense only) in different, nay, in opposite senses. If there ever was a case, in which uniformity of interpretation might well be deemed a necessary postulate, it would seem to be that of a fundamental law of a government. It might otherwise follow,

(*s*) The Federalist, No. 33.

that the same individual, as a magistrate, might be bound by one rule, and in his private capacity by another, at the very same moment.

"§ 384. There would be neither wisdom nor policy in such a doctrine; and it would deliver over the constitution to interminable doubts, founded upon the fluctuating opinions and characters of those, who should, from time to time, be called to administer it. Such a constitution could, in no just sense, be deemed a law, much less a supreme or fundamental law. It would have none of the certainty or universality, which are the proper attributes of such a sovereign rule. It would entail upon us all the miserable servitude, which has been deprecated, as the result of vague and uncertain jurisprudence. *Misera est servitus, ubi jus est vagum aut incertum.* It would subject us to constant dissensions, and perhaps to civil broils, from the perpetually recurring conflicts upon constitutional questions. On the other hand, the worst, that could happen from a wrong decision of the judicial department, would be, that it might require the interposition of congress, or, in the last resort, of the amendatory power of the states, to redress the grievance.

"§ 385. We find the power to construe the constitution expressly confided to the judicial department, without any limitation or qualification, as to its conclusiveness. Who, then, is at liberty, by general implications, not from the terms of the instrument, but from mere theory, and assumed reservations of sovereign right, to insert such a limitation or qualification? We find, that to produce uniformity of interpretation, and to preserve the constitution, as a perpetual bond of union, a supreme arbiter or authority of construing is, if not absolutely indispensable, at least, of the highest possible practical utility and importance. Who, then, is at liberty to reason down the terms of the constitution, so as to exclude their natural force and operation?

"§ 386. We find that it is the known course of the judicial department of the several states to decide in the last resort upon all constitutional questions arising in judgment;* and that this has always been maintained as a

* [So in Virginia in the case of *Kemper* v. *Hawkins*, 1 Virginia Cases, p. 20.]

rightful exercise of authority, and conclusive upon the whole state.(*t*) As such, it has been constantly approved by the people, and never withdrawn from the courts by any amendment of their constitutions, when the people have been called to revise them. We find, that the people of the several states have constantly relied upon this last judicial appeal, as the bulwark of their state rights and liberties; and that it is in perfect consonance with the whole structure of the jurisprudence of the common law. Under such circumstances, is it not most natural to presume, that the same rule was intended to be applied to the constitution of the United States? And when we find, that the judicial department of the United States is actually entrusted with a like power, is it not an irresistible presumption, that it had the same object, and was to have the same universally conclusive effect? Even under the confederation, an instrument framed with infinitely more jealousy and deference for state rights, the judgments of the judicial department appointed to decide controversies between states was declared to be final and conclusive; and the appellate power in other cases was held to overrule all state decisions and state legislation.(*u*)

"§ 387. If, then, reasoning from the terms of the constitution, and the known principles of our jurisprudence, the appropriate conclusion is, that the judicial department of the United States is, in the last resort, the final expositor of the constitution, as to all questions of a judicial nature; let us see, in the next place, how far this reasoning acquires confirmation from the past history of the constitution, and the practice under it.

"§ 388. That this view of the constitution was taken by its framers and friends, and was submitted to the people before its adoption, is positively certain. The Federalist(*v*) says, 'Under the national government, treaties and articles of treaties, as well as the law of nations, will always be expounded in one sense, and executed in the same

(*t*) 2 Elliot's Debates, 248, 328, 329, 395; Grimke's speech in 1828, p. 25, &c.; Dane's Append. § 44, 45, p. 52 to 59; Id. § 48, p. 62.

(*u*) Dane's App. § 52, p. 65; *Penhallow* v. *Doane*, 3 Dall. 54; Journals of Congress, 1779, vol. 5, p. 86 to 90; 4 Cranch 2.

(*v*) The Federalist, No. 3.

manner; whereas, adjudications on the same points and questions in thirteen states, or three or four confederacies, will not always accord, or be consistent; and that as well from the variety of independent courts and judges appointed by different and independent governments, as from the different local laws, which may affect and influence them. The wisdom of the convention in committing such questions to the jurisdiction and judgment of courts appointed by, and responsible only to, one national government, cannot be too much commended.' Again, referring to the objection taken, that the government was national, and not a confederacy of sovereign states, and after stating, that the jurisdiction of the national government extended to certain enumerated objects only, and left the residue to the several states, it proceeds to say:(*w*) 'It is true, that in controversies between the two jurisdictions (state and national) the tribunal, *which is ultimately to decide*, is to be established under the general government. But this does not change the principle of the case. The decision is to be impartially made according to the rules of the constitution, and all the usual and most effectual precautions are taken to secure this impartiality. Some such tribunal is clearly essential to prevent an appeal to the sword, and a dissolution of the compact. And that it ought to be established under the general, rather than under the local governments, or, to speak more properly, that it could be safely established under the first alone, is a position not likely to be combated.'(*x*)

"§ 389. The subject is still more elaborately considered in another number,(*y*) which treats of the judicial department in relation to the extent of its powers. It is there said, that there ought always to be a constitutional method of giving efficacy to constitutional provisions; that if there are such things as political axioms, the propriety of the judicial department of a government being co-extensive with its legislature, may be ranked among the number;(*z*) that

(*w*) The Federalist, No 39.
(*x*) See also the Federalist, No. 33.
(*y*) The Federalist, No. 80.
(*z*) The same remarks will be found pressed with great force by Mr. chief justice Marshall, in delivering the opinion of the court in *Cohens* v. *Virginia*, (6 Wheat. 264, 384.)

the mere necessity of uniformity in the interpretation of the national law decides the question; that thirteen independent courts of final jurisdiction over the same causes is a hydra of government, from which nothing but contradiction and confusion can proceed; that controversies between the nation and its members can only be properly referred to the national tribunal; that the peace of the whole ought not to be left at the disposal of a part; and that whatever practices may have a tendency to disturb the harmony of the states, are proper objects of federal superintendence and control.(*a*)

(*a*) In The Federalist, No. 78 and 82, the same course of reasoning is pursued, and the final nature of the appellate jurisdiction of the supreme court is largely insisted on. In the convention of Connecticut, Mr. Ellsworth (afterwards chief justice of the United States) used the following language: "This constitution defines the extent of the powers of the general government. If the general legislature should at any time overleap their limits, the judicial department is the constitutional check. If the United States go beyond their powers; if they make a law, which the constitution does not authorize, it is void; and the judicial power, the national judges, who, to secure their impartiality, are to be made independent, will declare it void. On the other hand, if the states go beyond their limits; if they make a law, which is a usurpation upon the general government, the law is void, and upright and independent judges will declare it. Still, however, if the United States and the individual states will quarrel; if they want to fight, they may do it, and no frame of government can possibly prevent it." In the debates in the South Carolina legislature, when the subject of calling a convention to ratify or reject the constitution was before them,* Mr. Charles Pinckney (one of the members of the convention) avowed the doctrine in the strongest terms. "That a supreme federal jurisdiction was indispensable," said he, "cannot be denied. It is equally true, that in order to ensure the administration of justice, it was necessary to give all the powers, original as well as appellate, the constitution has enumerated. Without it we could not expect a due observance of treaties; that the state judiciaries would confine themselves within their proper sphere; or that a general sense of justice would pervade the Union, &c. That to ensure these, extensive authorities were necessary; particularly so, were they in a tribunal, constituted as this is, whose duty it would be, not only to decide all national questions, which should arise within the Union; but to control and keep the state judiciaries within their proper limits, whenever they should attempt to interfere with the power."

* Debates in 1788, printed by A. E. Miller, 1831, Charleston, p. 7.

"§ 390. The same doctrine was constantly avowed in the state conventions, called to ratify the constitution. With some persons it formed a strong objection to the constitution; with others it was deemed vital to its existence and value.(*b*) So, that it is indisputable, that the constitution was adopted under a full knowledge of this exposition of its grant of power to the judicial department.(*c*)

"§ 391. This is not all. The constitution has now been in full operation more than forty years; and during this period the supreme court has constantly exercised this power of final interpretation in relation, not only to the constitution, and laws of the Union, but in relation to state acts and state constitutions and laws, so far as they affected the constitution, and laws, and treaties of the United States.(*d*) Their decisions upon these grave questions have never been repudiated, or impaired by congress.(*e*) No state has ever deliberately or forcibly resisted the exe-

(*b*) It would occupy too much space to quote the passages at large. Take for an instance, in the Virginia debates, Mr. Madison's remarks. "It may be a misfortune, that in organizing any government, the explication of its authority should be left to any of its co-ordinate branches. There is no example in any country, where it is otherwise. There is no new policy in submitting it to the judiciary of the United States." 2 Elliot's Debates, 390. See also Id. 380, 383, 395, 400, 404, 418. See also North Carolina Debates, 3 Elliot's Debates, 125, 127, 128, 130, 133, 134, 139, 141, 142, 143; Pennsylvania Debates, 3 Elliot's Debates, 280, 313. Mr. Luther Martin, in his letter to the Maryland convention, said: "By the third article the judicial power is vested in one supreme court, &c. These courts, and *these only*, will have a right to decide upon the laws of the United States, and *all questions arising upon their construction*, &c. Whether, therefore, any laws, &c. of congress, or acts of its president, &c. are contrary to, or warranted by the constitution, rests only with the judges, who are appointed by congress to determine; *by whose determinations every state is bound.*" 3 Elliot's Debates, 44, 45; Yates's Minutes, &c. See also the Federalist, No. 78.

(*c*) See Mr. Pinckney's observations, cited in Grimke's speech in 1828, p. 86, 87.

(*d*) Dane's App. § 44, p. 53, 54, 55; Grimke's speech, 1828, p. 34 to 42.

(*e*) In the debates in the first congress organized under the constitution, the same doctrine was openly avowed, as indeed it has constantly been by the majority of congress at all subsequent periods. See 1 Lloyd's Debates, 219 to 596; 2 Lloyd's Debates, 284 to 327.

cution of the judgments founded upon them; and the highest state tribunals have, with scarcely a single exception, acquiesced in, and, in most instances, assisted in executing them.(*f*) During the same period, eleven states have been admitted into the Union, under a full persuasion, that the same power would be exerted over them. Many of the states have, at different times within the same period, been called upon to consider, and examine the grounds, on which the doctrine has been maintained, at the solicitation of other states, which felt, that it operated injuriously, or might operate injuriously, upon their interests. A great majority of the states, which have been thus called upon in their legislative capacities to express opinions, have maintained the correctness of the doctrine, and the beneficial effects of the power, as a bond of union, in terms of the most unequivocal nature.(*g*) Whenever any amend-

(*f*) Chief justice M'Kean, in *Commonwealth* v. *Cobbett*, (3 Dall. 473,) seems to have adopted a modified doctrine, and to have held, that the supreme court was not the common arbiter; but if not, the only remedy was, not by a state deciding for itself, as in case of a treaty between independent governments, but by a constitutional amendment by the states. But see, on the other hand, the opinion of chief justice Spencer, in *Andrews* v. *Montgomery*, 19 Johns. R. 164.

(*g*) Massachusetts, in her resolve of February 12, 1799, (p. 57,) in answer to the resolutions of Virginia of 1798, declared, "that the decision of all cases in law and equity, arising under the constitution of the United States, and the construction of all laws made in pursuance thereof, are exclusively vested by the people in the judicial courts of the United States;" and "that the people in that solemn compact, which is declared to be the supreme law of the land, have not constituted the state legislatures the judges of the acts or measures of the federal government, but have confided to them the power of proposing such amendments," &c.; and "that by this construction of the constitution, an amicable and dispassionate remedy is pointed out for any evil, which experience may prove to exist, and the peace and prosperity of the United States may be preserved without interruption." See also Dane's App. § 44, p. 56; Id. 80. Mr. Webster's speech in the senate, in 1830, contains an admirable exposition of the same doctrines. Webster's Speeches, 410, 419, 420, 421. In June 1821, the house of representatives of New Hampshire passed certain resolutions, (172 yeas to 9 nays,) drawn up (as is understood) by one of her most distinguished statesmen, asserting the same doctrines. Delaware, in January 1831, and Connecticut and Massachusetts held the same in May 1831.

ment has been proposed to change the tribunal, and substitute another common umpire or interpreter, it has rarely received the concurrence of more than two or three states, and has been uniformly rejected by a great majority, either silently, or by an express dissent. And instances have occurred, in which the legislature of the same state has, at different times, avowed opposite opinions, approving at one time, what it had denied, or at least questioned, at another. So, that it may be asserted with entire confidence, that for forty years three fourths of all the states composing the Union have expressly assented to, or silently approved, this construction of the constitution, and have resisted every effort to restrict, or alter it. A weight of public opinion among the people for such a period, uniformly thrown into one scale so strongly, and so decisively, in the midst of all the extraordinary changes of parties, the events of peace and of war, and the trying conflicts of public policy and state interests, is perhaps unexampled in the history of all other free governments.(*h*) It affords as satisfactory a testimony in favour of the just and safe operation of the system, as can well be imagined; and, as a commentary upon the constitution itself, it is as absolutely conclusive, as any ever can be, and affords the only escape from the occurrence of

(*h*) Virginia and Kentucky denied the power in 1798 and 1800; Massachusetts, Delaware, Rhode Island, New York, Connecticut, New Hampshire and Vermont disapproved of the Virginia resolutions, and passed counter resolutions. (North American Review, October 1830, p. 500.) No other state appears to have approved the Virginia resolutions. (Ibid.) In 1810 Pennsylvania proposed the appointment of another tribunal than the supreme court to determine disputes between the general and state governments. Virginia, on that occasion, affirmed, that the supreme court was the proper tribunal; and in that opinion New Hampshire, Vermont, North Carolina, Maryland, Georgia, Tennessee, Kentucky and New Jersey concurred; and no one state approved of the amendment. (North American Review, October 1830, p. 507 to 512; Dane's App. § 55, p. 67; 6 Wheat. R. 358, note.) Recently, in March 1831, Pennsylvania has resolved, that the 25th section of the judiciary act of 1789, ch. 20, which gives the supreme court appellate jurisdiction from state courts on constitutional questions, is authorized by the constitution, and sanctioned by experience, and also all other laws empowering the federal judiciary to maintain the supreme laws.

civil conflicts, and the delivery over of the subject to interminable disputes.(*i*)

(*i*) Upon this subject the speech of Mr. Webster in the senate, in 1830, presents the whole argument in a very condensed and powerful form. The following passage is selected as peculiarly appropriate: "The people, then, sir, erected this government. They gave it a constitution, and in that constitution they have enumerated the powers, which they bestow on it. They have made it a limited government. They have defined its authority. They have restrained it to the exercise of such powers, as are granted; and all others, they declare, are reserved to the states or the people. But, sir, they have not stopped here. If they had, they would have accomplished but half their work. No definition can be so clear, as to avoid possibility of doubt; no limitation so precise, as to exclude all uncertainty. Who, then, shall construe this grant of the people? Who shall interpret their will, where it may be supposed they have left it doubtful? With whom do they repose this ultimate right of deciding on the powers of the government? Sir, they have settled all this in the fullest manner. They have left it with the government itself, in its appropriate branches. Sir, the very chief end, the main design, for which the whole constitution was framed and adopted, was to establish a government, that should not be obliged to act through state agency, or depend on state opinion and state discretion. The people had had quite enough of that kind of government, under the confederacy. Under that system, the legal action—the application of law to individuals, belonged exclusively to the states. Congress could only recommend—their acts were not of binding force, till the states had adopted and sanctioned them. Are we in that condition still? Are we yet at the mercy of state discretion, and state construction? Sir, if we are, then vain will be our attempt to maintain the constitution, under which we sit.

"But, sir, the people have wisely provided, in the constitution itself, a proper, suitable mode and tribunal for settling questions of constitutional law. There are, in the constitution, grants of powers to congress; and restrictions on these powers. There are, also, prohibitions on the states. Some authority must, therefore, necessarily exist, having the ultimate jurisdiction to fix and ascertain the interpretation of these grants, restrictions and prohibitions. The constitution has itself pointed out, ordained and established that authority. How has it accomplished this great and essential end? By declaring, sir, that '*the constitution and the laws of the United States, made in pursuance thereof, shall be the supreme law of the land, any thing in the constitution or laws of any state to the contrary notwithstanding.*'

"This, sir, was the first great step. By this, the supremacy of the constitution and laws of the United States is declared. The people so will it. No state law is to be valid, which comes in conflict with the constitution, or any law of the United States

20

"§ 392. In this review of the power of the judicial department, upon a question of its supremacy in the interpretation of the constitution, it has not been thought necessary to rely on the deliberate judgments of that department in affirmance of it. But it may be proper to add, that the judicial department has not only constantly exercised this right of interpretation in the last resort; but its

passed in pursuance of it. But who shall decide this question of interference? To whom lies the last appeal? This, sir, the constitution itself decides, also, by declaring, '*that the judicial power shall extend to all cases arising under the constitution and laws of the United States.*' These two provisions, sir, cover the whole ground. They are, in truth, the keystone of the arch. With these, it is a constitution; without them it is a confederacy. In pursuance of these clear and express provisions, congress established, at its very first session, in the judicial act, a mode for carrying them into full effect, and for bringing all questions of constitutional power to the final decision of the supreme court. It then, sir, became a government. It then had the means of self-protection; and, but for this, it would, in all probability, have been now among things, which are past. Having constituted the government, and declared its powers, the people have further said, that since somebody must decide on the extent of these powers, the government shall itself decide; subject, always, like other popular governments, to its responsibility to the people. And now, sir, I repeat, how is it, that a state legislature acquires any power to interfere? Who, or what, gives them the right to say to the people, 'We, who are your agents and servants for one purpose, will undertake to decide, that your other agents and servants, appointed by you for another purpose, have transcended the authority you gave them!' The reply would be, I think, not impertinent—'Who made you a judge over another's servants? To their own masters they stand or fall.'

"Sir, I deny this power of state legislatures altogether. It cannot stand the test of examination. Gentlemen may say, that in an extreme case, a state government might protect the people from intolerable oppression. Sir, in such a case, the people might protect themselves, without the aid of the state governments. Such a case warrants revolution. It must make, when it comes, a law for itself. A nullifying act of a state legislature cannot alter the case, nor make resistance any more lawful. In maintaining these sentiments, sir, I am but asserting the rights of the people. I state what they have declared, and insist on their right to declare it. They have chosen to repose this power in the general government, and I think it my duty to support it, like other constitutional powers."

See also 1 Wilson's Law Lectures, 461, 462.—It is truly surprising, that, Mr. vice-president Calhoun, in his letter of the 28th of August 1832, to governor Hamilton, (published while the present work was passing through the press,) should have thought, that a whole course of reasonings and operations has proceeded upon the ground, that, once made, the interpretation was conclusive, as well upon the states, as the people.(*k*)

"§ 393. But it may be asked, as it has been asked, what is to be the remedy, if there be any misconstruction of the constitution on the part of the government of the United States, or its functionaries, and any powers exercised by

proposition merely offered in the convention, and referred to a committee for their consideration, that "the jurisdiction of the supreme court shall be extended to all controversies between the United States and an individual state, or the United States and the citizens of an individual state,"* should, in connection with others, giving a negative on state laws, establish the conclusion, that the convention, which framed the constitution, was opposed to granting the power to the general government, in any form, to exercise any control whatever over a state by force, veto, or judicial process, or in any other form. This clause for conferring jurisdiction on the supreme court in controversies between the United States and the states, must, like the other controversies between states, or between individuals, referred to the judicial power, have been intended to apply exclusively to suits of a civil nature, respecting property, debts, contracts, or other claims by the United States against a state; and not to the decision of constitutional questions in the abstract. At a subsequent period of the convention, the judicial power was expressly extended to all cases arising under the *constitution*, *laws* and *treaties* of the United States, and to all controversies, to which the United States should be a party,† thus covering the whole ground of a right to decide constitutional questions of a judicial nature. And this, as the Federalist informs us, was the substitute for a negative upon state laws, and the only one, which was deemed safe or efficient. The Federalist, No. 80.

(*k*) *Martin* v. *Hunter*, 1 Wheat. R. 304, 334, &c., 342 to 348; *Cohens* v. *The State of Virginia*, 6 Wheat. R. 264, 376, 377 to 392; Id. 413 to 423; *Bank of Hamilton* v. *Dudley*, 2 Peters's R. 524; *Ware* v. *Hylton*, 3 Dall. 199; 1 Cond. R. 99, 112. The language of Mr. chief justice Marshall, in delivering the opinion of the court in *Cohens* v. *Virginia*, (6 Wheat. 384 to 390,) presents the argument in favour of the jurisdiction of the judicial department in a very forcible manner. "While weighing arguments drawn from the nature of government, and from the general spirit of an instrument, and urged for the purpose of narrowing the construction, which the words of that instrument seem to require, it is proper to place in the opposite scale those principles, drawn from the same sources, which go to sustain the words in their full operation and natural import. One of these, which has been pressed with great force by the counsel for the plaintiffs in error, is, that

* Journal of Convention, 20th August, p. 265.
† Journal of Convention, 27th August, p. 298.

them, not warranted by its true meaning? To this question a general answer may be given in the words of its early expositors: 'The same, as if the state legislatures should

the jndicial power of every well constituted government must be co-extensive with the legislative, and must be capable of deciding every judicial question which grows out of the constitution and laws.

"If any proposition may be considered as a political axiom, this, we think, may be so considered. In reasoning upon it, as an abstract question, there would, probably, exist no contrariety of opinion respecting it. Every argument, proving the necessity of the department, proves also the propriety of giving this extent to it. We do not mean to say, that the jurisdiction of the courts of the Union should be construed to be co-extensive with the legislative, merely because it is fit, that it should be so; but we mean to say, that this fitness furnishes an argument in construing the constitution, which ought never to be overlooked, and which is most especially entitled to consideration, when we are enquiring, whether the words of the instrument, which purport to establish this principle, shall be contracted for the purpose of destroying it.

"The mischievous consequences of the construction, contended for on the part of Virginia, are also entitled to great consideration. It would prostrate, it has been said, the government and its laws at the feet of every state in the Union. And would not this be its effect? What power of the government could be executed by its own means, in any state disposed to resist its execution by a course of legislation? The laws must be executed by individuals acting within the several states. If these individuals may be exposed to penalties, and if the courts of the Union cannot correct the judgments, by which these penalties may be enforced, the course of the government may be, at any time, arrested by the will of one of its members. Each member will possess a *veto* on the will of the whole.

"The answer, which has been given to this argument, does not deny its truth, but insists, that confidence is reposed, and may be safely reposed, in the state institutions; and that, if they shall ever become so insane, or so wicked, as to seek the destruction of the government, they may accomplish their object by refusing to perform the functions assigned to them.

"We readily concur with the counsel for the defendant in the declaration, that the cases, which have been put, of direct legislative resistance for the purpose of opposing the acknowledged powers of the government, are extreme cases, and in the hope, that they will never occur; but we cannot help believing, that a general conviction of the total incapacity of the government to protect itself and its laws in such cases, would contribute in no inconsiderable degree to their occurrence.

"Let it be admitted, that the cases, which have been put, are extreme and improbable, yet there are gradations of opposition to the laws, far short of those cases, which might have a baneful inviolate their respective constitutional authorities.' In the first instance, if this should be by congress, 'the success of the usurpation will depend on the executive and judi-

fluence on the affairs of the nation. Different states may entertain different opinions on the true construction of the constitutional powers of congress. We know, that at one time, the assumption of the debts, contracted by the several states during the war of our revolution, was deemed unconstitutional by some of them. We know, too, that at other times, certain taxes, imposed by congress, have been pronounced unconstitutional. Other laws, have been questioned partially, while they were supported by the great majority of the American people. We have no assurance, that we shall be less divided, than we have been. States may legislate in conformity to their opinions, and may enforce those opinions by penalties. It would be hazarding too much to assert, that the judicatures of the states will be exempt from the prejudices, by which the legislatures and people are influenced, and will constitute perfectly impartial tribunals. In many states the judges are dependent for office and for salary on the will of the legislature. The constitution of the United States furnishes no security against the universal adoption of this principle. When we observe the importance, which that constitution attaches to the independence of judges, we are the less inclined to suppose, that it can have intended to leave these constitutional questions to tribunals, where this independence may not exist, in all cases where a state shall prosecute an individual, who claims the protection of an act of congress. These prosecutions may take place, even without a legislative act. A person, making a seizure under an act of congress, may be indicted as a trespasser, if force has been employed, and of this a jury may judge. How extensive may be the mischief, if the first decisions in such cases should be final!

"These collisions may take place in times of no extraordinary commotion. But a constitution is framed for ages to come, and is designed to approach immortality, as nearly as human institutions can approach it. Its course cannot always be tranquil. It is exposed to storms and tempests, and its framers must be unwise statesmen indeed, if they have not provided it, as far as its nature will permit, with the means of self-preservation from the perils it may be destined to encounter. No government ought to be so defective in its organization, as not to contain within itself the means of securing the execution of its own laws against other dangers, than those which occur every day. Courts of justice are the means most usually employed; and it is reasonable to expect, that a government should repose on its own courts, rather than on others. There is certainly nothing in the circumstances, under which our constitution was formed; nothing in the history of the times which would justify the opinion, that the confidence reposed in the states was so implicit as to leave in them and their tribunals the power of resisting or defeating, in the form of law, the legitimate measures of the Union. The requisitions of congress, under the confedera

ciary departments, which are to expound, and give effect to the legislative acts; and, in the last resort, a remedy must be obtained from the people, who can, by the election of

tion, were as constitutionally obligatory, as the laws enacted by the present congress. That they were habitually disregarded, is a fact of universal notoriety. With the knowledge of this fact, and under its full pressure, a convention was assembled to change the system. Is it so improbable, that they should confer on the judicial department the power of construing the constitution and laws of the Union in every case, in the last resort, and of preserving them from all violation from every quarter, so far as judicial decisions can preserve them, that this improbability should essentially affect the construction of the new system? We are told, and we are truly told, that the great change, which is to give efficacy to the present system, is its ability to act on individuals directly, instead of acting through the instrumentality of state governments. But, ought not this ability, in reason and sound policy, to be applied directly to the protection of individuals employed in the execution of the laws, as well as to their coercion? Your laws reach the individual without the aid of any other power; why may they not protect him from punishment for performing his duty in executing them?

"The counsel for Virginia endeavour to obviate the force of these arguments by saying, that the dangers they suggest, if not imaginary, are inevitable; that the constitution can make no provision against them; and that, therefore, in construing that instrument, they ought to be excluded from our consideration. This state of things, they say, cannot arise, until there shall be a disposition so hostile to the present political system, as to produce a determination to destroy it; and, when that determination shall be produced, its effects will not be restrained by parchment stipulations. The fate of the constitution will not then depend on judicial decisions. But, should no appeal be made to force, the states can put an end to the government by refusing to act. They have only not to elect senators, and it expires without a struggle.

"It is very true, that, whenever hostility to the existing system shall become universal, it will be also irresistible. The people made the constitution, and the people can unmake it. It is the creature of their will, and lives only by their will. But this supreme and irresistible power to make, or to unmake, resides only in the whole body of the people; not in any sub-division of them. The attempt of any of the parts to exercise it is usurpation, and ought to be repelled by those, to whom the people have delegated their power of repelling it.

"The acknowledged inability of the government, then, to sustain itself against the public will, and, by force or otherwise, to control the whole nation, is no sound argument in support of its constitutional inability to preserve itself against a section of the nation acting in opposition to the general will.

more faithful representatives, annul the acts of the usurpers. The truth is, that this ultimate redress may be more confided in against unconstitutional acts of the federal, than of the state legislatures, for this plain reason, that, as every act of the former will be an invasion of the rights of the latter, these will ever be ready to mark the innovation, to sound the alarm to the people, and to exert their local influence in effecting a change of federal representatives. There being no such intermediate body between the state legislatures and the people, interested in watching the conduct of the former, violations of the state constitution are more likely to remain unnoticed and unredressed.(*l*)

"§ 394. In the next place, if the usurpation should be by the president, an adequate check may be generally found, not only in the elective franchise, but also in the controlling power of congress, in its legislative or impeaching capacity, and in an appeal to the judicial department. In the next place, if the usurpation should be by the judiciary, and arise from corrupt motives, the power of impeachment would remove the offenders; and in most other cases the legislative and executive authorities could interpose an efficient barrier. A declaratory or prohibitory law would, in many cases, be a complete remedy. We have, also, so far

"It is true, that if all the states, or a majority of them, refuse to elect senators, the legislative powers of the Union will be suspended. But if any one state shall refuse to elect them, the senate will not, on that account, be the less capable of performing all its functions. The argument founded on this fact would seem rather to prove the subordination of the parts to the whole, than the complete independence of any one of them. The framers of the constitution were, indeed, unable to make any provisions, which should protect that instrument against a general combination of the states, or of the people, for its destruction; and, conscious of this inability, they have not made the attempt. But they were able to provide against the operation of measures adopted in any one state, whose tendency might be to arrest the execution of the laws, and this it was the part of true wisdom to attempt. We think they have attempted it."

See also *M'Culloch* v. *Maryland*, (4 Wheat. 316, 405, 406.) See also the reasoning of Mr. chief justice Jay, in *Chisholm* v. *Georgia*, (2 Dall. 419, S. C. 2 Peters's Cond. R. 635, 670 to 675.) *Osborn* v. *Bank of the United States*, (9 Wheat. 738, 818, 819;) and *Gibbons* v. *Ogden*, (9 Wheat. 1, 210.)

(*l*) The Federalist, No. 44; 1 Wilson's Law Lectures, 461, 462; Dane's App. § 58, p. 68.

at least as a conscientious sense of the obligations of duty, sanctioned by an oath of office, and an indissoluble responsibility to the people for the exercise and abuse of power, on the part of different departments of the government, can influence human minds, some additional guards against known and deliberate usurpations; for both are provided for in the constitution itself. 'The wisdom and the discretion of congress, (it has been justly observed,) their identity with the people, and the influence, which their constituents possess at elections, are, in this, as in many other instances, as, for example, that of declaring war, the sole restraints; on this they have relied, to secure them from abuse. They are the restraints, on which the people must often solely rely in all representative governments.'(*m*)

"§ 395. But in the next place, (and it is that, which would furnish a case of most difficulty and danger, though it may fairly be presumed to be of rare occurrence,) if the legislative, executive and judicial departments should all concur in a gross usurpation, there is still a peaceable remedy provided by the constitution. It is by the power of amendment, which may always be applied at the will of three fourths of the states. If, therefore, there should be a corrupt co-operation of three fourths of the states for permanent usurpation, (a case not to be supposed, or if supposed, it differs not at all in principle or redress from the case of a majority of a state or nation having the same intent,) the case is certainly irremédiable under any known forms of the constitution. The states may now by a constitutional amendment, with few limitations, change the whole structure and powers of the government, and thus legalize any present excess of power. And the general right of a society in other cases to change the government at the will of a majority of the whole people, in any manner, that may suit its pleasure, is undisputed, and seems indisputable. If there be any remedy at all for the minority in such cases, it is a remedy never provided for by human institutions. It is by a resort to the ultimate right of all

(*m*) *Gibbons* v. *Ogden*, 9 Wheat. R. 1, 197.—See also, on the same subject, the observations of Mr. justice Johnson, in delivering the opinion of the court, in *Anderson* v. *Dunn*, 6 Wheat. R. 204, 226.

human beings in extreme cases to resist oppression, and to apply force against ruinous injustice.(*n*)

(*n*) See Webster's Speeches, p. 408, 409; 1 Black. Comm. 161, 162. See also 1 Tucker's Black. Comm. App. 73 to 75.

The following is the letter of Mr. Madison to Mr. Edward Everett, dated August 1830, referred to by judge Story in his Commentaries, and published as a note to page 375, of the first volume:

"In order to understand the true character of the constitution of the United States, the error, not uncommon, must be avoided, of viewing it through the medium, either of a consolidated government, or of a confederated government, whilst it is neither the one, nor the other; but a mixture of both. And having, in no model, the similitudes and analogies applicable to other systems of government, it must, more than any other, be its own interpreter according to its text and *the facts of the case.*

"From these it will be seen, that the characteristic peculiarities of the constitution are, 1, the mode of its formation; 2, the division of the supreme powers of government between the states in their united capacity, and the states in their individual capacities.

"1. It was formed, not by the governments of the component states, as the federal government, for which it was substituted was formed. Nor was it formed by a majority of the people of the United States, as a single community, in the manner of a consolidated government.

"It was formed by the states, that is, by the people in each of the states, acting in their highest sovereign capacity; and formed consequently, by the same authority, which formed the state constitutions.

"Being thus derived from the same source as the constitutions of the states, it has, within each state, the same authority, as the constitution of the state; and is as much a constitution, in the strict sense of the term, within its prescribed sphere, as the constitutions of the states are, within their respective spheres: but with this obvious and essential difference, *that being a compact among the states in their highest sovereign capacity*, and constituting the people thereof one people for certain purposes, it cannot be altered, or annulled at the will of the states individually, as the constitution of a state may be at its individual will.

"2. And that it divides the supreme powers of government, between the government of the United States, and the governments of the individual states, is stamped on the face of the instrument; the powers of war and of taxation, of commerce and of treaties, and other enumerated powers vested in the government of the United States, being of as high and sovereign a character, as any of the powers reserved to the state governments.

"Nor is the government of the United States, created by the constitution, less a government in the strict sense of the term, within the sphere of its powers, than the governments created by the constitutions of the states are, within their several spheres. It is like them, organized into legislative, executive and judiciary departments. It operates, like them, directly on persons and things. And, like them, it has at command a physical force for executing the powers committed to it. The concurrent operation in certain cases is one of the features marking the peculiarity of the system.

"Between these different constitutional governments, the one operating in all the states, the others operating separately in each, with the aggregate powers of government divided between them, it could not escape attention, that controversies would arise concerng the boundaries of jurisdiction; and that some provision ought to be made for such occurrences. A political system, that does not provide for a peaceable and authoritative termination of occurring controversies, would not be more than the shadow of a government; the object and end of a real government being, the substitution of law and order for uncertainty, confusion and violence.

"That to have left a final decision, in such cases, to each of the states, then thirteen, and already twenty-four, could not fail to make the constitution and laws of the United States different in different states, was obvious; and not less obvious, that this diversity of independent decisions must altogether distract the government of the Union, and speedily put an end to the Union itself. A uniform authority of the laws, is in itself a vital principle. Some of the most important laws could not be partially executed. They must be executed in all the states, or they could be duly executed in none. An impost, or an excise, for example, if not in force in some states, would be defeated in others. It is well known, that this was among the lessons of experience, which had a primary influence in bringing about the existing constitution. A loss of its general authority would moreover revive the exasperating questions between the states holding ports for foreign commerce, and the adjoining states without them; to which are now added, all the inland states, necessarily carrying on their foreign commerce through other states.

"To have made the decisions under the authority of the individual states, co-ordinate, in all cases, with decisions under the authority of the United States, would unavoidably produce collisions incompatible with the peace of society, and with that regular and efficient administration, which is of the essence of free governments. Scenes could not be avoided, in which a ministerial officer of the United States, and the correspondent officer of an individual state, would have rencounters in executing conflicting decrees; the result of which would depend on the comparative force of the local posses attending them; and that, a casualty depending on the political opinions and party feelings in different states.

"To have referred every clashing decision, under the two authorities, for a final decision, to the states as parties to the constitution, would be attended with delays, with inconveniences, and with expenses, amounting to a prohibition of the expedient; not to mention its tendency to impair the salutary veneration for a system requiring such frequent interpositions, nor the delicate questions, which might present themselves as to the form of stating the appeal, and as to the quorum for deciding it.

"To have trusted to negotiation for adjusting disputes between the government of the United States and the state governments, as between independent and separate sovereignties, would have lost sight altogether of a constitution and government for the Union; and opened a direct road from a failure of that resort, to the *ultima ratio* between nations wholly independent of, and alien to each other. If the idea had its origin in the process of adjustment between separate branches of the same government, the analogy entirely fails. In the case of disputes between independent parts of the same government, neither part being able to consummate its will, nor the government to proceed without a concurrence of the parts, necessity brings about an accommodation. In disputes between a state government, and the government of the United States, the case is practically, as well as theoretically different; each party possessing all the departments of an organized government, legislative, executive and judiciary; and having each a physcial force to support its pretensions. Although the issue of negotiation might sometimes avoid this extremity, how often would it happen among so many states, that an unaccommodating spirit in some would render that resource unavailing? A contrary supposition would not accord with a knowledge of human nature, or the evidence of our own political history.

"The constitution, not relying on any of the preceding modifications, for its safe and successful operation, has expressly declared, on the one hand, 1, 'that the constitution, and the laws made in pursuance thereof, and all treaties made under the authority of the United States, shall be the supreme law of the land; 2, that the judges of every state shall be bound thereby, any thing in the constitution and laws of any state to the contrary notwithstanding; 3, that the judicial power of the United States shall extend to all cases in law and equity arising under the constitution, the laws of the United States, and treaties made under their authority,' &c.

"On the other hand, as a security of the rights and powers of the states, in their individual capacities, against an undue preponderance of the powers granted to the government over them in their united capacity, the constitution has relied on, (1,) the responsibility of the senators and representatives in the legislature of the United States to the legislatures and people of the states; (2,) the responsibility of the president to the people of the United States; and (3,) the liability of the executive and judicial functionaries of the United States to impeachment by the representatives of the people of the states, in one branch of the legislature of the United States, and trial by the representatives of the states, in the other branch: the state functionaries, legislative, executive and judicial, being, at the same time, in their appointment and responsibilty, altogether independent of the agency or authority of the United States.

"How far this structure of the government of the United States is adequate and safe for its objects, time alone can absolutely determine. Experience seems to have shewn, that whatever may grow out of future stages of our national career, there is, as yet, a sufficient control, in the popular will, over the executive and legislative departments of the government. When the alien and sedition laws were passed, in contravention to the opinions and feelings of the community, the first elections, that ensued, put an end to them. And whatever may have been the character of other acts, in the judgment of many of us, it is but true, that they have generally accorded with the views of a majority of the states and of the people. At the present day it seems well understood, that the laws which have created most dissatisfaction, have had a like sanction without doors: and that, whether continued, varied, or repealed, a like proof will be given of the sympathy and responsibility of the representative body to the constituent body. Indeed, the great complaint now is, against the results of this sympathy and responsibility in the legislative policy of the nation.

"With respect to the judicial power of the United States, and the authority of the supreme court in relation to the boundary of jurisdiction between the federal and the state governments, I may be permitted to refer to the thirty-ninth number of the Federalist* for the light, in which the subject was regarded by its writer at the period, when the constitution was depending; and it is believed that the same was the prevailing view then taken of it; that the same view has continued to prevail; and that it does so at this time, notwithstanding the eminent exceptions to it.

"But it is perfectly consistent with the concession of this power to the supreme court, in cases falling within the course of its functions, to maintain, that the power has not always been rightly exercised. To say nothing of the period, happily a short one, when judges in their seats did not abstain from intemperate and party harangues, equally at variance with their duty and their dignity; there have been occasional decisions from the bench, which have incurred serious and extensive disapprobation. Still it would seem, that, with but few exceptions, the course of the judiciary has been hitherto sustained by the prominent sense of the nation.

"Those who have denied, or doubted the supremacy of the judicial power of the United States, and denounce at the same time a nullifying power in a state, seem not to have sufficiently adverted to the utter inefficiency of a supremacy in a law of the land, without a supremacy in the exposition and execution of the law: nor to the destruction of all equipoise between the federal government and the state governments, if, whilst the functionaries of the federal government are directly or indirectly elected by, and responsible to the states, and the functionaries of the states are in their appointment and responsibility wholly independent of the United States, no constitutional control of any sort belonged to the United States over the states. Under such an organization, it is evident, that it would be in the power of the states, individually,

[*"It is true, that in controversies relating to the boundary between the two jurisdictions, the *tribunal which is ultimately to decide is to be established under the general government.* Some such tribunal is clearly essential to prevent an appeal to the sword and a dissolution of the compact, and that it ought to be established under the *general* rather than under the local governments." Fed. No. 39.]

to pass unauthorized laws, and to carry them into complete effect, any thing in the constitution and laws of the United States to the contrary notwithstanding. This would be a nullifying power in its plenary character; and whether it had its final effect, through the legislative, executive or judiciary organ of the state, would be equally fatal to the constituted relation between the two governments.

"Should the provisions of the constitution as here reviewed, be found not to secure the government and rights of the states, against usurpations and abuses on the part of the United States, the final resort within the purview of the constitution, lies in an amendment of the constitution, according to a process applicable by the states.

"And in the event of a failure of every constitutional resort, and an accumulation of usurpations and abuses, rendering passive obedience and non-resistance a greater evil, than resistance and revolution, there can remain but one resort, the last of all; an appeal from the cancelled obligations of the constitutional compact, to original rights and the law of self-preservation. This is the *ultima ratio* under all governments, whether consolidated, confederated, or a compound of both; and it cannot be doubted, that a single member of the Union, in the extremity supposed, but in that only, would have a right, as an extra and ultra constitutional right, to make the appeal.

"This brings us to the expedient lately advanced, which claims for a single state a right to appeal against an exercise of power by the government of the United States, decided by the state to be unconstitutional, to the parties to the constitutional compact; the decision of the state to have the effect of nullifying the act of the government of the United States, unless the decision of the state be reversed by three fourths of the parties.

"The distinguished names and high authorities, which appear to have asserted, and given a practical scope to this doctrine, entitle it to a respect, which it might be difficult otherwise to feel for it.

"If the doctrine were to be understood as requiring the three fourths of the states to sustain, instead of that proportion to reverse the decision of the appealing state, the decision to be without effect during the appeal, it would be sufficient to remark, that this extra-constitutional course might well give way to that marked out by the constitution, which authorizes two thirds of the states to institute, and three fourths to effectuate an amendment of the constitution, establishing a permanent rule of the highest authority, in place of an irregular precedent of construction only.

"But it is understood, that the nullifying doctrine imports, that the decision of the state is to be presumed valid, and that it overrules the law of the United States, unless overruled by three fourths of the states.

"Can more be necessary to demonstrate the inadmissibility of such a doctrine, than, that it puts it in the power of the smallest fraction over one fourth of the United States, that is, of seven states out of twenty-four, to give the law, and even the constitu-

21

tion to seventeen states, each of the seventeen having, as parties to the constitution, an equal right with each of the seven, to expound it, and to insist on the exposition? That the seven might, in particular instances be right, and the seventeen wrong, is more than possible. But to establish a positive and permanent rule giving such a power, to such a minority, over such a majority, would overturn the first principle of free government, and in practice necessarily overturn the government itself.

"It is to be recollected, that the constitution was proposed to the people of the states as *a whole*, and unanimously adopted by the states as *a whole*, it being a part of the constitution, that not less than three fourths of the states should be competent to make any alteration in what had been unanimously agreed to. So great is the caution on this point, that in two cases where peculiar interests were at stake, a proportion even of three fourths is distrusted, and unanimity required to make an alteration.

"When the constitution was adopted as a whole, it is certain, that there were many parts, which, if separately proposed, would have been promptly rejected. It is far from impossible, that every part of a constitution might be rejected by a majority, and yet taken together as a whole, be unanimously accepted. Free constitutions will rarely, if ever, be formed, without reciprocal concessions; without articles conditioned on, and balancing each other. Is there a constitution of a single state out of the twenty-four, that would bear the experiment of having its component parts submitted to the people, and separately decided on?

"What the fate of the constitution of the United States would be, if a small proportion of the states could expunge parts of it particularly valued by a large majority, can have but one answer.

"The difficulty is not removed by limiting the doctrine to cases of construction. How many cases of that sort, involving cardinal provisions of the constitution, have occurred? How many now exist? How many may hereafter spring up? How many might be ingeniously created, if entitled to the privilege of a decision in the mode proposed.

"Is it certain, that the principle of that mode would not reach further than is contemplated? If a single state can, of right, require three fourths of its co-states to overrule its exposition of the constitution, because that proportion is authorized to amend it, would the plea be less plausible, that, as the constitution was unanimously established, it ought to be unanimously expounded?

"The reply to all such suggestions, seems to be unavoidable and irresistible; that the constitution is a compact; that its text is to be expounded, according to the provisions for expounding it—making a part of the compact; and that none of the parties can rightfully renounce the expounding provision more than any other part. When such a right accrues, as may accrue, it must grow out of abuses of the compact releasing the sufferers from their fealty to it."

www.ingramcontent.com/pod-product-compliance
Lightning Source LLC
Chambersburg PA
CBHW021542260326
41914CB00001B/126

* 9 7 8 1 5 8 4 7 7 4 5 3 2 *